FOURTH EDITION

An Introduction to Holistic
Enterprise Architecture

Scott A. Bernard

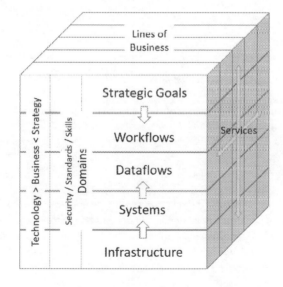

authorHOUSE®

AuthorHouse™
1663 Liberty Drive
Bloomington, IN 47403
www.authorhouse.com
Phone: 1 (800) 839-8640

Published by AuthorHouse 04/16/2020

ISBN: 978-1-7283-5805-5 (sc)
ISBN: 978-1-7283-5804-8 (e)

Contents

This book is dedicated to my children:
Bill, Kristine, and Katie

Preface

Intended Audience

An Introduction to Holistic Enterprise Architecture is intended for all levels of practitioners in business and government who want to know more about how large, complex organizations can be understood and improved. No prior subject knowledge is required, the book is written using plain terminology.

Why I Wrote This Book

An Introduction to Holistic Enterprise Architecture allows me to share almost forty years of experience as a business and technology manager, architect, consultant, and teacher. This includes being a Chief Information Officer, a decade of service as the U.S. Federal Chief Enterprise Architect, and graduate-level teaching at two universities. I wrote this book to help move business and technology planning by moving from a program-level, system-specific view to a more strategy-driven enterprise-level perspective. This is needed when large, complex organizations seek to be more mission effective and cost efficient in the face of constant change.

The response to this book since it was first published in 2004 has been overwhelmingly positive, which I am grateful for.[1] The changes presented in the 4th edition include updates to each chapter that reflect new business and technology practices, use of the term "holistic" Enterprise Architecture (EA), updates to the Cube Framework, and new chapters on doing solution architecture projects and on how EA can help in mergers and acquisitions.

Use in Business Transformation

Organizations are ever-changing in response to internal and external influences that include leadership priorities, market conditions, innovations, regulations, and social trends. Holistic architecture helps to manage this change at the macro and detailed levels through integrated analysis and design methods that are informed by goal setting, workflow optimization, resource stewardship, and risk management.

The term "business transformation" is often used to indicate that significant changes in structure and function are needed for an organization to remain competitive. These changes will likely include what types of work will be prioritized, how and by whom that work is done, what the reward system will be, and what the key performance measures and resource dependencies are. Holistic architecture helps by mapping strategic goals to enabling workflows and supporting technologies... organization wide.

The approach to holistic architecture that is presented in this book hopefully provides a clear explanation of the relationship between strategic, business, and technology planning. In its simplest form, strategic goals drive business workflows, which are often enabled by various technologies.

As many types of technology, especially information technology (IT), have become more available and affordable, they are built into most of the organization's mission and support functions, which make them tremendously important to organizational health. In recognition of this, the identification of integrated IT solutions to organization-wide (crosscutting) and mission-specific (vertical) requirements is one of the focal points of this book. Strategic goals and business requirements should drive IT solutions, and holistic architecture's contribution to this alignment is another focal point of the book. Finally, this book provides specific documentation techniques that create strategy and business-driven views of the enterprise, which in turn can help to identify gaps in performance that IT solutions can often help to close.

Why is it important to emphasize the *holistic* aspect of this approach to enterprise architecture? Because in my experience, the various types of business and technology planning/improvement/delivery methods that arose over the past two decades do not play well together. Please forgive the acronyms, but this includes ITIL, TOGAF, DODAF, FEAF, MDA, SOA, LEAN, 6 Sigma, TQM, BPR, BPI, SaaS, PaaS, IaaS, Cloud, CMMI, RMF, RUP, CORBA, OO, CPIC, PMP, and TBM.

Can you tell me if, when, and where these methods (best practices) should be used in the organization? I have found that most people can't. This is too bad because some of the methods are very good at planning, improvement, and service delivery in *specific areas* of the organization. EA moves the perspective to the *whole organization* and includes all aspects – nothing is left out. The framework identifies domains and uses the existing organization chart, asset inventory, and service catalog to create an over-arching model of the entire enterprise – in a cube geometry.

There is a place for each of the methods mentioned above; a sub-architecture domain wherein a method is used, sometimes extending across several domains. This largely eliminates the "battle of the best practices" and "architecture competition". It is not helpful to the organization when the supporters of various methods are vying for attention, support, resources, and influence. This unhelpful competition is made worse when proprietary commercial products and methods are added to the mix. This competition can set executives, managers, and staff against each other, which significantly detracts from organizational performance and morale.

So, the value proposition of the holistic EA approach presented in this book is that it is free to use and is proven through use in government and industry for nearly two decades. Think of EA as a neutral meta-method for viewing the organization. This can help you improve control and better be able to choose where, when, how to use domain-specific best practices. I encourage readers to subordinate and align domain-level architectures and best practices by inserting a holistic architecture to serve as the over-arching context for business transformation in an increasingly global operating environment.

Basic Terms for the Reader

As mentioned, I have tried to express concepts in this book using plain language so that readers without prior knowledge of enterprise architecture (EA) can understand them more clearly and without hype. After all, the title starts with *"An Introduction to…"* so the objective is to provide the first book you can use to understand enterprise architecture. A full glossary of terms and definitions can be found at the end of the book, but to get started here are the book definitions of frequently used terms, provided in the context of EA:

Holistic:	All levels, elements, and groups are included in one architecture.
Enterprise:	A large, complex organization, similar parts of several organizations.
Architecture:	A way of describing and drawing something (e.g., an organization).
Organization:	A social system of people/things that is formed to achieve goals.
Framework:	A method and/or geometry to show a relationship of parts.
Scope:	What's included.
Domain:	A sub-part of a concept or method.
Component:	A sub-part of a product or service.
Roadmap:	A drawing or description that shows a sequence.
Executive:	Someone who has top-level seniority and decision power.
Manager:	Someone who directs a specific area or function in the organization.
Staff:	Someone who performs work for a manager or with a team.
Stakeholder:	Someone who has a vested interest in a concept, practice, or product.
Customer:	Someone who actually uses a product or service.
Workflow:	An individual or group process or activity to accomplish something.
Requirement:	What stakeholders/customers need in a product or service.
Scaling:	Moving an activity in a consistent way to a larger or smaller scope.

I try not to use terms that are vague, stylish, or promote a particular group or something for sale. These "buzzword" terms include:

> Cloud, Transformation, Disruption, Digitization, Metering, Virtualization, Show-back, Provisioning, Optimization, Agile, Black-Belt, Hosting, Gamification, Revenue Sharing, Engagement, Big Data, Blockchain, Machine Learning, Dashboard, Crowdsource, Bot, Data Wrangling, Business Intelligence, Lean, Green, Exit Strategy, Helicopter View, Elevator Pitch, Low-Hanging Fruit, Win-Win, Blue Sky Thinking, Schema, Unpack, Abstract, Vector, Best Practice, Endgame, Core Competence, Re-skilling, Resilience, Net-Net, Bootstrap, Value-Add, Delta, Deep Dive, Actionable, KoolAid, Monetize, Synergy, Pivot, Leverage, Bleeding Edge, Seamless, Move the Needle, and Big Data.

I will mention a buzzword if I am trying to explain it, like "business transformation" on the prior page, or "battle of the best practices" in the first Chapter where I am saying that organizations often have to deal with unhelpful and expesive competitions between proprietary/popular/ preferred products, services, and vendors…. and that "holistic enterprise architecture" is a higher-level concept that can help to maintain control over these items. I encourage readers to see through the sales hype and power grabs that accompany the use of buzzwords. To underscore this in a hopefully entertaining way, I provide a "buzzword bingo" vignette at the end of each Case Study scene. The Case Study is intended to reinforce EA concepts in the context of common organizational situations as they face challenges with efficiency and changes in their operating environment.

Organization of This Book

An Introduction to Holistic Enterprise Architecture is organized into four sections of material, a case study, and several appendices of amplifying or reference material. The case study is presented at the beginning of each section and before selected chapters to reinforce the application of the concepts in a variety of settings. The four sections are intended to sequentially develop the reader's understanding of the concepts of holistic architecture and methods for implementation.

Section I provides an overview and context for the book, identifies the value and risk of doing holistic architecture, discusses the structure and changing nature of enterprises, and shows how holistic architecture helps to link strategic, business, and technology planning.

Section II defines and describes what a holistic architecture framework is, presents a step-by-step methodology to implement it through the documentation of current and future views of resources, and describes how to communicate changes in the architecture through an Architecture Transition Roadmap that also can serve as a "blueprint" for modernization.

Section III discusses how to use and maintain EA information in an on-line repository within the enterprise, and how governance processes can be integrated, as well as the author's thoughts on holistic architecture as a profession and opinions on future trends. The Appendices amplify or extend the material presented in all Sections and are intended to be primarily for student reference. A full glossary of key terms is provided along with examples of the documentation models described in various chapters. Examples of each type of artifact are available at www.btmgllc.com.

Here's a little secret. I know that everyone is busy, so you can get the major concepts of the book by just reading the Preface and Chapter 1. More details and examples on each concept are provided in the following chapters.

The *EA3 and EA6 Frameworks, Holistic Enterprise Architecture*, and *Living Enterprise* are registered trademarks. The concepts and graphics in this book were originally presented in lectures given by Dr. Bernard at universities, agencies, and public events beginning in 2001.

Acknowledgements

I would like to thank my colleagues and former student for their encouragement to me in writing about holistic architecture and its predecessors enterprise architecture and IT systems architecture. In particular, I would like to thank one of my mentors, John Zachman, who provided a Foreword to the early editions of this book and in doing so he gives new students to the subject the best possible beginning for their studies. In the view of many, John Zachman is the founder of Enterprise Architecture as it has come to be known, and I sincerely thank him for his mentorship.

John got it right when he introduced the Information Systems Architecture in a co-authored article in the *IBM Systems Journal* in 1987, and he has continued to provide on-target architecture consulting, training, and mentoring on a global basis ever since, remaining an active teacher, lecturer, and practitioner in 2020 as this edition is published.

I would also like to thank and remember Dr. Steven Spewak who helped start the profession of EA. Steve was an inspirational mentor to me during my initial years as an architect. He passed away in March 2004 a few months before the first edition of this book was published…. he is sorely missed by many in our profession. It is both exciting and challenging to be part of a maturing profession, and I salute those who endeavor to develop holistic enterprise architectures for public and private sector organizations. To them I would say good luck, the work ahead of you will be frustrating at times, and yet fulfilling as the contribution of EA to organizational success is fully realized.

My kids are my joy. They know that this book's creation and updates have been a lot of work and I have enjoyed chatting with them about it along the way. William (Bill) is now a Marine Corps pilot protecting the Nation. Kristin is finishing her degree at Johnson & Wales University in Rhode Island (I spelled her name wrong in the 1st Edition's dedication – bad dad!). Katherine (Katie) is studying at Rochester institute of Technology… she said recently "It used to be that electronics were an escape from the world, but now the world is an escape from electronics." So perceptive, so true.

One more thought. My father was a successful land developer and home builder who learned the essentials of traditional architecture on his own. There were many parallels in our lives, and the duality of traditional and organizational architecture is yet another. Dad passed away a few years ago, Mom died when I was in college and I miss them. I took drafting classes in high school and used to watch Dad work with traditional architects on the designs of the houses he was building and there was a wonderful creative energy that I came to appreciate. As I became more interested in organizational design, I felt some of the same creative energy, which is part of why I continue to focus on this area. When I was a CIO, I found that I needed some way to organize the perpetual chaos of systems development and upgrade projects, ongoing operations, and more than occasional surprises. Because of this, I learned about organization-wide architecture, which helped to establish a reference framework for planning and decision-making. Now, with greater appreciation, I enjoy being part of the growth of this field, which in many ways is like the one that my father came to know… a nice blessing in the journey of life.

About the Author

Scott Bernard has nearly forty years of experience in information technology management, including work in the academic, federal government, military, and private sectors. Dr. Bernard has served as the United States Federal Chief Enterprise Architect at the Executive Office of the President in their Office of Management. He served as the Chief Enterprise Architect for the State of Maryland and prior to that held positions as a Chief Information Officer, IT management consultant, line-of-business manager, network operations manager, telecommunications manager, and project manager for several major IT systems installations. He has developed enterprise architectures for several public and private sector organizations, started an enterprise architecture practice for an IT management firm, developed his own consulting practice, and taught enterprise architecture at a number of universities, businesses, and government agencies. In 2002, Dr. Bernard created the EA3 Cube Framework and method, since updated to the EA6 Framework featured in this book, as well as the design for an on-line EA repository that is called Living Enterprise. In 2005, 2012, and 2020 he updated this book.

Dr. Bernard has served for over two decades on the faculty of the School of Information Studies at Syracuse University. Since 2005, he has also served as a Senior Lecturer in the Executive Program of the Institute for Software Research at Carnegie Mellon University's School of Computer Science. Dr. Bernard was the founder of the Association of Enterprise Architects, and first editor of the *Journal of Enterprise Architecture* (from 2005-2010) which is still published to a world-wide readership.

Dr. Bernard earned his Ph.D. at Virginia Tech in Public Administration and Policy; a master's degree in Business and Personnel Management from Central Michigan University, a master's degree in Information Management from Syracuse University, and a bachelor's degree in Psychology from the University of Southern California. He is a graduate of the Naval War College and earned a CIO Certificate and an Advanced Management Program Certificate from the National Defense University. Dr. Bernard was designated a member of the Federal Government's Senior Executive Service from 2011-2018. He is also a former career naval aviator who served onboard aircraft carriers and with shore squadrons, led IT programs, and was the Director of Network Operations for the Joint Chiefs of Staff.

Section I

The Concept of Enterprise Architecture

Case Study (Scene 1) - **Possible Need for an EA Program**
Introduces the Danforth Manufacturing Company and several business and technology challenges that will cause the organization to consider using EA to improve planning, decision-making, and solution implementation.

Introduction – Will this be an *Architected* Organization?
EA is increasingly recognized as the only management and technology discipline that can produce holistic designs for organizations that are agile and all-encompassing. Whether an organization uses EA in this way becomes the question, and if not, what are the consequences.

Chapter 1 - An Overview of Enterprise Architecture
Provides the student with an overview of the emerging profession and practice of holistic EA. The chapter's discussion introduces the concept that EA provides a comprehensive view of an enterprise. This differs from the more system-centric or process-centric views that previous analysis and planning approaches have emphasized.

Chapter 2 – How Culture Affects Architecture
Discusses why it is important that enterprise architects understand how an organization's culture affects structure and function. Enterprises are types of social organizations and as such, the concepts of organizational theory presented in this chapter are applicable to the practice of holistic enterprise architecture.

Case Study (Scene 2) - **Considering an EA Program**
Continues with the Chief Information Officer (CIO) of Danforth Manufacturing Company who makes a presentation regarding how an EA approach can help to evaluate several requests for IT systems and coordinate their implementation.

Chapter 3 - Value / Risk of Creating an Enterprise Architecture

Chapter 3 discusses the value and risk of creating an enterprise-wide architecture. The main concepts of this chapter are (1) that EA represents a different way of looking at resources across the enterprise, and (2) that the significant cost of creating an EA must be justified by the value that it brings to the enterprise by linking strategy, business, and technology. Another key concept is (3) that an integrated set of planning, decision-making, and implementation processes can better identify and resolve performance gaps across the enterprise, and that EA promotes this type of integrated governance.

The Danforth Manufacturing Company (DMC) develops, produces, and sells several lines of photovoltaic storage cells (solar-powered batteries) for use in various consumer, business, and aerospace products. Richard "Rick" Danforth, the President and Chief Executive Officer (CEO) of DMC, has called a meeting of the Executive Committee to review several recent capital investment requests. The largest two of these was a request by Kate Jarvis, the Chief Operating Officer (COO), for a new sales and inventory tracking system and a request by Jose Cruz, the Chief Financial Officer (CFO) to invest in a new cost accounting system. Also invited to the meeting were Roberta Young, the company's first Chief Information Officer (CIO) who joined the company two weeks before, and Gerald Montes, the company's Chief Counsel.

Rick Danforth was the last one to enter the executive boardroom. He smiled at his top management team and said, "Thank you all for coming by to talk a bit more about several investment requests that came out of our annual planning meeting last month. Sarah, you hadn't joined the company yet, so I'm particularly interested in your thoughts today. Mainly, I want to better understand from the group why our current capabilities are insufficient and how these new systems will help bottom-line performance. Kate, why don't you go first and then we'll hear from Jose."

Kate rose and walked to an easel that held several charts and diagrams. "As mentioned at the planning meeting, my request for a new Sales and Inventory Tracking System (SITS) is based on an insufficient current ability to match inventory and production information with customer orders. We are also experiencing excessive turnaround time for orders in the industrial product lines, as compared to our competition. Our sales representatives in the field are beginning to lose orders. They can't provide on-the-spot quotes based on real-time checks of available inventory and current pricing. The Same goes for our representatives. They are not able to see when the custom and small job production runs are being scheduled. This would help sales in this high-profit area which we will be expanding. Our major competitor fielded this information capability almost a year ago. While I was skeptical at the time about the impact it would have on their sales, I now believe that it's a successful model for them and is going to make or break us in the industrial product line."

Rick leaned forward. "Kate, this sounds quite serious. Even so, from a cost perspective I am concerned about the return on investment (ROI) for SITS. Last month you stated that initial cost estimate for the development of SITS was over three million dollars. We have tight budgets for the next two years... have you looked at ROI?" "Yes," responded Kate. "These charts show the level of investment and payback period for SITS, which I estimate to be two years, depending on how quickly and thoroughly the sales force adopts it. The lifecycle for SITS should be seven years, with positive ROI seen in years three through seven, and an average of about 12% per year."

Rick turned to Roberta, "What do you think? Isn't part of the problem here that many of our information systems don't talk to each other?" Roberta grimaced slightly and said, "I think you're right, from what I've seen in my initial survey of IT capabilities, a lot of our systems were built as individual projects based on what then were unique requirements. We now have some duplication of functionality and evidence of inefficient support for evolving business processes." Robert responded quickly, "Isn't the SITS proposal just more of the Same?" "Perhaps" said Roberta, "I'm EAring that Kate wants to integrate information exchanges across the sales, inventory, and production lines of business. This represents a somewhat higher-level approach to meeting several business requirements."

Rick turned to Jose, "What do you think about Kate's problem? Jose answered with a pensive look, "Well, I agree that we need to address our competition's capability. While our aerospace product line is the most profitable, the industrial product line brings in the most revenue, so there would be a significant impact on the entire company if we lose market share in the industrial product area." Rick then turned to Gerald, "So what does the Chief Counsel think?" Gerald paused for a moment and then said, "I think that we must act decisively to protect market share in the industrial product line, but I'm not sure that SITS is the answer. You might be right

Rick, the proposal that Kate is making might be more of the same type of technology solution that Roberta says got us in this situation."

Rick leaned back in his chair and said, "Before going further on this proposal, let's talk about Jose's investment request. I wonder if there are any parallels." Jose turned on the conference room's projector and brought up a set of briefing slides. "My request is for a cost accounting system that would replace the current accounting system. As Rick mentioned, there are tight budgets the next two years, and having the ability to more readily see spending and profit generation within each line of business will help us to manage the budget more effectively. This system is one module of "WELLCO" a proven commercial enterprise resource planning (ERP) product. We can utilize this product by expanding it if other back office requirements emerge. The cost of the investment is just under $600,000. According to the vendor, the historical payback period for this cost accounting module is eighteen months, with an average annual ROI of sixteen percent during the subsequent years."

"Jose, can this new accounting capability support what Kate is looking for?" said Gerald. Jose responded, "The WELLCO module can handle some of the things Kate is probably looking for, including price and volume information in sales, inventory, and production activities, but this module is not configured to specifically support all of the information I believe she will need." "Can it be modified?" Interjected Rick. "Possibly so," said Jose, "and if not, I would think that other modules of WELLCO could handle it. Roberta, help me out with this one if you can." Roberta responded, "I know that WELLCO is one of the leading ERP products designed to support many front and back office functions. It might be possible to get enough functionality to support both Jose's and Kate's requirements. I am concerned that we are still looking at requirements from a program-level and systems-level viewpoint… essentially bottom-up planning. Wouldn't the company benefit more from a more strategic approach that evaluates requirements and proposed solutions across the entire enterprise in the context of our strategic goals?"

The group was silent for a moment, and then Gerald spoke. "Our annual planning retreat is where most of the company's strategic planning happens. We look at our current strategic goals and initiatives. We look at what changes are needed to keep us competitive. As you saw from the meeting last month, new proposals are also surfaced during the retreat and then followed-up on.

That is to say, if they merit consideration for funding and implementation." Roberta asked, "Is there some model of the enterprise that is used to support these discussions?" "Well, if you mean our annual business plan, we have that" said Jose. "More than that" said Roberta, "A model of strategy, business, and technology that enables you to see what we have now and what is planned for the future. Something that gives us the ability to play with the model to see what other future investment and operating scenarios would look like." "We don't have anything as fancy as that" said Kate, "Though a model like that would have helped me analyze what we could do to help the field."

Rick stood up and walked to the window. "Roberta, you are new to the team, but sometimes a fresh look at a situation can provide valuable insights. What I believe you are telling us is that we lack a true top-down, strategy-driven capability to surface requirements and solutions... is that right?" "Yes" responded Roberta. "DMC is not alone. Many companies have the Same problem because they still support program-level decision- making. We tend to let it occur in a relative vacuum with few overarching goals and standards to guide analysis, planning, documentation, and decision-making. I am going to propose that both Kate's and Jose's proposals be reviewed through a different lens, that of an enterprise-wide architecture."

Roberta continued, "If we had this type of model, we could see current capabilities, future requirements, and gaps in our ability to meet those requirements. We could also see duplicative current capabilities and future solutions. From what I have EArd at this meeting we may have some overlapping requirements which probably should not be met with separate solutions if we are to optimize our financial and technology resources."

"Interesting" said Rick. "Sounds like a silver bullet, and I am wary of those" said Gerald. Rick spoke again, "Roberta, would an enterprise-wide architecture really help us? If it is doable, that's great, but why haven't we heard about it before? I know there are no free lunches and where is the ROI in such an architecture?" Kate added "While I appreciate the idea, I don't have time to wait for the entire company to be modeled, I need a new capability now."

"Well," said Roberta. "You are right, establishing a holistic enterprise architecture will not be free and it will take time. Fortunately, there are approaches being used by the public and private sector that support the modeling of requirements and solutions in a standardized way between multiple lines of business, which are referred to as architecture segments. So, as each segment is completed it adds to the architecture as a whole. By treating Jose's area as the company's financial segment, and Kate's area as the production segment, we can just address these areas first, thereby reducing the time for completion of the architecture part of the larger project that may implement a combined solution. We can do this by modeling only those strategic drivers, business services, and technology solutions that apply to those two segments. Eventually though, for the architecture to be the most valuable to DMC, the entire company should be modeled in its current state, and several possible future states."

"As far as our return on investment" continued Roberta, "that is more difficult to pinpoint since the cost of doing the analysis and modeling depends on the amount of existing information and the degree of cooperation that is achieved with stakeholders. By the way, these stakeholders include our executives, managers, and support staff. But let's say that a top-down architectural analysis reveals that there are common requirements between Kate and Jose, and we can meet those requirements either through adding functionality to SITS or by buying several more modules of the commercial WELLCO product and doing some customization. We potentially could save several hundred thousand dollars, or perhaps millions of dollars compared to doing SITS and WELLCO separately... all of which become ROI from the architecture effort. You probably haven't heard about enterprise architecture because when a company is doing it well, it can become a strategic asset that makes the company more efficient and agile. That type of capability is normally not broadcasted."

"So, what's the downside?" asked Gerald. "Holistic enterprise architecture tends to be viewed as a hostile takeover by program managers and executives who have previously had a lot of independence in developing solutions for their own requirements" said Roberta. "Also, architecture brings a new language and planning processes, which like any type of change can be seen as threatening to those involved and therefore may be resisted. Strong executive sponsorship and ongoing stakeholder involvement can overcome much of this."

"Roberta, the organization-wide architecture approach seems to make sense, but I am not completely sold yet" said Rick. "Let's do a pilot project. I want you to work with Kate and Jose and bring me a plan and business case within two weeks to develop the part of an architecture for DMC that addresses their current capabilities and stated future requirements. We'll use this as the test for whether we want to go forward with an enterprise-wide architecture. Thanks, see you in two weeks."

Buzzword Bingo

"Hey guys, the DMC leadership team is thinking in silos and we have to transform our business to become world-class" says the CEO. "Spot-on" says the COO "We are neither agile or resilient, our service catalog is vaporware, and I need a leading-edge business intelligence system that draws from our data lake". "I'm with you" says the CFO, but the data lake has to live in the cloud and give me analytics on the fly, not to mention a clean audit at the drop of a hat." "Bingo" says the CEO, "One team – one fight." "You bet" says the COO "But I need the BI system asap or we won't launch the new product on time next quarter with enough oomph." "Roger that" says the CFO "But I can't pivot to this until next fiscal year because the Feds are crawling up my backside with the accounting audit." "We have to be more agile and we can mitigate this risk" says the CEO, "You two do a mind-meld before my podcast next week…. I want an integrated and aligned strategy for going forward… give it a snappy name like WELLCO and be sure to include our new CIO … a bunch of this is on her turf." "Already on it" says the CIO, "This isn't my first rodeo, I have a solution architecture in my hip pocket". "You are a Rockstar!" says the COO. "My new BFF!" says the CFO. "Wahoo! – see everyone next week" says the CEO on his way out the door to catch a bus to Abilene.

Author's Note

As mentioned in the Preface, I have added a "buzzword bingo" vignette at the end of each DMC case study scene to point out and poke fun at the sales and techno-hype that often accompanies and confuses many important discussions about how an organization can improve itself. I hope that highlighting this phenomenon will help to build authentic conversations and flexible organizations with healthy cultures that can change when needed.

Introduction

Will this be an *Architected* Enterprise?

Basically, I am asking whether an enterprise (an organization) is going to be structured and run based on an over-arching set of standards for how work is done and technology employed - or is the enterprise going to consist of a collection of un-coordinated processes, programs, and systems?

If the organization decides to develop and maintain a *holistic and authoritative* enterprise-wide architecture to serve as a primary reference for planning and decision-making, then leadership and management must embrace and implement this decision by properly resourcing the EA function and seeing that it is incorporated into how the organization is run.

A similar question is faced when an enterprise considers making a major, holistic commitment to a quality assurance (QA) approach that will be consistently applied throughout all lines of business. To date, many enterprises have decided to do this only to find that their effort fails when leadership does not continually back it, especially if that enterprise is not used to standard processes and metrics. We saw how beginning in the 1980's QA made a tremendous difference in the competitiveness of major automotive industry players – with Japanese manufacturers being the first to take the QA plunge. Now, QA is baked into the culture of auto manufacturers around the world – and the products of the surviving companies are much better as a result. Some companies could not adapt to higher quality standards and are no longer in business or lost major market shares. It should therefore be no surprise that many of these surviving companies began embracing EA during the past decade along the Same path that their QA initiatives were implemented. Other industry sectors are doing this too – insurance, retail, and aerospace to name a few. For some governments, including the U.S. Federal Government, it is a legal mandate that agencies develop and maintain an enterprise architecture.

The existence of an organization chart, documentation on processes and resources, or employees who hold architect titles do not necessarily mean that the enterprise is "architected." The litmus test for this is similar to the key question for QA adoption – does the enterprise consider the architecture to be an authoritative reference and are the associated methods baked into how things are done every day… in other words, is EA part of the culture? If not, then there is a paper architecture that may provide one-time or occasional value – but not a living architecture culture that contributes to high levels of agility and performance on an ongoing basis across all lines of business, business units, and program offices.

Let's say that an enterprise decides to not have an architecture, for whatever reason. The main problems that I see are that leadership will not have the ability to generate clear, consistent views of the overall enterprise on an ongoing basis, they won't be able to effectively compare business units, and the locus of power for planning and decision-making will be at the line-of-business, program, and/or system owner levels – with significant differences in how things are done and high potential for overlapping or duplicative functions and resources… waste and duplication.

Now let's say that an enterprise decides to have an EA and is prepared to maintain leadership backing and put resources behind it. This would allow the enterprise to avoid the problems just described and create a culture of ongoing controlled adaptation and optimization in response to changes in external and internal drivers. This sounds to me like a more of a recipe for success, especially in highly dynamic operating environments – but to take the test for your own enterprise – go ahead and ask "what would happen if we did not become an architected organization" and play out the costs and benefits, then ask "what if we do go with EA" and try to identify the cost, benefits, risks, and mitigation strategies.

On significant benefit for large private sector companies that decide to be an architected enterprise is that EA can play a key role in evaluating merger and acquisition (M&A) opportunities, whether that company is acquiring or being acquired. In that EA helps to rationalize and align strategic, business, and technology plans – and associated processes and resources – the architecture can clarify the capabilities, assets, and value of that company – potentially adding tens or hundreds of millions of dollars to the valuation and reducing risk in the post- merger/acquisition period as the resulting company makes dozens or hundreds of decisions about what business capabilities, systems, and groups should go forward, and which should be eliminated. A historical stumbling block to M&A efforts is a lack of understanding of the culture and capabilities of the companies being brought together – and EA can help with this throughout the M&A lifecycle – from initial due diligence research, to valuation negotiations, to post merger/acquisition streamlining and new product/service rollouts.

This book is for orgnizations that decide to take the plunge and embrace holistic enterprise architecture to better understand themselves and their potential, and to eliminate the battle of the best practices. In so doing, the organization will have a new source of unique competitive advantage.

Finally, it is worth recognizing that the term enterprise architecture is seen as a negative by many CXOs and managers because the practice of EA had not delivered as promised or they hear it from their peers. In my opinion, this is an unfair characterization, just as it would be to say that the field of quality assurance (QA) is without value or merit. Just as with any management or technology area of practice, the first decade is when the initial set of concepts and methods emerge and evolve. The most valuable survive, the others fade away, the Same is true with practitioners who are marginal and/or charge too much for their work. I would ask that you read this book with an open mind, not buying into negative hype – and remember that EA is trying to do something very difficult – making sense of large, complex organizations.

Chapter 1

Overview of Enterprise Architecture

The main concept of this chapter is that EA is a strategy and business driven activity that supports management planning and decision-making by providing coordinated views of an entire organization. These views encompass strategy, business, and technology, which is different from technology-driven, systems-level, process-centric or quality control approaches. Implementing a holistic architecture involves establishing a management program and utilizing a framework-based documentation method that guides analysis and design throughout the organization.

Key Term: *Enterprise*
An organization or sub-activity whose boundary is defined by commonly-held goals, processes, and resources. This includes whole organizations in the public, private, or non-profit sectors, part(s) of an organization such as business units, programs, and systems, or part(s) of multiple organizations such as consortia and supply chains.

Key Term: *Enterprise Architecture*
The analysis and documentation of an enterprise in its current and future states from an integrated strategy, business, and technology perspective.

Learning Objectives

- ➢ Understand the purpose of EA.
- ➢ Understand the elements of an EA management program.
- ➢ Understand the elements of an EA documentation method.
- ➢ Understand differences to other analysis / planning approaches.

Introduction

EA is a noun and a verb... it is a design model and a set of analysis/design activities. The purpose of creating an EA is to improve the performance of organizations by enabling them to see themselves in terms of a clear, comprehensive view of their strategic direction, business practices, information flows, and enabling technology resources. By developing current and future versions of this integrated view, an organization can manage the transition from current to future operating states.

Home Architecture Analogy: Building a house one room at a time without the blueprints for the whole house can lead to a poor result. It is analogous to developing organizations, business units, programs, and systems without an enterprise-wide architecture for reference, as duplication and inefficiency in resources, and a lack of overall agility can result.

The strategic use of resources is increasingly important to the success of public, private, and non-profit sector enterprises, including extended enterprises involving multiple internal and external participants (i.e., supply chains). How to get the most from business, technology, and human resources requires an enterprise to think in terms of enterprise-wide solutions, rather than individual systems and programs (Figure 1-1). Doing this requires a new approach to planning and systems development, an approach that has come to be known as Enterprise Architecture. The word "enterprise" implies a high-level, strategic view of the entire entity, while the word "architecture" implies a structured framework for the analysis, planning, and development of all resources in that entity. Adding the word "holistic" implies that the architecture covers all aspects of the organization, serving as a meta-context.

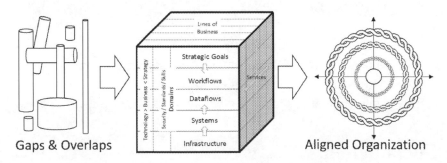

Figure 1-1: The Organizing Value of EA
(yes, this a "magic silver bullet" picture)

Regarding resources, one of the greatest challenges that many enterprises continue to face is how to identify the business and technology components of strategic initiatives. A big part of this challenge is that technology, information technology (IT) in particular, has historically not been viewed as a strategic asset. As such, planning activities often have focused on the development of individual technology solutions to meet specific organizational requirements.

The following "bumper sticker" captures what holistic EA is all about... documenting how an organization's strategic goals drive its business activities, and how various types of IT enable many of those activities.

$$EA = S \rightarrow B \leftarrow T$$

Strategy *drives* Business, *enabled* by Technology

Enterprise Architecture is a Noun and a Verb

Holistic EA is about analyzing and designing big virtual things... organizations and their capabilities, whereas traditional architecture is focused on designing physical things. There are many parallels in these two disciplines and there are several intersecting areas such as creating work environments that promote productivity and support agility.

EA is both a noun and a verb. The architecture of an enterprise is a noun... a thing... a collection of models and information. Creating an enterprise-wide architecture is a verb... an activity... that is performed using a standardized process that is sustained through an ongoing management program. EA provides a strategy and business-driven approach to policy, planning, decision-making, and resource development that is useful to executives, line managers, and support staff.

Governance is Oversight

To be effective, a holistic EA program must be part of a group of management practices that form an integrated governance structure, as shown in Figure 1-2. Governance is primarily about the oversight of planning and decision-making across the organization. The most important areas of oversight include strategic planning, enterprise architecture, capital investment planning, workforce planning, knowledge management, program management, risk management, and operations/security.

Holistic Enterprise Architecture as a Meta-Discipline

An enterprise-wide architecture should serve as an authoritative reference, source of standards for processes / resources, and provider of designs for future operating states. An EA is most effective when it is recognized as *the* architecture of the enterprise, covering *all* elements and aspects. Having a single source of reference is essential to avoiding waste and duplication in large, complex organizations. It also resolves the "battle of best practices" and competitions between sub-architectural domains, which can be problematic for organizations that are trying to become more effective.

Developing an enterprise-wide architecture using the methods in this book is a unique and valuable undertaking for organizations, in that the EA is holistic and serves as an umbrella or "meta-context" for all other management and technology best practices. The EA also creates views, analyses, and models of a current or future enterprise that helps people make better plans and decisions. EA extends beyond technology planning, by adding strategic planning as the primary driver of the enterprise, and business planning as the source of most program and resource requirements.

There is still a place for technology planning, which is to design systems, applications, networks, call centers, networks, and other capital resources (e.g. buildings, equipment) to meet the business requirements... which are the "heart" of the enterprise's activities... creating and delivering products and services that accomplish the strategic goals of the organization.

Regarding the "battle of the best practices", organizations in the public and private sectors are often faced with decisions about which practices to adopt as they pursue quality, agility, efficiency; manage risk, and adopt new technologies. There are dozens of best practices out there, and most of them were created in isolation – relative to the other best practices. I call this the "battle of the best practices" and it creates an expensive dilemma for organizations – what to adopt? Because the implementation and maintenance methods for many of the best practices are very resource intensive, and the scope is not all-inclusive, the organization is faced with the challenge of deciding which to adopt, how to do it, and what overlaps, contradictions, and gaps are produced from the resulting collection.

When EA is the architecture of an organization, it becomes the over-arching, highest level discipline and the authoritative reference for standards and practices. When EA is used in this way, organizations can make rational decisions about which best practices need to be adopted, what they will cover, and how they can relate to each other.

What is a "Complete" Architecture Approach?

For an EA approach to be considered *complete*, the six core elements shown in Figure 1-3 must be present and work synergistically together.

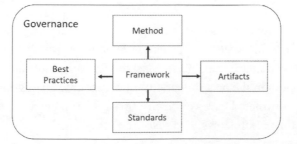

Figure 1-3: The Six Basic Elements of a "Complete" EA Approach

The first core element is <u>Governance</u> which identifies the planning, decision-making, and oversight processes and groups that will determine how the EA is developed and maintained, accomplished as part of an organization's overall governance.

The second core element is <u>Method</u> which are specific steps to establish and maintain an EA program, via the selected approach.

The third core element is <u>Framework</u> which identifies the scope of the overall architecture and the type and relationship of the various sub-architecture levels and threads. Not all frameworks allow for sub-domains or are able to integrate strategy, business, and technology planning.

The fourth core element is <u>Artifacts</u> which identifies the types and methods of documentation to be used in each sub-architecture area, including strategic analyses, business plans, internal controls, security controls, and models of workflow, databases, systems, and networks. This core element also includes the online repository where artifacts are stored.

The fifth core element is <u>Standards</u> which identify business and technology standards for the enterprise in each domain, segment, and component of the EA. This includes recognized international, national, local, and industry standards as well as enterprise-specific standards.

The sixth core element is <u>Associated Best Practices</u> which are proven ways to implement parts of the overall architecture or sub-architectures, in context of the over-arching EA.

Enterprise Architecture Activities

Enterprise Architecture is both a noun and a verb: a thing and an activity. EA work is accomplished through a *management program* and an *analysis/design method* that are scalable… consistently repeatable at various levels of scope. Together, the program and method provide an ongoing capability and useful coordinated views of an enterprise's strategic direction, business services, information flows, and resource utilization.

As a **management program**, EA provides:

- ➢ Strategic Alignment: Connects goals, activities, and resources
- ➢ Standardized Policy: Resource governance and implementation
- ➢ Decision Support: Financial control and configuration management
- ➢ Resource Oversight: Lifecycle approach to development/ management

As an **analysis/design method**, EA provides:

- ➢ Holistic Approach: The framework, analysis/design method, and artifact set
- ➢ Current Views: Views of as-is strategies, processes, and resources
- ➢ Future Views: Views of to-be strategies, processes, and resources
- ➢ Management Plan: A plan to move from the current to the future architecture

Architecture as a Management Program

EA an ongoing management program that provides a strategic, integrated approach to capability and resource planning / decision-making. An EA program is part of an overall governance process that determines resource alignment, develops standardized policy, enhances decision support, and guides development activities. EA can help to identify gaps in the capabilities of business activities and supporting IT services and systems.

Standardized Policy

EA supports the implementation of standardized policy to align strategic goals, business processes and enabling IT solutions. EA does this by:

- Identifying strategic and operational requirements
- Determining the strategic alignment of activities and resources
- Developing enterprise-wide business and technology resources
- Prioritizing the funding of programs and projects
- Overseeing the management of programs and projects

- Identifying performance metrics for programs and projects
- Identifying and enforcing standards and configuration management

Policy documents include those which can be categorized as general guidance such as high-level directives and memos; specific program guidance such as plans and manuals; and detailed process guidance such as standard operating procedures. By using these hierarchical categories of documents, succinct and meaningful policy is established. It does so in a way that no single policy document is too long and therefore not too burdensome to read. It is also important to understand how the various areas of policy are inter-related so that program implementation across the enterprise is coordinated.

Decision Support

EA provides support for IT resource decision-making at the executive, management, and staff levels of the enterprise. At the executive level, the architecture provides visibility for large IT initiatives and supports the determination of strategic alignment. At the management level, the architecture supports design and configuration management decisions, as well as the alignment of IT initiatives with technical standards for voice, data, video, and security. At the staff level, the architecture supports decisions regarding the full lifecycle of IT resources and services.

Resource Oversight

EA supports standardized approaches for overseeing the development of capabilities and optimizing supporting resources. Depending on the scope of the resources involved and the available timeframe for development, various system development lifecycle methods can be used to reduce the risk that cost, schedule, or performance parameters may not be met. EA further supports standardized, proven approaches to project management that promote the comprehensive and effective oversight of ongoing programs and new development projects. Finally, EA supports the use of a standardized process for selecting and evaluating investment in IT resources from a business and financial perspective.

Architecture as an Analysis and Design Method

References to enterprise-level architecture practices began to emerge in the late 1980's in various management and academic literatures, with an early focus on technical or systems architectures and schemas for organizing information. The concept of holistic enterprise architecture followed this and included views of strategic goals, business services, information flows, systems and applications, networks, and the supporting infrastructure as well as "threads" that pervade every level: standards, security, and skills. EA analysis and design projects are accomplished through the following three general steps :

1. Understand what the organization has now. (*Current Architecture*)
2. Determine what the organization wants. (*Future Architecture*)
3. Identify the migration sequence. (*Transition Roadmap*)

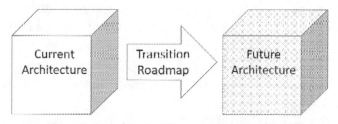

Figure 1-4: Basic Steps of EA Projects

The Architecture Framework.

The EA framework identifies the scope of the architecture to be developed and establishes relationships between sub-architecture areas, also called "domains". The framework's scope is reflected through its geometric design and the areas that are identified for documentation. The framework creates an abstracted (model) set of "views" of an enterprise through the way that it collects and organizes architecture information. An example that will be used throughout the book is the framework that is illustrated in Figure 1-5, which has a cubic shape whose six faces relate to fundamental aspects of the organization (see Chapter 5 for more details).

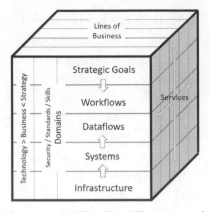

Figure 1-5: The EA6 Framework

Known as the EA6 "Cube" Framework, the levels of this example framework are hierarchical so that the different sub-architectures (that describe distinct functional areas) can be logically related to each other. This is done by positioning high-level strategic goals/initiatives at the top, business products/services and data/information flows in the middle and supporting systems/applications and technology/infrastructure at the bottom. In this way alignment can be also be shown between strategy, information, and technology, which aids planning and decision-making.

To lower risk and promote efficient, phased implementation methods, the EA framework is divided into segments of distinct activity, referred to as *Lines of Business* (LoBs). For example, each LoB has a complete sub-architecture that includes all five hierarchical levels of the framework. The LoB therefore can in some ways stand alone architecturally within the enterprise except that duplication in data, application, and network functions would occur if each LoB were truly independent. An architecture encompassing all five framework levels that is focused on one or more LoBs can be referred to as a *segment* of the overall EA.

Architecture Components

EA components are *changeable* goals, processes, standards, and resources that may extend enterprise-wide or be contained within a specific line of business or segment. Examples of components include strategic goals and initiatives; business products and services; information flows, knowledge warehouses, and data objects; information systems, software applications, enterprise resource programs, and web sites; voice, data, and video networks; and supporting infrastructure including buildings, server rooms, wiring runs/closets, and capital equipment. Figure 1-6 below provides examples of *vertical* and *crosscutting* EA components at each level.

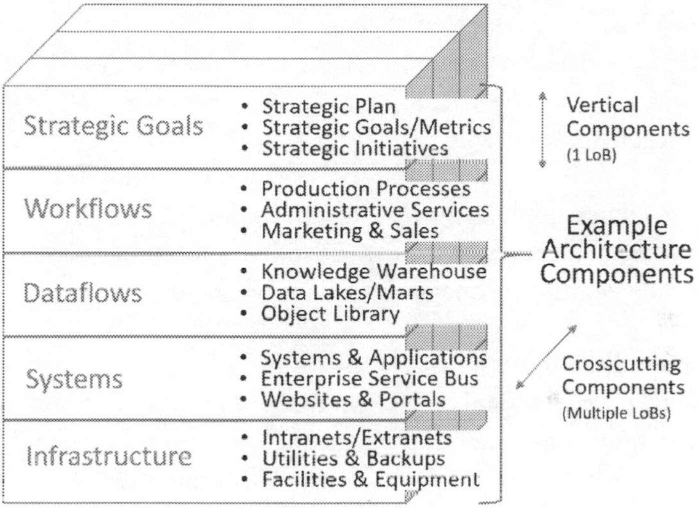

Figure 1-6: Examples of EA Components

Key Term: *Vertical Component*
A vertical component is a changeable goal, process, program, or resource (equipment, systems, data, etc.) that serves one line of business.

Key Term: *Horizontal Component*
A horizontal (or crosscutting) component is a changeable goal, process, program, or resource that serves several lines of business. Examples include email and administrative support systems that serve the whole enterprise.

Current Architecture

The current architecture contains those EA components that currently exist within the enterprise at each level of the framework. This is sometimes referred to as the "as-is" view. The current view of the architecture serves to create a 'baseline' inventory of current resources and activities that is documented in a consistent way with the future view of the architecture so that analysts can see gaps in performance between future plans and the current capabilities. Having an accurate and comprehensive current view of EA components is an important reference for project planning, asset management, and investment decision-making. The current view of the architecture is composed of 'artifacts' (documents, diagrams, data, spreadsheets, charts, etc.) at each level of the framework, which are archived in an on-line repository to make them useable by stakeholders.

Future Architecture

The future architecture documents the new/modified components that are needed by the enterprise to close an existing performance gap or support a new strategic initiative, operational requirement, or technology solution.

As is shown in Figure 1-7, the future architecture is driven at both the strategic and tactical levels in three ways: new directions and goals; changing business priorities; and emerging technologies. The EA cannot reflect these changes in the future architecture unless the enterprise's leadership team provides the changes in strategic direction and goals; unless the line of business managers and program managers provide the changes in business processes and priorities that are needed to accomplish the new goals; and unless the support/delivery staff identifies viable technology and staffing solutions to meet the new business requirements.

Figure 1-7: Drivers of Architectural Change

The future architecture should cover planned changes to architecture components in the near term (tactical changes in the next 1-2 years), as well as changes to EA components that are a result of the implementation of long-term operating scenarios that look 3-10 years into the future. These scenarios incorporate different internal and external drivers and can help to identify needed changes in processes, resources, or technology that translate to future planning assumptions, which in turn drive the planning for new components. An example future scenario and additional details on the future architecture are provided in Chapter 8.

Architecture Transition Roadmap

The Architecture Transition Roadmap (Roadmap) summarizes the EA approach and provides descriptions of current and future views of the architecture, as well as a sequencing plan for managing the transition to the future business and technology operating environment. The Roadmap is a living document that is essential to realizing the benefits of the EA as a management program. How the enterprise is going to continually move from the current architecture to the future architecture is a significant planning and management challenge, especially when IT resources supporting key business functions are being replaced or upgraded. Chapter 9 provides additional details on the development of the Roadmap.

Architecture Threads

EA documentation includes 'threads' of common activity that are present in all levels of the framework. These threads include IT-related security, standards, and skill methods and considerations.

Security. Security is most effective when it is an integral part of the EA management program and documentation methodology. A comprehensive IT Security Program has several focal areas including information, personnel, operations, and facilities. To be effective, IT security must work across all levels of the EA framework and within all the components. Chapter 11 provides additional details.

Standards. One of the most important functions of the holistic architecture is to provide technology-related standards at all levels of the framework. The architecture standards for each domain and component draw on accepted international, national, and industry standards, and when possible, promote the use of non-proprietary solutions. This enhances the integration of EA components, as well as better supporting the switch-out of components when needed.

Skills. Perhaps the greatest resource that an enterprise has is people. It is therefore important to ensure that staffing, skill, and training requirements are identified for business unit and support service activities at each level of the architecture framework, and appropriate solutions are reflected in the current and future architectures.

Domain, Reference, Segment, Solution Architectures

These are sub-sets of the holistic enterprise architecture, with examples:

- Domain Architecture: a *level of the framework* (system, data, network).
- Reference Architecture: promotes a *standard method* (inventory control).
- Segment Architecture: covers a *particular group or area* (finance, HR).
- Solution Architecture: meets a *particular need* (supply chain integration).

The EA Repository

Providing easy access to EA documentation is essential for use in planning and decision-making. This can be accomplished through the establishment of an on-line repository to archive the documentation of architeecture components in the various area of the EA framework. The repository is essentially a website and database that stores information and provides links to software tools and other EA program resources. Figure 1-8 below provides an example of how a EA repository might be designed. This example is called *Living Enterprise* and it is designed to support documentation that is organized through the use of the EA6 Framework. Chapter 12 provides details on the design and function of an EA repository.

Current Architecture	EA Program	EA Standards	EA Tutorial	Site Map	Search

Enterprise Architecture Repository

Future Architecture						
Transition Plan	Goals & Initiatives	Products & Services	Data & Information	Systems & Apps	Networks & Infra.	Security Solutions
			Domains			
High Level View	Strategic Plan	Business Plan	Knowledge Warehouse	Business Systems	Wide-Area Network	Security Program
Mid Level View	Goals & Initiatives	Business Processes	Data/Info Flows	Support Systems	Local Area Network	System Approvals
Detailed View	Key Perf. Measures	Investment Portfolio	Data Dictionary	Application Inventory	Buildings & Equip.	System Controls

Figure 1-8: Example EA Repository Design – Living Enterprise

Fitting the Architecture Elements Together

While the basic elements of EA analysis and design provide holistic and detailed descriptions of the current and future architecture in all areas of the underlying framework, it is important to also be able to articulate these relationships in discussions and presentations with executives, managers, support staff, and other stakeholders. Being able to understand and relate how the architecture fits together is essential to being able to use the architecture in planning and decision-making throughout the enterprise. This communication is supported through two EA program resources: the Architecture Transition Roadmap and the artifact (model) repository. As was mentioned in the previous section, this Roadmap is a living document that is periodically updated so that it remains relevant as the ongoing primary reference for describing where the current and future architectures are at. The architecture repository should be the authoritative on-line archive for architecture documentation for the EA Program and projects.

Communicating with Stakeholders

The following is an example of how to communicate about holistic architecture with stakeholders. In this example, some questions are presented about how to apply an EA framework to an enterprise, which subsequent chapters of the book answer. These are the types of questions that should be answered in the first few sessions of architecture project and documentation meetings in order to promote an understanding of how the framework and documentation can reflect the enterprise. In the following example of how to talk about EA, the five levels and three threads of the framework are used for illustration. Notice how the questions build in a way that reflects the hierarchical relationships between the levels of the framework.

Provide context by saying that each area of the architecture framework represents a functional area of the enterprise. This framework can be used in a top-down, bottom- up, or single-component manner. To begin to use the framework in a top down-manner, a series of questions at each level should be asked in order to determine how information about the enterprise will fit within that level of the framework. This is different from asking requirements questions when doing a detailed analysis/design project.

The first questions to ask will relate to the top-most (hierarchical) domain: the "Strategic Goals and Initiatives" level of the framework. The questions are: (1) for what purpose does the enterprise generally exist (usually expressed in the mission statement) and (2) what kind of organization does the enterprise generally intend to be (often given in the vision statement)? What are the primary goals (strategic goals) of the enterprise? What then are the strategic initiatives (ongoing programs or new projects) that will enable the enterprise to achieve those goals? When will the enterprise know that it has successfully reached these strategic goals or is making progress toward these goals (outcome measures)? Finally, for this level of the framework, what are the standards, skills, and security controls that are needed?

The second set of questions relate to the "Business Products and Services" level of the framework, and it is important to first ask what are the ongoing activity areas (lines of business) that the enterprise must engage in to support and enable the accomplishment of both strategic initiatives and normal 'maintenance/housekeeping' functions? What then are the specific activities in each line of business (business services)? What are the products that are delivered in each line of business? How do we measure the effectiveness and efficiency of the line of business processes (input/output measures) as well as their contribution to strategic goals (outcome measures)? Do any of these business services or manufacturing processes need to be reengineered before they are made to be part of the future architecture? What are the standards, skills, and security controls that will be needed at the business level of the framework?

The third set of questions relate to the "Data and Information" level of the framework. When the lines of business and specific business service/products have been identified, it is important to ask what are the flows of information that will be required within and between activity areas in order to make them successful? How can these flows of information be harmonized, standardized, and protected to promote sharing that is efficient, accurate, and secure? How will the data underlying the information flows be formatted, generated, shared, and stored? How will data become useable information? What are the standards, skills, and security controls that will be needed at the datalevel of the framework?

The fourth set of questions relate to "Systems and Applications" level of the framework and it is important to ask which IT and other business systems and applications will be needed to generate, share, and store the data, information, and knowledge that the business services need? How can multiple types of IT systems, services, applications, databases, and web sites be made to work together where needed? How can configuration management help to create a cost-effective and operationally efficient 'Common Operating Environment' for systems and applications? What are the standards, skills, and security controls that will be needed at the systems and applications level of the framework?

The fifth set of questions relate to the 'Network and Infrastructure' level of the framework and it is important to ask what types of voice, data, and video networks or computing/telecom clouds will be required to host the IT systems/applications and to transport associate, data, images, and conversations, as well as what type of infrastructure is needed to support the networks (e.g. buildings, server rooms, other equipment). How can these networks be integrated to create a cost- effective and operationally efficient hosting and transport environment? Will these networks and clouds extend beyond the enterprise? What are the standards, skill, and security issues.at this level? What are the physical space and utility support requirements for these infrastructure resources? What are the standards, skills, and security controls that will be needed at the networks and infrastructure level of the framework?

Summary of Concepts

A program or systems-level perspective is not enough for the management and planning of technology and other resources across enterprises with significant size and complexity. EA is the one discipline that looks at systems holistically as well as provides a strategy and business context. EA was described as both a management process and an analysis and design method that helps enterprises with business and technology planning, resource management, and decision- making. The purposes of an EA management program were described: strategic alignment, standardized policy, decision support, and resource development. The six basic elements of an EA analysis and design method were presented: the documentation framework, components, current views, future views, an Architecture Transition Roadmap, and multi-level threads that include security, standards, and workforce planning. An example of how to communicate the various areas of the EA framework was also provided. The next several chapters provide additional details about the importance of organizational culture in holistic EA and its value to large, complex organizations, what the risks of doing EA are, and how to ensure that this enterprise-level architecture is driven by strategic goals and business requirements.

Chapter 1 Questions and Exercises

1. What are some of the differences between holistic enterprise architecture (EA) and a systems-level planning approach?
2. Why is EA described as both a management program and an analysis and design method?
3. What are the four elements of an EA management program and the six elements of an EA analysis and design method?
4. What are some of the EA components and documentation artifacts that would be included in current and future views at each framework level?
5. Can EA be used by all types of enterprises? If so, why?
6. How does an EA repository support the implementation methodology?
7. Choose a real-world large-sized enterprise and determine:
   a. Is information technology seen as a strategic asset?
   b. Does an enterprise architecture program exist?
   c. Are there gaps in business/technology performance that an enterprise architecture program could help identify and correct?

Chapter 2

How Culture Affects Architecture

Chapter Overview

It is important for enterprise architects to understand how an organization's culture affects its structure and function. Enterprises are types of social organizations and as such, the concepts of organizational theory presented in this chapter are applicable to the practice of holistic enterprise architecture.

Key Term: *Culture*
The beliefs, customs, values, structure, normative rules, and material traits of a social organization. Culture is evident in many aspects of how an organization functions.

Key Term: *Stakeholder*
Everyone who is or will be affected by a policy, program, project, activity, or resource. Stakeholders for the EA program includes executive sponsors, architects, program managers, users, and support staff.

Learning Objectives

> - Understand the cultural aspects of an enterprise
> - Understand the similarities and differences between an organization and an enterprise
> - Become familiar with models of organizations and enterprises
> - Be able to tie cultural aspects of an enterprise to architecture
> - Understand why architecture makes people uncomfortable.

Introduction

Enterprise architecture is as much about people and social interaction as it is about processes and resource utilization. Understanding each of these aspects of an enterprise is essential to the development of accurate views of the current architecture and options for the future.

> *Home Architecture Analogy:* A traditional architect needs to understand the characteristics and desires of the owners to produce an effective design for their new or remodeled home. How many people there are, their ages, work, leisure, entertaining, and storage needs are all factors to be considered.

Insight into the "people aspect" of enterprises is also important to the development of policy, standards, and transition plans that will be accepted by the organization. Change involves moving from what is familiar to something unfamiliar, which is uncomfortable and/or threatening to many people. Therefore, there may be resistance to initiatives that promote major changes in processes and resources throughout the enterprise.

Discussion

Organizations Exist for a Reason

An organization is a *collection of people and things, brought together to pursue common goals.* Examples of these goals are social companionship, providing/consuming products and services, making money, staying healthy, and pursuing a hobby. Each organization is formed and sustained through the verbal and/or written agreement of its members. This can be as informal as email or phone chats with friends to agree to regularly meet for a neighborhood book club, or as formal as military enlistment contracts and employment contracts with a company, university, hospital, government agency, or non-profit group. Usually, part of this agreement is an understanding of why the organization exists, its values, and your role.

The boundary of the organization is influenced by its purpose, goals, and activities. The purpose of the organization is usually written in a government law, an incorporation application, a business license, a mission statement, or "About Us" section of the organization's homepage.

I refer to these statements of existence and purpose as a "Charter." To understand an organization's culture, it is important for holistic enterprise architects to find and understand the original and current Charter documents.

People Are Often Self-Interested

People are biological creatures that have a built-in drive to survive and be social... it's part of our genetic makeup and controls our decision-making. Psychologist Abraham Maslow proposed a theory of human motivation in 1943 that included the famous "hierarchy of needs." This theory and model indicate that people are primarily driven to

survive their immediate surroundings, then to thrive among the group, and then go beyond.[2]

Basic survival concerns cause people to often think about themselves first. This is not to say that people cannot be altruistic, placing the welfare of others before themselves, but the research of Maslow and other social scientists indicate that people must feel safe and accepted before wanting to help others.

A person's survival needs start with that individual, but in the absence of physiological threat, the needs rapidly move to the level of the group. People can feel threatened in an organization when they perceive that they are not accepted or lose control. Examples include unpleasant surprises, not getting invited to meetings, not having a say in decisions, changes in work duties, and not getting properly rewarded. This me-first attitude is built-in, and people normally can't move to a level of unselfish sharing until they feel secure themselves. This is important for enterprise architects to understand – people crave consistency and control, they do not like surprises. Promoting a holistic architecture that is going to change many aspects of an organization can be very threatening to the people in that organization. More on this later.

Academic Influences on Enterprise Architecture

Developing an enterprise-wide architecture involves an evaluation and depiction of people, processes, and resources. Some of the areas of practice and theory that have influenced holistic architecture include business administration, public administration, operations research, sociology, organizational theory, management theory, information science, and computer science. Understanding the mission, goals, and culture of an enterprise is as important to implementing holitic architecture as is the selection of analytic methods and documentation techniques. The EA approach described in this book is based on theories of how social organizations are structured and how systems and activities function within enterprises. Figure 2-2 below shows the academic fields and areas of theory/practice that influence holistic EA.

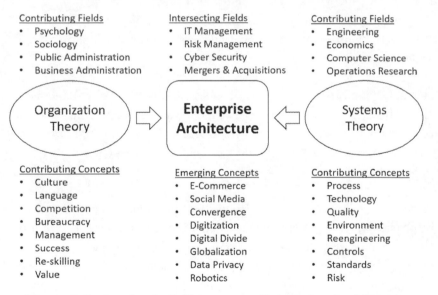

Contributing Fields
- Psychology
- Sociology
- Public Administration
- Business Administration

Intersecting Fields
- IT Management
- Risk Management
- Cyber Security
- Mergers & Acquisitions

Contributing Fields
- Engineering
- Economics
- Computer Science
- Operations Research

Organization Theory ⇒ **Enterprise Architecture** ⇐ Systems Theory

Contributing Concepts
- Culture
- Language
- Competition
- Bureaucracy
- Management
- Success
- Re-skilling
- Value

Emerging Concepts
- E-Commerce
- Social Media
- Convergence
- Digitization
- Digital Divide
- Globalization
- Data Privacy
- Robotics

Contributing Concepts
- Process
- Technology
- Quality
- Environment
- Reengineering
- Controls
- Standards
- Risk

Figure 2-2: Academic Influences on Enterprise Architecture

Throughout the book, there are many references to organizations instead of enterprises. This is because the word enterprise is used to indicate that a particular topic extends organization-wide. Accordingly, the terms are usually interchangeable, the exception being when enterprise refers to a discrete part of an organization or linked parts of several organizations. The concepts and methods on structure and function come from established organizational theory. Organizations are complex social systems, which regardless of mission, share many similarities in structure and functions.

The Structure of Enterprises (Organizations)

Sociologists were studying commonalities in organizational structure and function during the 1950s – 1970s starting with the work of Talcott Parsons who identified three levels of structure (institutional, managerical, and technical), which was extended other noted theorists including Harold Leavitt, Henry Minzberg, and Jay Galbraith as shown in Figure 2-3 below.

General models of factors affecting organizational structure that included technology began appearing in the 1960's, with the most prominent being the "Leavitt Diamond", which in 1965 implied that a change in any of the four primary elements will have an effect on the others and that the interation of all of the elements is what underlies organizational success.

Jay Galbraith was an organizational theorist who in 1973 presented a star-shaped model of how organizations function. He defined organizational design as "the alignment of the strategy of the business with process, rewards, and (people). An organization's design usually entails making trade-offs of one set of structural benefits against another.[3]

Management theorist Henry Mintzberg developed a model of organizational structure in 1979 that had six "basic parts": an ideology, a strategic apex, a technostructure, a support staff, middle "line" management, and the operating core (working base).[4] He also identified organizational types: simple, divisional, machine bureaucracy, professional bureaucracy, and innovative adhocracy.

Parsons/Thompson Levels

As mentioned, one of the first models of general organizational structure is a three-level view envisioned by sociologist Talcott Parsons in the 1950's and refined by sociologist James Thompson in the 1960's.[5] Parsons' research identified three general levels that are common to most social organizations (technical, managerial, and institutional), based on the observation that different types of activities occur at each level. Thompson built on Parsons' ideas by further identifying activity types occuring at each level.[6]

The geometry of the Parson/Thompson Model (PTM) has been adapted by the author to resemble a series of concentric circles. This may provide a more useful image for depicting a social organization that interacts with its environment via the model's Institutional Level, facilitates internal resources via the Managerial Level, and protects a "core" of essential processes and resources at the Technical Level. Figure 2-4 below shows this spherical version of the PTM, which also is useful showing how a holistic architecture framework can document organizational functions.

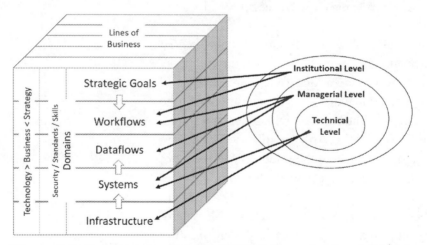

Figure 2-4: Relating the Cube and PTM Organizational Models

The value of the Parsons/Thompson Model is its use as an authoritative reference for developing architectural views of structure and process for an organization. Regardless of the model's wide acceptance in academia, the question of whether this fifty year old view would be relevant and useful to understanding the structure of current public and private sector organizations is answered by observing that many large and medium sized corporations and government agencies continue to be hierarchical, rule- based, and goal-oriented. These were some of the primary characteristics of the "rational" organization that Parsons and Thompson originally studied. Evidence of this still being a valid model is also seen in the rational nature of organizational charts, mission statements, strategic plans, operational plans, and business services of these types of organizations.

Figure 2-5 below provides the actual language tat Parsons and Thompson used to describe the activities at each level of the organization.

Organizational Level	Structure *Parson's* *Purpose of each Level*	Function *Thompson's* *Activities of the Level*
Institutional	Where the organization establishes rules and relates to the larger society as it derives legitimization, meaning, and higher-level support, thus making possible the implementation of organizational goals.	The organization is very open to the environment in order to determine its domain, establish boundaries, and secure legitimacy.
Managerial	Where mediation between the organization and the immediate task environment occurs, where the organization's internal affairs are administered, and where the organization's products are consumed and resources supplied.	A dynamic of mediation occurs where less formalized and more political activities occur.
Technical	Where the actual "product" of an organization is processed.	The organization is "rational" as it carries on production (input/output) functions and tries to seal off those functions from the outside to protect them from external uncertainties as much as possible.

Figure 2-5: Parson/Thompson Model of Enterprises

There are new types of organizations that have emerged due to technology-based changes in how people communicate and work. Global telecommunications and the Internet have made location a largely irrelevant factor in terms of where some types of work are being done (e.g., knowledge work and on-line services). Two primary changes related to organizational structure and function have resulted. First, more organizations are becoming regional or global in nature, and are relying on remote sub-groups to do significant amounts of the work. Second, more people are becoming self-employed knowledge workers who contract their services remotely to various enterprises depending on their interest, skills, and availability. Examples include people who process digitized EAlth care forms, software developers, web site developers, distance learning instructors, financial traders, insurance salespeople, and telemarketers. Because these organizations can get certain functions accomplished remotely, their structure may become less hierarchical and more collaborative.

While it can be argued that these new networked organizations exhibit many of the structural and functional characteristics found in the Parsons/ Thompson Model, there are enough differences to merit discussion of a variation of that model which may better describe how organizations operate in a more global on-line business environment.

The Organizational Network Model

New types of organizations and enterprises are appearing which are based on cooperative networks of local and remote individual workers and semi- autonomous teams who carry out key functions. In these enterprises, greater cost efficiency and more mission flexibility are achieved by removing layers of management that are not needed in a decentralized operating mode. These teams are actually sub-groups that have their own management level and technical level with core processes, and therefore will still exhibit some of the characteristics of the Parsons/Thompson Model. The difference presented here is that the organization/enterprise's structure is based on these teams and remote workers, whose goals and functions may change depending on internal and external influences.

Called the Organizational Network Model (ONM), an *Executive Team* sets policy and goals, approves resources, and evaluates results, while semi- autonomous *Functional Teams* and *Independent Workers* manage ongoing programs/lines of business, new development projects, and team-specific resources. The Functional Teams and Independent Workers receive policy, goals, and general direction from the Executive Team, yet carry out organizational functions in an independent and/or cooperative manner, depending on the goal(s). Workers can be located at organizational sites (within the boundary), can be teleworking independently, or be with remotely located functional teams. Figure 2-6 provides an illustration of the ONM.

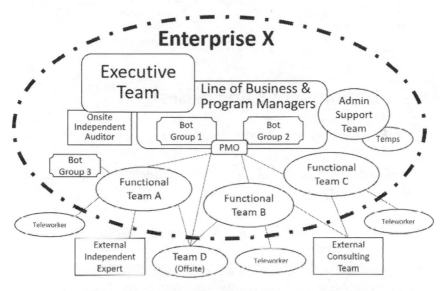

Figure 2-6: Organizational Network Model

Being less hierarchical, these "flatter" and more flexible ONM organizations can respond to changing requirements more quickly by creating, modifying, or eliminating Functional Teams and/or adjusting the number and type of Independent Workers and software or hardware robots (Bots) that can do repetitive tasks and engage in recursive or extended machine learning (called Robotic Process Automation – RPA). These types of ONM organizations and enterprises can also exist as extended supply chains or networks of teams from inside and outside the traditional organizational boundary. This includes trusted business partners and independent consultants who can share sensitive information and key resources with the enterprise as part of the activities of the Executive Core, Functional Teams, Independent Workers, and Bots. Figure 2-7 shows how ONM Functional Teams relate to an enterprise's Lines of Business.

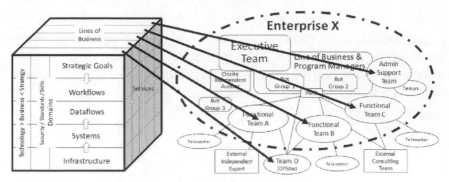

Figure 2-7: Relating Functional Teams to EA Lines of Business

Organizations and Enterprises

Organizations and enterprises are similar in that they are both types of social entities that have a culture, a formal and informal structure, goals, activities, and resources. The difference is that an enterprise can be defined as a subset of an organization or can involve multiple organizations.

Why isn't this book's title *An Introduction to **Organizational** Architecture*? Because that would largely limit the subject to architectures that encompass an entire organization, and while those architectures are important, a more versatile concept is an enterprise, which can cover part of the organization, all of the organization, or parts of multiple organizations.

Enterprises are normally made up of *vertical, horizontal,* and *extended* components. Vertical components (also known as *lines of business* or *segments*) are activity areas that are particular to one line of business (e.g., research and development). Horizontal components (also known as *crosscutting enterprises*) are more general areas of activity that serve multiple lines of business. Extended components comprise more than one organization (e.g., extranets and supply chains).

EA views of vertical components are complete stand-alone architectures in that they contain documentation from all levels of the framework. These types of vertical components are also known as "segments." When vertical segments are documented using the Same framework, they can be aggregated into a larger architecture picture that may cover several or all lines of business. This may be a preferable way to develop the first version of an enterprise's architecture as it allows them to undertake a more manageable amount of work at less initial cost (compared to attempting to do the architecture for the entire enterprise all at once, without prior experience). This is called a "segmented approach" to documenting the overall EA. The segmented approach is also useful in large and/or decentralized enterprises where parts of the architecture may need to be developed and maintained by several different groups.

Understanding Culture

Understanding the culture of an organization is essential to developing realistic views of how strategic goals come and go, how processes function, and how resources are used. Every organization is different, as are the vertical, horizontal, and/or extended components. This is due to the culture of an organization being a product of the values, beliefs, habits, and preferences of many people and many groups. The graphic to the right shows four different types of organizational culture (see Cameron, 2011).[7]

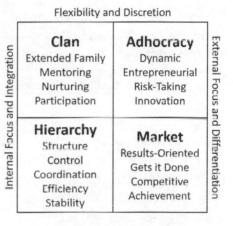

Figure 2-8. Culture Types

Managing Change

Changes within the enterprise will happen regardless of the presence of an EA program, however they will happen in a more disjointed or completely independent manner without a holistic architecture. The effect of the EA program is to coordinate change such that it is much more driven by new strategies and business requirements, and less by new technologies.

People can be resistant to changes in their environment, whether it is at home or the workplace. If the EA program promotes changes in the enterprise, and if people are often resistant to any type of change when they do not have some level of control, then the EA program will likely be resisted by stakeholders unless something is done to increase their level of control. This resistance can be reduced by:

- Involving stakeholders in the architecture program.
- Regularly communicating architecture activities to stakeholders.
- Allowing for stakeholder input to planning and decision-making.
- Managing stakeholder expectations as to what the EA program can do.
- Communicate with management and staff on how work processes and individual assignments will change, including new skills training.

Key Term: *Change Management*
The process of setting expectations and involving stakeholders in how a process or activity will be changed, so that the stakeholders have some control over the change and therefore may be more accepting of the change.

Those who are affected by the architecture program are called "stakeholders" and they are the ones most likely to resist the program and/or changes that are perceived to be the product of the architecture program. Therefore, one of the things that the architecture program manager needs to ensure is that there is stakeholder involvement in as many aspects as possible. This includes governance and oversight activities, the selection of a framework and methodology, participation in and reviews of documentation activities, and participation in the development of and updates to the Architecture Transition Roadmap.

Another aspect of managing change that is caused by the architecture program's projects is regular and effective communication on program activities with all stakeholders. This includes formal documents such as an Architecture Communication Plan, the Architecture Transition Roadmap, and email notices regarding the periodic update of the current and future views. It also includes informal communication on an ongoing basis with all stakeholders to ensure that their participation and support is maintained.

The details of EA program governance are discussed in Chapter 4. It is important to provide "a place at the table" for as many different types of stakeholders as can be accommodated. This increases buy-in for architecture policy, standards, and decision-making, as well as increasing the success chances for implementing big changes called for in the future architecture.

Managing stakeholder expectations is yet another way to promote the success of the architecture program and help stakeholders deal with change. Expectation management is about identifying realistic outputs and outcomes. It can be accomplished by collaboratively assessing the capability of the architecture program to document current and future architectures, the timeframe and resources that will take, and the obstacles to acceptance by stakeholders. This is an ongoing aspect of EA.

Globalization Drives Change

Ongoing advances in the speed of physical transportation and data transmission throughout the world make it possible to be anywhere in the world within one day and to interact with most anyone in real-time (voice, data, and/or video). The culture of organizations is increasingly affected by this "globalization" phenomenon as people's norms, ideas, and beliefs are continually brought into close contact. The Internet of Things (IoT) is driving change at an unprecedented rate.

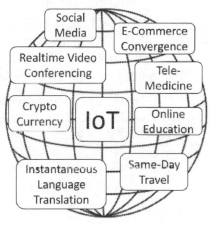

Summary of Concepts

This chapter described how enterprises are types of social organizations and discussed the importance of understanding the structure and culture of the enterprise that a holistic architecture is documenting. While it is also important to understand the enterprise's processes and supporting technologies, it is the people of the enterprise who make plans and decisions about strategic direction, business activities, and resource utilization. The chapter also covered influences on the field of holistic architecture and presented several models of organizations that can assist in the development of current and future views. Finally, the importance of managing change locally and globally was discussed, and the reality that EA activities may be resisted by stakeholders who feel a loss of control.

Chapter 2 Questions and Exercises

1. Why is it important to understand the "people side" of architecture?
2. Compare and contrast an organization and an enterprise.
3. What are some of the academic fields that influence the field of EA?
4. Describe the purpose of each level of the Parsons/Thompson Model.
5. How is the Organization Network Model different from the Parsons/ Thompson Model of organizations?
6. Who are stakeholders in EA and what might they want to resist?
7. What are four ways to manage change with stakeholders?
8. Select a large or mid-size enterprise and describe the following:
   a. What structural and cultural aspects should be captured by EA?
   b. Who are the potential stakeholders in an EA program?
   c. What strategies for gaining stakeholder buy-in could be used?

Case Study:
Danforth Manufacturing Company
Scene 2: Considering an EA Program

Rick Danforth, the President and CEO of DMC, has called a follow-on meeting of the Executive Committee to review several recent capital investment requests and the suggestion to use an enterprise architecture approach to evaluate these requests and coordinate potential implementation projects. COO Kate Jarvis has requested a new custom Sales and Inventory Tracking System (SITS), and CFO Jose Cruz, has requested a new cost accounting system that is part of a commercial software package. Also invited to the meeting is CIO Roberta Washington, who joined the company one month ago, and who is giving a briefing on how enterprise architecture can help in this review.

"Good morning everyone" said Rick. "I'm eager to hear what you have to say about the architecture initiative. Roberta, why don't you lead off, and then let's hear from Kate and Jose."

"Thank you, Rick" said Roberta as he handed out an 8-page document entitled *DMC Enterprise Architecture Plan – Financial and Production Segments*. "Kate, Jose, and I have spent a good deal of time together during the last two weeks and I believe that we have found several interesting things about their requirements and how an architecture approach can save us money and provide a more valuable long-term solution. We formed a working group to do the analysis and included an experienced enterprise architect and a senior systems analyst who I know from some past work, as well as several managers and staff from Kate and Jose's groups, including two sales representatives from the field. The architect, Raja Patil, provided some background on what enterprise architecture is all about and how to document and evaluate current and future views of resources and requirements. With that, the group documented the current business services and associated IT resources that might be replaced or modified by Kate's and Jose's proposals. Then, the group documented Kate's and Jose's requirements from a business process perspective and looked for areas of commonality or duplication. Finally, Raja and the systems analyst, Lily Jefferson, led the group in a scenario planning exercise that developed two plausible business and technology solutions that meet both of their requirements in an integrated manner. Either of these integrated solutions look to be less expensive to implement than it will be to do Jose's and Kate's systems independently."

Jose then spoke to the group. "I was really impressed with what the group did in only two weeks. Roberta is right about looking at these type of requirements from an architecture perspective. What I realized is that my back-office support systems can have more types of direct feeds of information from Kate's line of business systems. In fact, the more we do this, the timelier and more accurate the information across the company will be. The big thing here is that we eventually need to look at all of our business and technology requirements from a company-wide standpoint so that we can start to integrate and streamline our processes and capabilities."

Kate then spoke. "I agree with Jose that this was an eye-opener. There are flows of information between Jose's financial group and my business managers, but these flows and the supporting systems have been developed independently with no overarching plan in mind. Roberta and his associates showed me an architecture approach and implementation process that can be completed for our respective areas within the next two months and then be used to guide the implementation of a solution that I believe will meet my requirements and those that Jose has as well. This benefits everyone. Even the sales reps were getting into the game and provided a couple of ideas about automatically pushing sales and inventory data to them that I had not considered. I am recommending that we go with this approach to refine and select a solution so that I don't lose any more time on my competition."

Gerald leaned forward and looked at Roberta. "I remember you saying that enterprise architecture links strategy, business, and technology. I am not hearing about strategy.... was that left out?" "Good question Gerald" responded Roberta. "We did not go too much into company strategy because of the two-week timeframe for developing the initial architecture plan. However, that is an area that we will have to quickly address if the architecture plan for these two segments is approved for implementation.

The way that I would pursue this is to identify DMC's strategic goals that relate to Kate and Jose's requirements, and ensure that the solutions align with the accomplishment of those goals. For example, I see that the company will be opening a new custom order line of business next year that builds on what we are doing on an ad-hoc basis right now. I would want to see if the solution for Kate and Jose's requirements could also be able to support similar requirements for the custom order business."

Rick said "I always talk about value and risk before approving any project. I am seeing value through cost savings and potential scalability of the solution. So, what is the cost of doing these segments and then the whole architecture? And, what are the risks and how do we mitigate them?"

"The cost of doing a complete and detailed architecture for a mid-size company like DMC may be considerable" said Roberta. "And I therefore recommend this type of segmented approach to developing a company-wide architecture, where we take one line of business at a time."

Roberta continued, "In the plan we developed, you will see that the cost for the first two segments is $305,000, which covers analysis, modeling, documentation, and an EA tool. There is also a $51,600 cost for documenting and applying the general architecture methodology, framework, and standards, that is largely reused in subsequent segment efforts. The analysis of these two segments should take two to three weeks and depending on which of the two solutions is selected, the supporting documentation will take another month. So, this plan delays Jose and Kate approximately two months, but saves the company well over $356,600 if a combined solution is adopted."

Roberta leaned forward in his chair and said, "By having a standardized architecture approach, we ensure alignment in each completed segment and can also use it to guide each new development and upgrade projects throughout the company, so that architecture alignment occurs much more quickly. This approach is also a risk mitigation strategy, in that we are spreading out the cost and effort over time, involving stakeholders in the development of each segment, and incorporating lessons learned from each segment effort. Two of the most important success factors for doing an enterprise architecture are the strong support of executive leadership and buy-in from stakeholders. If you see value in having an architecture, and have a say in how it affects you, then the architecture can become a powerful planning and decision-making tool for DMC."

Rick thought for a moment about what Roberta had said and then addressed the group. "I am inclined to approve the plan to develop a standardized architecture and these first two segments, are there any objections?" There were no other comments. "Ok Roberta, let's proceed with the plan and get together every two weeks for a progress report."

Buzzword Bingo

"Hello most excellent Leadership Team!" says the CEO. I enjoyed the visioning retreat for CEOs out in Abeline last week, what good wilderness wandering! Your texts and tweets reflected our new aligned agility... bravo!" Thanks Boss, we are the disruptors... we are the transformers! says the COO. "One fight, one team, one solution" says the CFO. "My cloud solution heals all." says the CIO. "Any threat vectors?" asks the CEO. "Only the typical cyber stuff" says the CIO. "And some supply chain requirements adaptation on my end" says the COO. Are you happy from the financials perspective?" asks the CEO. "Absolutely" says the CFO. "Thursday's demo showed me what I needed to know; my threat surface is tiny." "I can contract for the cloud services in two weeks if you are good-to-go on this." says the CIO. "Launch-em... let's scrum again then" says the CEO has he heads toward the collaboration room to meet with interns.

Chapter 3

The Value and Risk of Creating an Enterprise Architecture

Chapter Overview

Chapter 3 discusses the value and risks associated with creating an enterprise-wide architecture. The main concepts of this chapter are that holistic architecture represents a different way of looking at resources across the enterprise, and that the significant cost of creating a holistic architecture must be justified in terms of the value it will bring to users of EA products in their planning and decision-making activities.

Learning Objectives

- ➢ Understand the potential value of a holistic architecture.
- ➢ Understand the risks associated with implementing EA.
- ➢ Learn an approach for measuring the costs and benefits of a EA program.
- ➢ Understand how holistic architecture helps integrate strategy, business, and technology.

Introduction

There is both value and risk associated with the establishment of an EA program in an enterprise. On the value side, holistic architecture has the unique capability to bring together views of strategy, business, and technology that allow an enterprise to see itself in current and future operating states. EA also supports the modeling of different future operating scenarios, which may help the enterprise survive (or thrive) as it responds to changes in the internal and external operating environment, some of which can be unexpected. Additionally, a EA program establishes an integrated set of IT resource planning, decision-making, and implementation processes that can better identify and resolve performance gaps across the enterprise.

> *Home Architecture Analogy:* It is important for a traditional architect to use proven engineering methods and meet frequently with the owners to make sure the design meets their taste, needs, and budget. Not doing these things introduces the risk of building failure and/or dissatisfaction with the layout.

On the risk side, creating a holistic architecture for an entire enterprise can be time consuming, costly, and disruptive to business services. Also, developing detailed documentation that covers strategy, business, and technology withn each area of the enterprise can be time consuming and costly. Hiring and/or training architects and supporting analysts is one element of the cost. Another cost element is the time it takes line of business managers and support staff away from their normal work. Finally, the cost of documentation tools and on-line repositories must be factored in as well. Further, there is the risk that the architecture will not be used by stakeholders if they do not buy-in to the concept of holistic architecture or perceived value.

On the value side, EA is unique in its ability to promote enterprise-wide thinking about resource utilization. Holistic architecture replaces the systems-level approaches to IT resource development that have characterized the last several decades and has left many enterprises with stovepipe and/or duplicative IT resources. Holistic architecture promotes the development of more efficient enterprise-wide common operating environments for business and technology, within which more capable and flexible business services and systems can be hosted. This in turn makes an enterprise more agile and able to respond to internal and external drivers of change, which promotes greater levels of competitiveness.

The benefits should outweigh the costs of doing holistic architecture, or the program should not be established. In the Case Study example, if an architecture program helps DMC's executives find a combined solution to two sets of business and technology requirements, then a significant amount of money can be saved. Multiply this by several of these situations each year, and the EA program may very well pay for itself. Further, holistic architecture helps to identify existing duplication in functional capability, which can generate additional savings. Finally, EA documentation helps to identify current and future performance gaps that may not be otherwise realized, which enables the enterprise to be more proactive and cost-efficient in addressing solutions.

Discussion

Overall Value

The value of holistic architecture is that it enhances resource-planning capabilities and supports better decision-making. This is accomplished through communication improvements in respect to current and future resources. Ideas are conveyed more rapidly while differences in interpretations and misunderstandings are reduced.

The overall value of holistic architecture will vary with the size and complexity of the enterprise, the type and number of IT-related performance gaps, duplication within current IT resources, and stakeholder acceptance. For those larger, less centralized enterprises that are regional or global in nature, EA can be an effective governance process for IT resources. For smaller more centralized enterprises, EA can help to ensure that the organization remains able to align business requirements with technology solutions, and enhance inventory, security, and configuration management activities.

Improved Planning

Holistic architecture enhances both top-down and bottom-up approaches to planning. Top- down planning begins with considerations for strategy and business, which are enhanced by the holistic perspectives of the enterprise that EA provides. Bottom-up planning is also enhanced, as EA coordinates what would otherwise be disparate and separate program-level planning activities. EA also enhances strategic planning as it helps to bring together multiple perspectives of business and technology at various levels of the enterprise. Finally, EA supports program and project management by providing a baseline of reference documentation for business alignment, standards, and configuration management.

Better Decision-Making

EA improves decision-making by providing comprehensive views of current capabilities and resources, as well as a set of plausible future operating scenarios that reveal needed changes in processes and resources (see Chapter 8 for additional details on future scenarios). By having an on- line repository of information that is updated at regular intervals, decision-makers have real-time access to higher-quality information at various levels of detail.

In that the EA program links to other areas of resource governance (e.g., capital planning, project management, and security), decision-makers can obtain coordinated information on operations, support, and development activities. Chapters 10 and 11 provide additional details on the relationship between architecture, capital planning, project management, and security.

Communications

Holistic architecture improves communication throughout the enterprise by providing a regularly updated baseline of integrated information on strategy, business, and technology. Also, the EA program and implementation methodology bring standardized approaches and terminologies for the development and management of enterprise resources. This standard architecture language and methodology is especially helpful in large, complex enterprises that are geographically dispersed, and which may have multiple social and work cultures that have promoted different ways of doing things. Holistic architecture should not stifle the creativity that cultural diversity can bring but should augment and enhance that creativity by improving the alignment of business and technology to the strategic goals and initiatives of the enterprise.

The old saying is that "a picture is worth a thousand words." Architecture drawings and data visualizations are some of the most important artifacts that architecture projects produce. Having an on-line repository of architecture models and information is like having a vault of models, analyses, and reports that can be useful in a variety of activities throughout the enterprise. It is tremendously valuable if the members of an enterprise can electronically call-up the Same set of architecture reference materials at financial planning meetings, research and development seminars, sales and marketing reviews, and daily operations and support activities. With an updated repository of architecture materials available, meetings can convey greater amounts of information in shorter periods of time, achieving higher levels of understanding based on a common set of architecture terms, models, and information.

Managing Risk

Risk is related to *uncertainty*, and in applied form is the potential source(s) for the failure or underperformance of a program or project. The management of risk involves lowering or eliminating the uncertainty that desired outcomes will not be realized. There are several types of risk that relate to the implementation and maintenance of a holistic architecture:

Financial. Implementing a holistic architecture involves establishing current and future views of enterprise resources. Like any implementation project, establishing the initial set of EA information will require start-up funding that is more than what will be required for the periodic updates. Even after the architecture is established, cuts in the ongoing maintenance budget can affect the program, to the point of making documentation of little use if it becomes too out of date.

Lack of Acceptance. Holistic architecture represents a new way of looking at enterprise resources by providing an integrated view of strategy, business, and technology that supports the consolidation or re-engineered of these resources to produce additional value. Former approaches to program management that supported systems level planning will be replaced with EA level planning that is promoted through the architecture program. This will most likely create some tensions between program various stakeholder groups.

Loss of Key Personnel. An effective EA program requires a team of experienced enterprise and domain architects. Each of these skill sets is important to the program and the loss of members of the EA team with those skills can create delays in program implementation, as well as effect implementation costs.

Schedule Delays. As with all implementation projects, the documentation of current/future architecture views and the creation of the Architecture Transition Roadmap are approached as projects that have sprints, milestones, and completion target date. Delays to the schedule can come from many sources and depending on the point at which a delay occurs during architecture implementation, and how long the delay is, the effect can go from being negligible to being catastrophic for a new EA program.

Documentation Tools. One of the greatest challenges for a Chief Enterprise Architect is to develop current and future views of the architecture that are rich in detail, easy to access, and which can support modeling and decision-making types of queries. The capabilities of architecture tools and supporting applications at present are such that intuitive and informative "management views" of architecture information are difficult to produce with these tools. Further, because more than one software application is normally required in a EA program, tool integration is an issue that must be dealt with. As new commercial tools are introduced a Chief Enterprise Architect must consider what the effect will be on overall documentation if that product does not integrate with other tools.

Mitigating Risk

Risk mitigation is a fancy term for avoiding or dealing with uncertaincies that can have a negative impact on the organization – minor or major. EA promotes planning, capabilities, and response actions that reduce the likelihood that sources of risk will emerge and negatively impact the organization. Actions that mitigate risk (lower uncertainty) include strengthening executive support for the EA program, solidifying budgets, not being the first adopter of EA tools and documentation techniques, ensuring there are trained back-ups on the EA team, and using a detailed EA implementation methodology to guide the overall program.

Additionally, basic program management skills address potential problems of key personnel turnover, cost and schedule overruns, performance issues, and stakeholder acceptance. Overcoming issues related to technology compatibility among EA products is usually achieved by using commercial tools that are based on open standards, are mature, and have significant market share. Risk identification and mitigation is not a one-time activity, it's an ongoing management review item that is core to an EA program.

Quantifying EA Program Value

How to translate value to the bottom line is one of the questions executives and Line of Business (LoB) managers have about EA programs. Building a business case that includes an alternatives analysis, cost-benefit analysis, and return on investment calculation is the primary measure for evaluating the contribution to profitability and/or mission success. Many aspects of EA value can be quantified, including the following areas:

Shortening Planning Cycles. EA can help shorten planning cycles by providing a robust repository of on-line information regarding current and future processes and resources. While EA does not replace strategic planning or business process improvement activities, it does enhance them through contribution of useful information that that would otherwise be gathered separately.

More Effective Planning Meetings. EA information allows for the presentation of a common baseline of planning and reference information. It reduces ambiguity and increases levels of common understanding.

Shorter Decision-Making Cycles. The time it takes to gather and cross-walk strategy, business, and technology information is greatly reduced by having a repository of EA information that was developed through the use of a logical framework and archiving method. Decision-making processes can be streamlined to reflect the availability of this new resource of integrated baseline information.

Improved Reference Information. By using an EA documentation framework and implementation methodology, information on processes and resources is gathered in a standardized method using the Same tools and applications. Additionally, the method for storing the information is coordinated through the use of the on-line EA repository, which requires the use of standardized data and document formats. This in turn creates the ability to perform queries for information across otherwise disparate activities and resources. It also supports a more robust data mining and business analysis capability.

Reduction of Duplicative Resources. One of the greatest contributions an EA makes to an enterprise is aiding the visualization of the value that current resources provide, where those value areas overlap, and where performance gaps exist. For example, duplicative data represents low-hanging fruit ready for elimination through the implementation of the future architecture. Subsequent improvements might then focus on the introduction of new technologies and improvements in efficiency.

Reduced Re-work. By approaching the planning and execution of new resources in a holistic manner, potential re-work that might have been created through individual program level initiatives (containing duplicative and/or conflicting capabilities) can be avoided. Also, re-work is reduced through the use of a step-by-step EA methodology and framework (see Chapters 4, 5), that call for standard approaches to documentation based on mature modeling and analysis techniques.

Improved Resource Integration and Performance. EA promotes integration through the planning and utilization of resources on an enterprise-wide basis. EA also helps to compare current and future requirements for business and technology, in order to identify performance gaps and solutions. This result is contrasted with stovepipe program-level inputs to provide incremental improvements within individual LoBs.

Fewer People in a Process. EA supports business process reengineering (BPR) and business process improvement (BPI) activities by encouraging planning in the context of both enterprise-wide crosscutting requirements and LOB requirements. Quantifying this includes the elimination of parts of a process that are repetitive. Also, streamlined processes that use resources more efficiently can equate to position requirement reductions and payroll savings.

Improved Communication. EA helps to promote a common language and central approach that can reduce misunderstandings of resource requirements and potential solutions. This can reduce re-work. Whole processes may require repetition due to misunderstandings of different interpretations of requirements and/or solutions.

Reduction in Cycle Time. EA can help an enterprise to reduce the time it takes to plan, develop, implement, and retire resources within its business and technology operating environment. By using an EA methodology and framework (see Chapters 4 and 5), each resource is evaluated from the Same holistic strategy, business and technology viewpoint, and is documented using the Same set of EA tools and techniques. Also, EA compliments capital planning and program management reviews of completed projects (see Chapters 10 and 11) so that the 'lessons learned' can be applied to subsequent efforts. In this way, the enterprise can improve efficiency and reduce the amount of time it takes to implement similar resources.

Quantifying Architecture Program Costs

The cost of EA should be approached from a program lifecycle view that centers on phases for implementation, maintenance, and refreshment. One way to estimate architecture program costs is to look at each area of the implementation methodology (see Chapter 4) and identify the direct and indirect costs to accomplish each of the steps. In general, this would include the following:

- Program administration and other tie-ins
- Salary/benefits for a Chief Architect and team staff
- Meetings, facilities, and materials for stakeholder planning sessions
- Platforms and web developers to establish the EA repository
- Interviews and materials to document current views
- Future scenario planning sessions with stakeholders
- Interviews and materials to document future views
- Development and documentation of the Transition Roadmap
- Architecture modeling software and hardware purchases and licences
- Regular updates to key documentation

The cost of establishing an initial version of the holistic architecture will be more than the cost of updating and maintaining it, due to the direct and indirect costs associated with establishing new EA processes and capabilities and gaining stakeholder support.

The recurring (annualized) cost of the EA program should be established and presented to the EA program sponsor, so that there is a clear understanding of the one-time costs for implementation of the EA and the ongoing costs for EA maintenance and refreshment activities. As with any program, this budget picture should be baselined relative to the EA program activities that are approved by the sponsor, so that any approved changes to the scope of those EA activities are accompanied by a change to the budget. If this is not done, the EA program may evolve to a position of being responsible for too much relative to the resources it has available.

In that EA is an advanced analytic type of activity, most of the cost of developing and maintaining EA documentation will be the cost of labor for trained architects. The second largest cost area will be the supporting technology (hardware, software, web applications, databases, tools, etc.). The other major cost area will be the facility costs for the EA team's work area and meetings with stakeholders.

Those who do holistic architecture for a living work under a variety of job titles, including Chief Architect, Solution Architect, Systems Architect, Data Architect, Network Architect, Security Architect, IT Consultant, Management Consultant, and a number of related analyst titles.

Furthermore, there tends to be a set of classifications for senior, mid-level, and junior positions for many of these jobs. From an informal survey of enterporise architecture-related salaries conducted by the author, a senior enterprise architect's position can command over $120,000 per year.10 Mid-level positions (3-5 years of experience) can earn in the range of $70,000 to $80,000.00 per year, and the junior positions for beginning architects can earn in the range of $40,000 to $60,000 per year.

As expensive as this seems, the cost to outsource these positions is even greater. The industry average for one work year is about 2,060 hours (this is Monday-Friday 8-hour days and accounts for time away for holidays and personal time off). Some government contract labor rates for the outsourcing of a Chief Architect and/or Senior Consultant position are over $200 per hour, which translates to over $400,000 per year. The rate for mid-level enterprise architects can range from $125 to $175 per hour, so at the upper end of this range the outsourcing of one of these positions can cost over $350,000. The rate for junior enterprise architects can range from $55 to $85 per hour, and at the upper end of this range the cost of outsourcing can be over $175,000. The cost of domain-specific architect positions is usually a bit lower because they are looking at only one area of the architecture (e.g., data, work processes, applications, networks), not how it all fits together – which requires knowledge and experience in all areas and this takes years to obtain.

This significant level of cost for enterprise architecture labor has caused some organizations to pause in considering the implementation of a EA program. However, when the potential savings generated by the architecture program are factored in, there can be a very high return on investment, especially in enterprises where EA can reduce duplicative capabilities and help identify common solutions to otherwise separate requirements. With costs for information systems in the many millions of dollars, the consolidation of even a few of those systems can make the EA program more than pay for itself, as well as enable the enterprise to re-direct the funding from duplicative resources to other business requirements.

Linking Strategy, Business, and Technology Planning

For EA to support an enterprise holistically, it must link (align) strategy, business and technology planning activities. Holistic EA is most effective when it simultaneously supports top-down executive planning and decision-making across the enterprise and bottom-up management planning and decision-making within each LoB. In this way, EA helps to ensure that strategy drives business and technology planning. From a business perspective EA provides the context and purpose of business activities by ensuring technology is implemented only after business requirements are identified. From a technology perspective, EA provides the strategy and business context for resource planning. This can be critical when working with multiple organizations to create common resources such as integrated supply chains, or in the case of mergers and acquisitions.

Linking Holistic Architecture and Organizational Strategy

The framework and methodology organizes planning and documentation in a way that allows strategy to influence business and technology planning and decision-making. This is important especially in the documentation of future EA views. By first identifying what changes are anticipated in strategic goals and initiatives, subsequent documentation of business activities and technology resources can be completed in such a way as to promote alignment, efficiency, and effectiveness. Documenting strategy involves the identification of goals, initiatives, and outcome measures. The following are related key terms and concepts:

Strategic Goals. These are the primary objectives of the enterprise. Strategic goals typically require several years to accomplish. Changes in strategic goals are made in response in internal and external business and technology drivers and/or changes in laws and regulations.

Strategic Initiatives. These are the business and technology activities, programs, and projects that enable accomplishment of strategic goals, such that they can affect the fundamental direction of the enterprise.

Strategic Measures. These are outcome measures that identify when a strategic initiative has successfully met a strategic goal. Outcome goals define when an enterprise is accomplishing its mission.

Linking Holistic Architecture and Business Planning

As is reflected in the design of the EA framework, strategy creates business requirements and technology supports solutions for meeting those requirements. EA documents three primary issues at the business level:

Supporting Strategic Goals. Touch points between strategic initiatives and business activities need to be clearly documented. Not all business activities are strategic, and it is important to distinguish in the EA documentation between those that directly link to strategic initiatives and those that provide general support functions for the enterprise.

Documentation of Business Activities. Documenting the creation and delivery of business products and services is important in supporting Business Process Improvement (BPI) and Business Process Reengineering (BPR) projects, and in documenting business activities to show inputs, outputs, outcomes, and other elements of influence regarding each business process. It's also important to identify how business processes are linked to one another.

Identifying Supporting Technologies. Analyzing business requirements and activities can reveal critical supporting technologies. Examples of this include marketing activities that require trend analysis data or a manufacturing process that requires various types of resources including raw materials, facilities, labor, computers, data, and robotics. EA helps to identify and document workflows and supporting technologies.

Linking Holistic Architecture and Technology Planning

Technology is a type of resource that enables information and other resource flows to support the creation and delivery of business products and services, which in turn enables the achievement of strategic goals. It is important that technology not drive business and strategy planning, especially in resource-constrained enterprises, where the expense of duplicative non-strategic technologies cannot be afforded. Bottom-up planning (e.g. where technology is the catalyst for change) is a viable use of EA; however, it's not the normal process for resource implementation. It's more important for the enterprise to understand its primary directions and priorities, plan necessary business activities, and then identify the supporting resources, including various types of information technology.

Summary of Concepts

This chapter provided a detailed discussion of the value and risk of establishing a holistic EA program. A clear articulation of the business case for EA is needed to obtain executive sponsorship and resources for EA program implementation and maintenance. Quantifying the areas of value that the EA program will contribute is important, and those include improved communication, planning, and decision-making. A total lifecycle approach to estimating costs is used to differentiate the one-time direct and indirect costs associated with program start-up and initial EA documentation from the ongoing costs of EA program management and documentation updates. Comparisons were made in the area of EA labor costs between in-house salaries and the expense of paying for external EA consulting support. In concluding the discussion of EA value, the linkage between EA, strategy, business, and technology was shown.

Chapter 3 Questions and Exercises

1. What are some of the areas of value that are generated by EA?
2. What are some of the risks associated with implementing EA?
3. How does EA help an enterprise to view its strategic direction/goals?
4. How does EA help an enterprise to view its business services?
5. How does EA help an enterprise to view technology resources?
6. What is meant by managing risk?
7. Identify two methods to manage risk.
8. How does EA link to strategy, business, and technology?
9. Select a real-world business and identify the following:
   a. Areas of potential value that a holistic EA program would provide.
   b. Areas of potential risk to the implementation and acceptance of a holistic EA program, and strategies to mitigate those risks.
   c. How EA can help develop views of this business' strategic direction and goals; business services; and supporting resources.

Section II

Developing a Holistic Enterprise Architecture

Section II defines and describes how to accomplish and implement a holistic architecture. It covers what an architecture framework is, presents a step-by-step methodology for implementation, discusses how to document current and future views of the architecture, and describes how to articulate the path forward in an "Architecture Transition Roadmap" which also serves as a transition and sequencing plan from current to future capabilities.

Foundational elements of an EA program are the documentation framework and the implementation methodology. The documentation framework defines _what_ the EA program will document, and the implementation methodology defines _how_ that documentation will be gathered and used. By documenting current and future views, along with an Architecture Transition Roadmap, the architecture improves planning agility, helps to prioritize resource utilization, and helps to lower the risk of project failures. Section II is organized as follows:

Case Study (Scene 3) - The Importance of a Methodology

The Case Study continues the scenario at Danforth Manufacturing Company that was presented in Section I. Now that the CEO has decided to proceed with a EA program, this part of the Case Study will focus on how the EA program and the implementation methodology will be executed. The CIO has hired a Chief Architect, who describes the need for and purpose of a holistic methodology.

Chapter 4 - The Implementation Methodology

Chapter 4 describes the procedure for establishing the EA program and developing/maintaining a holistic architecture. The necessity of using a "complete" architecture approach and a holistic framework are disussed, as is the need for documentation at an appropriate level of detail to reduce cost and the risk of producing an architecture that is not useful.

Chapter 5 - The Documentation Framework

Describes the purpose of a holistic documentation framework and how it establishes the scope of the architecture. The EA6 Framework is presented in detail, as it becomes the basis for further discussion about how a holistic framework links strategy, business, and technology areas together to help improve resource planning and decision-making throughout the organization.

Chapter 6 - Components and Artifacts

Architecture components are processes and resources that provide capabilities at each level of the framework. Examples include strategic goals and measures, business services, information objects, software applications, and network hardware. Artifacts are models that describe architecture components.

Case Study (Scene 4) - Developing Current / Future Views

Illustrates how current and future architecture views will be developed. The context is that of evaluating several proposed IT systems and looking for common requirements and combined solutions. Following this evaluation, two segments of the DMC architecture will be developed that cover several lines of business.

Chapter 7 - Developing Current Architecture Views

Covers the development of artifacts that reflect current views of components in the context of the EA6 Framework and the related implementation methodology. Current architecture views are important to an organization because they establish and/or verify what resources (including IT) are being used in the lines of business to support the achievement of strategic goals. The current views become a reference baseline much like an inventory that then supports planning and decision-making regarding the future architecture and option paths.

Chapter 8 - Developing Future Architecture Views

Covers the development of future views of components in the context of the framework. The chapter also provides a description of a method for developing future views that is called "scenario planning." Future scenarios can help the enterprise to envision one or more potential future business and technology operating states.

Chapter 9 - Developing an Architecture Transition Roadmap

Discusses the development of an Architecture Transition Roadmap, which is the document that describes how an enterprise will manage the transition of its current processes and resources to those which will be needed in the future.

Case Study:
Danforth Manufacturing Company
Scene 3: The Importance of a Methodology

At a meeting of the Executive Committee several weeks before, Rick Danforth, the President and CEO of Danforth Manufacturing Company (DMC), had approved the request of CIO Roberta Washington to use an EA approach to evaluate two sets of IT system requirements that COO Kate Jarvis and CFO Jose Cruz had brought to the executive leadership group. Roberta is now moving forward on a plan and a business case to develop an architecture for several lines of business related to Kate and Jose's requirements. These "segments" of the DMC enterprise architecture will help Kate and Jose to evaluate their recent requests for new information systems to see if there were overlapping requirements.

To properly provide leadership and resources for the project, Roberta worked with DMC's Executive Committee during the past week to obtain approval to establish an EA Program that would be led by a qualified Chief Architect. The newly appointed Chief Architect reports to Roberta. She selected Raja Patil, whom he had known from earlier work. Also, Roberta was given a budget for this initial architecture project and a working area that can accommodate several people who will be hired and/or "borrowed" from other business areas for the period of the project.

This initial architecture effort is the test case for considering the development of a company-wide EA for DMC. Scene 3 describes the first meeting of the EA Working Group, which includes Roberta, Kate, Jose, Raja, several line of business managers, Lily Jefferson a senior systems analyst at DMC, and several end users of DMC's current sales and finance systems.

"Hello, and welcome to the Enterprise Architecture Working Group" said Roberta. We are going to develop two segments of the company's enterprise architecture, which cover several lines of business. These are lines of business that need more IT support. Before we can do that, we need to have a detailed methodology that will guide our efforts and reduce the risk that we will not be successful in developing the architecture segments. I have handed out a one-page outline of a methodology that I used with another organization and it helped tremendously. The four phases of the methodology cover program establishment, methodology development, documentation activities, and maintenance. During the past several weeks, I have worked with the Executive Committee to formally establish the program and bring Raja Patil on board as our new Chief Enterprise Architect. Raja, congratulations and welcome. Raja was with me during the prior project that we used this methodology, so I am going to turn it over to him to tell us about that and guide the Architecture Working Group through a review to see if we want to make any changes."

"Thank you, Roberta." said Raja. "It is a pleasure to be at DMC and to be working with you again on an architecture program, especially one that promises to bring great value to this organization. The first thing I would like you to know is that as Chief Architect, I will be very inclusive regarding stakeholder involvement in the development of the enterprise architecture program and all segments. This is because I have seen that down-road acceptance can only be gained through the ongoing participation of those who will be using the information, and those who are impacted by the ongoing program and specific solution architecture projects. Second, I'd like to tell you briefly about my very first enterprise architecture project, one where we did not use a methodology. This project started ok but lost its way as the segments were being developed. Why? Because the team did not have anything to keep designs standardized and aligned, or promote stakeholder interest, and we ended up with segments that did not integrate into an overall architecture... so the project did not produce the amount of value that was expected, and the information was rarely used." "Since then, I've learned to let the business requirements drive the architecture, and to develop segments collaboratively with those who will use them, so they can ensure that the types of information are there when they need it.... not just the items we think they will need."

Raja continued. "What you received several weeks ago was the *DMC Enterprise Architecture Plan – Financial and Production Segments* report that Roberta and I developed with Jose, Kate, and several members of this EA Working Group. That report lays out the business case for this project, which is to evaluate the business and technology requirements for two proposed systems. To do that type of analysis, we need several segments of an overall DMC enterprise architecture, to provide reference views of the current and planned process and resources involving DMC's strategic goals, business activities, and technology capabilities. To develop these segments for the finance and production lines of business, we need a methodology. As Roberta said, this methodology will help keep us on track and reduce the risk of project failure."

Jose asked, "What do I need to do to help with this methodology?" Roberta answered, "Look at the outline and tell us if there is something that you as a business executive might also need to have as part of our architecture program or documentation process. Also, when we get to the modeling steps, we need to know from you, Kate, and your respective staff what kind of planning and decision-making information you need in your lines of business. We also need to know the formats you would require. From that, the Architecture Working Group can refine the requirements that we will use to select modeling techniques and tools."

Roberta continued, "Once we get the current views established for your and Kate's segments, we can develop some future operating scenarios and identify planning assumptions. This is the baseline of architecture information that we can finally use to evaluate your proposals for separate system. We'll see if they fit into the future architecture as proposed, or we will be able to determine if there is a better way to meet your requirements."

Raja spoke up. "Roberta, you talked about a lot of interdependent parts, which hopefully reinforces our comments about the value of having a methodology to guide our activities. Also, Roberta alluded to different types of architecture information that we will be gathering, and you may be wondering what that is and how it is organized? The short answer is that we will use a holistic architecture framework. One of the foundational elements of any enterprise-wide architecture program is the selection of a framework that defines the scope of the overall architecture and its sub-segments. Further, the graphic depiction of the framework provides a visual image of the areas of the architecture and how they relate. So, let's go ahead with the review of the implementation methodology."

The Architecture Working Group meeting finished its review of the implementation methodology and selected documentation framework. Raja said "Let's get together on Thursday morning to talk about how this methodology and framework will be used to document current and future views of the segment. Roberta will brief the selected methodology and framework to the Executive Committee at the next bi-monthly status meeting." With that the working group meeting adjourned.

Buzzword Bingo

"A big DMC hello to the new Architecture Working Group!" said the CIO, "The AWC is going to rock this place with transformative ideas and super-charged collaboration between silo'd legacy islands of production. Let's give our own hello to my new Chief Enterprise Architect – he's a rock star!" "Bravo!" said the COO. "Howdy!" said the CFO. "Ok, the AWC has to hit the deck running and scrum on the requirements that Kate and Jose have so we can rationalize, consolidate, and align them in our first sprint." "Sounds like a plan." said the COO. The CIO continued, "We are also going to run a parallel sprint to flesh-out the company's first overall architecture and must-have stanadards so we have something to bounce the solution off of." "Awesome" said the CFO. The CEA spoke up, "Thanks for the warm welcome, I am so looking forward to taking this journey with all of you, we will be the best-of-breed in no time!" "Yep" said the CIO, "The new reference architecture is going to be a positive disruptor and we need that to break down the silos and have the agility and resilience we need to out hustle the competition." See everyone on Thursday, the CEO will drop by too."

Chapter 4

The Implementation Method Chapter Overview

This chapter describes the purpose and value of using a comprehensive, proven implementation methodology (method), which is a detailed procedure for establishing an ongoing architecture program that conducts analysis and design projects in a coordinated manner. Using a mature method reduces the risk of creating an ineffective architecture.

Key Term: *Enterprise Architecture Method*   "How"
The method defines how the architecture will be implemented and used, including the selection of a framework, standards, tools, and repository.

Key Term: *Enterprise Architecture Framework*   "What"
A graphical structure and description that shows the scope of the architecture (what is included) and relationship of its parts (domains and components).

Learning Objectives

➢ Understand the purpose of an EA method.
➢ Understand what it means for an EA method to be complete.
➢ Understand the steps of the EA6 method's phases and steps.
➢ Understand the relationship between a method and framework.

Introduction

The EA method is a step-by-step description of how the program is to be established and run, and how current/future architecture views are to be developed, maintained, and used. The EA method presented in this book uses an enterprise-wide approach and framework, that should incorporate other domain-specific solution architecture methods and operating best practices. Other existing architecture approaches (e.g., TOGAF, MDA, DODAF, ITIL) are useful for specific analysis and design projects, but do not provide a holistic organizational context or comprehensive business/ technology baseline. This enterprise-level context is the unifying aspect of EA6... all other best practices are utilized *within* the framework.

Home Architecture Analogy: An EA method is like the standard approach that architects are taught for designing and constructing a home. There are things that must be done in a certain order and way for the design to be successful and for the home to be properly constructed.

Discussion

An EA program has many elements and a key to success is to use a detailed implementation method to get started and guide projects. The method described in this book is generalized so it can be used by any type of organization. The organization should discuss the following before starting:

- All aspects of the organization are included in the architecture.
- Governance is a mix of centralized standards and decentralized execution.
- The products of the program are analyses, designs, and recommendations.
- Policy on standards and methods will be needed and must be supported.
- Resources will be needed (e.g., people, tools, funding, training, facilities).
- The organization owns its architecture, not consultants or vendors.
- Some products require regular updates (overviews, standards, inventories).

The following are the major phases and steps of the *EA6 Implementation Method*:

Phase I: Program Establishment
Step 1: Designate the executive who champions the EA Program.
Step 2: Establish governance and links to other management processes.
Step 3: Launch the EA Program Office and hire a Chief Architect.
Step 4: Chief Architect hires or contracts for EA team members.
Step 5: Develop an Implementation Plan and communicate it to stakeholders.

Phase II: Preparation to Conduct Projects
Step 6: Conduct training on program objectives, schedule, and approach.
Step 7: Select documentation methods appropriate for the framework.
Step 8: Select the software tools that enable EA analysis and design.
Step 9: Establish an architecture repository and policy/standards catalog.
Step 10: Identify components and the order of documentation.

Phase III: Documentation of Current and Future Views
Step 11: Harvest/assess existing business and technology documentation.
Step 12: Document current views of existing components.
Step 13: Develop several future business/technology operating scenarios.
Step 14: Identify future planning assumptions for each future scenario.
Step 15: Use the scenarios to drive the design of future components.

Phase IV: Use and Maintain the Architecture
Step 16: Develop/maintain the Architecture Transition Roadmap.
Step 17: Use EA information to support planning and decision-making.
Step 18: Regularly update current and future views of components.
Step 19: Maintain a repository for modeling and analysis products.
Step 20: Release annual updates to the Roadmap.

This implementation method addresses the establishment of a new EA program, adopting the book's approach, creating the organization's first holistic architecture, and using it to support planning/decision-making. The following are more detailed descriptions of each phase and step.

Phase I: Program Establishment

Phase I activities are designed to get the EA program initially started, identify key players, and communicate the *EA Implementation Plan* to the *executive sponsor* and other stakeholders in order to gain buy-in and support. These pre-documentation activities are important to ensuring that the EA program has clear goals, remains focused, and is accepted throughout the enterprise.

Step 1: Executive Ownership.

The critical first step is for the organization's most senior leadership to formally designate the executive who will be responsible for and champion the EA Program. The designation document should signal the importance of the program and require support and alignment from all business units.

Step 2: Establish Governance

The second step is for the executive sponsor and Chief Architect to co-develop an approach to architecture oversight (governance) that enables effective policy, planning, and decision-making within the program. This approach to governance should include links to other key oversight processes (e.g., strategic planning, capital planning, project management, security, and workforce planning).

Step 3: Launch the EA Program.

The third step is for the executive sponsor to establish an EA program and hire a qualified Chief Enterprise Architect to lead the EA Program. The EA Program's establishment activity begins as a start-up project that becomes an ongoing program when the team is hired and a schedule of forthcoming projects is established. The executive sponsor must provide the Chief Architect with enough resources (e.g., budget, personnel, hardware/software, and facilities) and have the authority to establish the EA program. The Chief Architect should be accountable for EA program resources and results. Another of the Chief Architect's first actions should be to determine with the executive sponsor what the operating model for the EA Program Office will be. The options are: (1) for the office to only do audits and promulgate standards; (2) do limited design and analysis work in support of business unit projects; (3) conduct architecture projects themselves; or (4) a mix of these options – sometimes advising, sometimes doing it all themselves.

Step 4: Create the EA Team.
In step four, the Chief Architect hires or contracts for EA team members in key skill areas (e.g., business process analysis, systems design, data architecture, web applications, network engineering, security controls). How many there are depends on the operating model. Some team members are organizational employees, while others may come from outside organizations (e.g., consultancies) or be independent contractors.

Step 5: Architecture Program Implementation Plan
The first step of Phase II is to develop an *Architecture Program Implementation Plan* (Plan) that articulates the EA development method and a schedule for establishment and projects. The Plan should be written in plain language to gain stakeholder buy-in from non-technical executives, line of business managers, support staff, and other potential end users of EA documentation. The Plan should include statements about the purpose and vision of the EA, examples of how the EA will bring value to the enterprise, where EA documentation will be available for access, a summary of the methodology used, and the general principles that will be used for EA development.

Phase II: Preparation to Conduct Projects

Phase II activities solidify the EA team's readiness to start providing architecture services (audits, standards, analysis, and design). This begins with team and stakeholder training, then moves to confirming the artifact documentation methods and tools that are appropriate for the framework and finishes with the establishment of an on-line repository for documentation and an update of the Architecture Implementation Plan to set the order of analysis and design projects throughout the organization.

Key Term: *EA Artifact*
An EA artifact is a documentation product, such as a text document, system specification, application interface information, diagram, spreadsheet, briefing slides, and/or video clip.

Step 6: Conduct Training.

This step focuses on training to get the EA Program Office ready to offer services and inform customers and other stakeholders. The training covers EA Program objectives, schedule, and approach, including the areas of the enterprise that the EA will focus on first. For example, the training should summarize the scope and relationships of the framework areas by identifying the five sub-architecture domains and three 'thread' areas, what the lines of business are (from the org chart) and how they relate to the business and technology components (e.,g., data, systems, processes, equipment, facilities).

Step 7: Select documentation methods.

The next step is to select the methods that will be used to gather and develop EA documentation artifacts. For example, the following are methods for modeling in the eight sub-architecture domain areas of the framework (five levels and three threads). The following are examples of EA artifacts that are used in each area:

Strategic Level:	Strategic Plan, Scenarios, Balanced Scorecard
Business Level:	IDEF-0 Diagrams, Flowcharts, Swim Lane Charts
Data Level:	Data Models, Object Diagrams, Data Dictionary
Systems Level:	System Diagrams, Web Service Models, APIs
Network Level:	Voice/Data/Video Network Diagrams/Documents
Vertical Threads:	Security Diagrams, Standards, Workforce Skills

It is important to choose documentation techniques that will provide the information that is needed for resource planning and decision-making. Therefore, the Chief Architect should consult with EA stakeholders and the EA team in selecting the methods for artifact development and what type of information will need to be gathered to be able to create artifacts.

Step 8: Tool Selection

Select the software applications that enable EA analysis and design. Once the lines of business and components are are known, EA documentation and artifact modeling requirements can be established. For example, if object-oriented methods are being used to develop artifacts at the data level of the framework, then a modeling tool that has capability with the Unified Modeling Language (UML) is called for. Software applications in the current (legacy) operating environment may use a variety of old and new programming languages, including COBOL, Java, C, C++, Ruby, PERL, Visual Basic, PHP, SQL, and Pascal (see Tiobe or GitHub for a list). Tools will also be needed to model processes, databases and flows, networks, and facilities. Office automation tools are also needed, including graphics, spreadsheets, and word processing. Consideration should be given to obtaining a robust architecture documentation suite of tools to enable the automated "rippling" of changes among linked models and databases.

Step 9. Establish the Architecture Repository/Standards Catalog.
The EA Repository is the place on the organization's internal network (private cloud) where architecture models, analyses, standards, policies, and project information are stored and made available to those who need them. A significant element of the repository is a listing of business and IT policies and standards. Begin by selecting a document management and storage application/database. Then determine what the archiving taxonomy (storage categories) will be, including file tags and metadata. The organization is then ready to upload content and promote its use to support planning and decision-making. Chapter 12 provides more information on the design of the EA repository/catalog.

Step 10: Identify the EA components to be documented.
Identify the EA components that will have to be documented in each area of the framework (strategy, business, information, services, networks, and vertical threads). Each of these areas represents a distinct set of activities and resources across the enterprise, which are represented by EA components. EA components are plug-and-play goals, processes, measures, projects, data, services, and IT resources in the various functional areas. An EA component therefore is unique in the capability and resources that it represents within the EA framework. Each EA component is documented using information gathering methods and modeling techniques that are appropriate for the type of things that are contained in the EA component. For example, at the strategic level the enterprise's strategic goals, activities, and

outcome measures are the primary items to be documented. At the business level, the line-of business services and associated measures are documented. At the information level, the flows of information, databases, knowledge warehouses, and data standards are documented. At the services and applications level, the various web services, office automation services, and software applications are documented. At the technology infrastructure level the voice, data, and video networks, as well as associated cable plants and equipment facilities are documented. For the vertical threads, IT security information, IT standards, and IT workforce information are gathered for associated activities and resources in each of the five other functional areas.

Phase III: Documentation of the EA

Phase III activities are where the actual development of the EA occurs in the form of documentation artifacts. This involves analyzing and documenting the current strategy, business, information, services, and infrastructure of the enterprise. It also involves the development of artifacts that reflect changes in resources in the short-term and the development of a group of long-term future scenarios to identify possible courses of action and resource changes that would be needed in response to different internal and external influences. The activities in this phase of the EA documentation methodology conclude with the development of an Architecture Transition Plan that summarizes the current and future views of the architecture and provides a transition and sequencing plan for short- and long-term changes.

Step 11: Harvest and Assess Existing Documentation.

The first step of Phase III is the beginning of actual EA documentation activities. Preceding activities established what would be documented, how it would be documented, and who would do the documentation. The current view of EA components is what is now being documented through the identification of what the EA components are at each level of the framework and then using existing and new artifacts to document the EA components that currently exist. In many ways this activity is like taking an "inventory" of the components (strategic goals, business services, measures, data, services, and IT resources) that already exist in the enterprise and mapping them to existing documentation (harvest).

Step 12: Document current views of existing EA components.
The second step of Phase III is the development of new artifacts to complete the documentation of all existing components. The documentation methods and tools identified in Step 8 are used to gather and standardize existing artifacts, as well as to develop new artifacts. These documentation artifacts are organized by levels of the framework and are stored in the EA repository that was established in Step 10. Additional details on developing the current architecture are provided in Chapter 7.

Step 13: Develop future business/technology operating scenarios.
Prior to developing future views of EA components, it is helpful to gain a high-level understanding of the possible future directions that the enterprise could take, depending on how it responds to internal and external influences. Three or more future scenarios should optimally be developed with EA and line of business stakeholders to reflect what may occur if (1) the status quo is maintained; (2) an optimal business/technology operating environment is encountered; and (3) a high threat survival situation. There are several beneficial outcomes from the development of the scenarios. First, the enterprise is more prepared and organized to handle future situations and plan needed resources. Second, a number of planning assumptions are identified in each scenario that reveal what the priorities of the enterprise might be if that scenario is pursued. Third, the planning for future capabilities is more coordinated, as opposed to simply gathering separate inputs from line of business managers and technology managers. Separate inputs are known to perpetuate stovepipe capabilities. Chapter 8 provides additional details and an example about how to develop future scenarios and the future architecture.

Step 14: Identify future planning assumptions for scenarios.
Each future scenario describes, in story form, a possible business/ technology operating environment that the enterprise might pursue or face. In this step, the key elements of each future scenario are analyzed to reveal what things are important to the enterprise and what changes

have to occur for the scenario to become reality. For the purposes of the EA, these key elements become the planning assumptions that can then be grouped together to represent changes in each of the functional areas of the framework. One of the benefits of having the scenario and planning assumptions is that they were developed with stakeholder buy-in, which will help when future changes are implemented.

Step 15: Use scenarios to drive the design of future components.
This step involves the documentation of changes to EA components in the near term (1-2 years) and the longer term (3-5 years). These changes should be derived from the input by the leadership team (CXOs) via the operating scenarios' planning assumptions, and from program and project managers who know what the future business requirements are, as well as planned system implementations, upgrades, and retirements. By doing it this way, the changes are more coordinated and aligned with the strategic direction of the enterprise. Future views of EA components should be developed using the Same artifact documentation and modeling techniques that were used to develop the current views. This helps to more clearly identify what the changes are in each of the functional levels of the EA framework, which helps in planning and decision-making.

Phase IV: Use and Maintain the EA

Phase IV focuses on the implementation and use of the architecture as a whole by all stakeholders and establishes an annual cycle for updates. This is where the value of the EA Program is realized, as planning and decision-making throughout the enterprise are supported. This value is maintained through the development and maintenance of an Architecture Transition Roadmap, the regular updates of the current and future views of the architecture. Value is also gained in the maintenance of the EA repository and the maintenance of all associated software licenses for modeling and archiving.

Step 16: Develop the Architecture Transition Roadmap.
The first step in Phase IV is the development of the Architecture Transition Roadmap. This Roadmap serves to articulate how the EA was developed and provides a synopsis of the current and future

views. The Roadmap also provides a transition and sequencing sub-plan for the near-term changes, which may already be in the project pre-implementation stage. Also, a long-range sequencing sub-plan is provided that covers the potential changes associated with the future scenarios. Chapter 9 provides more detail on the development of an Architecture Transition Roadmap.

Step 17: Use the EA to support planning/decision-making.
During Phase III activities, current and future views of the architecture were stored in the EA repository and are ready to be used by the enterprise to support planning and decision-making. These stored artifacts become a baseline of reference information that can be used in a wide variety of executive, management, and staff activities. When this is done, a greater level of understanding is developed of capabilities and performance gaps among a wider group within the enterprise. Further, by having the EA documentation in an on-line repository, this information can be called up and referred to in meetings, which reduces the time it takes to convey an idea, increases comprehension, and reduces interpretation errors among meeting participants. For example, if in a planning meeting, one of the participants wanted to show needed improvements in information exchange within a particular line of business, EA documentation on the current and possible future views of that information flow could be called up from the repository and projected at the meeting. This, along with information on the associated business services, support applications, and networks can be referenced meaningfully. The time to convey the ideas is significantly reduced when diagrams and text are being shown to everyone at the meeting. This can stimulate more productive discussions and informed decisions.

Step 18: Update current and future views of EA Components.
The information in the EA repository is valuable for planning and decision-making only as long as it is comprehensive and accurate. Therefore, it is important to regularly update the current and future views of EA components in all areas of the framework. Further, it is helpful to users of EA information if the updates are made on a regular schedule: once or twice a year. Also, it is important to maintain version control in between updates, so that all of the users of the EA information know that they are conducting planning and decision-making activities

based on the Same information. Since what is planned in the future EA views will eventually become the current architecture (at least some of it), it should be recognized that EA updates are ongoing activities that do not cease. Future EA plans will continue as an organization grows and changes. Consider a time when the enterprise no longer needs changes in future capabilities and resources. Should this occur, the EA program transitions from focusing on the establishment of the EA to maintaining the EA and seeing that it continually brings value to the enterprise.

Step 19: Maintain the EA repository and modeling capabilities.
The Chief Architect and EA team need to ensure that the EA repository and support applications/tools are kept current in terms of licensing and functionality. The requirements for archiving and modeling should be reviewed annually, and new products should be regularly reviewed to ensure that the EA team has the right application support capability. The team should be on the lookout for new improvements in tool functionality so that these improvements can be applied to the advantage of the enterprise. The costs for software purchases and license renewals should be part of the annual EA program budget.

Step 20: Release annual updates to the Transition Roadmap.
The Chief Architect needs to regularly inform EA stakeholders about the status of the architecture. This is done through the annual release of an updated Architecture Transition Roadmap that discusses changes that were made to the current and future views of the EA during the past year. The communication should provide a transition and sequencing plan for changes anticipated during the coming year. Also, the ongoing value of the EA needs to be communicated through the citation of examples of where EA documentation supported planning and decision-making, helped reduce duplicative capabilities, saved costs, improved alignment, and increased communication.

Summary of Concepts

This chapter presented a comprehensive method for the implementation of an EA program and associated documentation activities. The four phases and twenty steps of the example EA method are generalized so they can be used in many types of public and private sector enterprises. Phase I activities serve to establish the EA program, identify a Chief Architect to lead the program, create an EA governance capability to run the EA program in a way that integrates with other IT management processes, and issue an EA Communication Plan to gain stakeholder buy-in and support. Phase II activities serve to select an EA framework that defines the scope of the architecture, the EA components that will make up the architecture in each functional area, and software applications/tools to automate the documentation of EA components. Phase III is where the actual documentation of current and future views of the architecture occurs. The final Phase IV activities are where the EA is used throughout the enterprise to support planning and decision-making and regular updates are performed to the Roadmap to keep the EA adding value.

Chapter 4 Questions and Exercises

1. What is an EA implementation method?
2. What is the role of an EA framework within the EA method?
3. What is the purpose of Phase I activities in the EA method?
4. Why are Phase III activities dependent on the completion of Phase II?
5. Compare and contrast the purpose of Phase II and Phase IV activities.
6. Can the steps of the EA method be changed for different enterprises?
7. Who is responsible for execution of the EA program and method?
8. How often should an EA be updated? Why?
9. Select a real-world medium or large size enterprise and provide:
    a. The phases/steps of an EA implementation method.
    b. The way that EA stakeholder support will be obtained.
    c. The recommended schedule for updating the EA.

Chapter 5

The Analysis and Documentation Framework

Chapter Overview

Chapter 5 defines and describes the purpose of the EA analysis and documentation framework, provides examples of existing frameworks and discusses the EA6 Framework which is a generalized framework that is suitable for use in public and private sector enterprises.

Learning Objectives

- ➢ Understand the purpose of an EA framework as part of a complete EA approach
- ➢ Understand the framework in the implementation method.
- ➢ Understand how the framework establishes an EA's scope.
- ➢ Be familiar with the origin of EA frameworks and examples.
- ➢ Understand the design of the EA6 Framework.

Introduction

The foundational elements of an EA program are the analysis and documentation framework (EA framework), and the implementation methodology (EA method). The EA framework defines _what_ the EA program will document, and the EA method defines _how_ that documentation will be developed and used. By defining what parts of the enterprise are included in the EA, the framework defines the scope of the architecture. The design of the framework communicates the relationship of the areas of the EA that are documented.

> _Home Architecture Analogy:_ The EA documentation framework is like the structural skeleton of a home. It is the framing that defines the size and relationship of parts of the house and individual rooms.

Discussion

The EA analysis and documentation process is accomplished through an EA implementation method that includes (1) the framework, (2) components, (3) current architectural views, (4) future architectural views, a plan for managing the ongoing transition between these views, and vertical threads that effect the architecture at all levels.

Analysis and documentation, as organized through an EA framework, provides standardized, hierarchical views of the enterprise from an integrated strategy, business, and technology perspective, shown below.

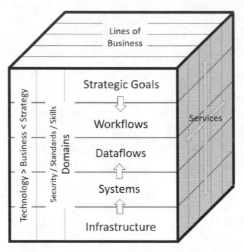

Figure 5-1. The EA6 Framework

The Origin of Frameworks

IT modeling and documentation frameworks emerged during the era of mainframe computing as data, software, and hardware requirements became more complex and multifaceted, and as the types of end-users increased and their locations became more distant. Reflecting the nature of that era, most early architectures were technically oriented, often vendor and/or product specific. Vendors of software and hardware products increasingly touted their own proprietary solutions, standards, and product lines under the banner of information or systems architectures. While this vendor-driven approach to architecture did serve to advance the capability of computing in general, it also created significant incompatibility problems for enterprises that operated many IT products from multiple vendors.

In addition to the issue of product incompatibility, there was a focus on developing and operating individual information systems versus the creation of an overall IT capability within an enterprise. Furthermore, systems-level IT planning grew out of an approach to analysis and design that focused on meeting a specific set of requirements within the enterprise. For example, many enterprises introduced IT in response to a perceived need for automated support for accounting, payroll, and administrative business functions. This often grew to include manufacturing, service, and sales support. In most cases, each of these business requirements were met by individual system solutions based on proprietary vendor approaches and products. The result was a heterogeneous collection of IT resources that independently supported business areas but could not exchange information outside of a particular system or business area. It was this scenario that gave rise to terms like "stovepipe systems" and "islands of computing capability."

This scenario was increasingly problematic to enterprises that sought to share information between lines of business and support functions. Further, the duplication in systems capability and cost of operating and maintaining a myriad of independent systems became a focal point for improvement. A desire to create interoperability, reduce costs, and increase capability was the organizational driver that changed things.

During the mid-1970's and 1980's this change came in two main areas: database and network design. First, an approach to information systems analysis and design that was based on the enterprise's information requirements came about through the introduction of standardized methods for modeling data, structure, and process. Second, the era of distributed client-server computing came into being as "dumb" mainframe terminals began to be replaced by "smart" desktop computers that could be networked in a client-server design that reached throughout an enterprise.

In the first area, an approach to database design, now known as the "structured" approach, was developed for modeling the processing and structure of data. Data Flow Diagramming (DFD) techniques allowed enterprises to identify how an information system would process data in support of a business function. The Entity-Relationship Diagram (ERD) technique allowed analysts to identify the types of data items that an enterprise wanted to collect along with the attributes and relationships of those data items. Through these two analysis methods, enterprises could design more efficient and capable "relational" databases that used procedural programming languages (e.g., COBOL, FORTRAN, C) which were capable of serving multiple information systems and business processes. Further, this shifted the analysis and design focus from proprietary solutions to generic information requirements.

In the second area, the movement from mainframe to distributed computing also served to change the way that information systems and networks were designed. While structured information modeling techniques promoted new relational database designs, networked computing promoted the hosting of these databases in multiple locations on smaller computer "servers" that could be located closer to the end-user. Information systems standards based on international and industry agreements emerged, as did new designs for the hosting and transport of the information. Important examples include the Open Systems Interconnection (OSI) Reference Model for information networks that was proposed by J.D. Day and H. Zimmerman in 1983.[8] This model has seven layers that address services, interfaces, and protocols. Prior to that, in 1974 the Transport Communications Protocol (TCP) was proposed by Vinton Cerf and Robert Kahn[9] that led to work on a private research network that connected universities and selected military and business enterprises throughout the nation (known as the ARPANET). In 1978, version of TCP was split into two inter-related protocol sets, one for data communications and another for inter-network (internet) addressing – the Internet Protocol (IP). The acceptance of TCP/IP on a broad scale in the late 1980's and early 1990's promoted the integration of telecommunications and data network infrastructures and provided the catalyst for the dramatic growth of the global Internet. Other standards for data transfer emerged in the late 1980's and early 1990's including a standard that defined "Ethernet" local area networks and Asynchronous Transport Mode (ATM) networks that promoted integrated voice, data, and video transmission.

Data hosting also changed as developments in computer micro processors, hard drive storage, removable disk storage, and telecommunications interfaces all made the desktop computer, also known as the personal computer (PC), a viable candidate to support print, file, and application hosting functions. Since the early 1980's the performance capability of PCs has risen dramatically each year, while the cost of PCs has dropped. This dynamic boosted the movement away from mainframe computing to networked computing based on 'client' and 'server' PCs working together to share data and applications. Standardized approaches to application development began to emerge as a result, along with protracted competitive battles among vendors to develop products that would dominate in the new networked and converged computing environment.

The early 1990's also saw the introduction of a new approach to designing databases. Focusing on the problem of separating structure from process in modeling relational databases, an "object-oriented" approach was developed that took advantage of new programming languages (i.e., Java, C++) that could support data objects that had attributes and behaviors. Additionally, these data objects could encapsulate (prohibit changes to) certain areas of their code to protect them from alteration. This was significant in that objects then represented reusable code whose quality in key areas was assured. Finally, the non-encapsulated areas of code offered users the ability to customize or add attributes and behaviors such that objects became a building block for application and database development.

It was during this time that some of the first writing on information architecture frameworks began to emerge. In 1987, Dennis Mulryan and Richard Nolan (he later developed the Balanced Scorecard) wrote about "Undertaking and Architecture Program"[10] and in 1991 Brandt Allen and Andrew Boynton wrote an article entitled "Information Architecture: In Search of Efficient Flexibility."[11] In 1987 [12] and 1992,[13], John Zachman published seminal articles in the IBM Systems Journal about an idea for an Information Systems Architecture (ISA) that used a matrix to hierarchically organize business and technology documentation to identify what, how, where, by whom, when, and why were processes occurring.

Zachman's work served to elevate the discussion of architectures to the level of the enterprise and stimulated additional writing on enterprise-wide information architectures that was to continue throughout the 1990s. Significantly, in 1992 Steven Spewak built upon Zachman's work and developed the concept of 'Enterprise Architecture Planning' (EAP).[14] The EAP method represented a distinct departure from the technically-oriented architectures of previous years, as it focused on how IT would be used to support business functions on an enterprise-wide (enterprise) basis. It is the combined work of John Zachman and Steven Spewak that form the basis of most of the enterprise architecture frameworks that are in use today throughout business and government, including the EA6 Framework.

Examples of EA Frameworks

The Zachman ISA Framework

In the late-1980's John Zachman observed that the data processing requirements of many of his IBM clients were becoming more complex. There was a need to show information systems from several perspectives that addressed this complexity and promoted planning, design, and configuration management. Zachman drew from both the aircraft and construction industries in developing a highly intuitive and comprehensive schema for documenting information systems architecture (ISA) in the context of several hierarchical perspectives characteristics. Zachman's ISA framework is a schema with rows and columns that functions much like a relational database in that he calls for the development of basic or "primitive" architectural artifacts for each of the 30 cells in the schema, such that none of these artifacts are repeated in other cells or combined to create what Zachman calls "composite" products. By documenting the ISA (now known as the Zachman EA Framework) in detail at each level of the EA framework, an enterprise develops multiple views of their processes and resources that are useful to senior executives, line managers, and support staff. Further, Zachman's approach addresses the what, how, where, who, when, and why questions about an enterprise. Figure 5-2 provides the current version of the Zachman Framework for EA (v3.0).[15]

The Spewak EA Planning Method — Zachman Framework grid

	What	How	Where	Who	When	Why	
Executive Perspective (Scoping)	Inventory Identification	Process Identification	Distribution Identification	Responsibility Identification	Timing Identification	Motivation Identification	Scope Contexts
Management Perspective (Owners)	Inventory Definition	Process Definition	Distribution Definition	Responsibility Definition	Timing Definition	Motivation Definition	Business Concepts
Architect Perspective (Designers)	Inventory Representation	Process Representation	Distribution Representation	Responsibility Representation	Timing Representation	Motivation Representation	System Logic
Engineer Perspective (Builders)	Inventory Specification	Process Specification	Distribution Specification	Responsibility Specification	Timing Specification	Motivation Specification	Technology Physics
Technician Perspective (Implementers)	Inventory Configuration	Process Configuration	Distribution Configuration	Responsibility Configuration	Timing Configuration	Motivation Configuration	Tool Components
Enterprise Perspective (Users)	Inventory Instantiations	Process Instantiations	Distribution Instantiations	Responsibility Instantiations	Timing Instantiations	Motivation Instantiations	Operational Instances
	Inventory Sets	Process Flows	Networks	Assignments	Timing Cycles	Motivations	

Since 1992, John Zachman has gone on to influence a number of different EA frameworks and writings on the EA, including the author's initial EA6 and current EA6 frameworks, as well as this textbook. While Zachman's basic ISA approach is evident in his current schema, many new concepts have been addressed such as how IT security is an implicit element in each cell's artifact(s). Zachman has written a number of papers that are available through his website on how his approach to EA addresses a number of old and new issues and how it is used in current work with organizations worldwide.

The Spewak EA Planning Method (1992)

About the time that John Zachman was releasing his second article to expand the original ISA Framework, Steven Spewak was further extending these ideas into a planning-oriented framework that incorporated new features including a focus on business, an implementation approach that includes principles and values, a migration strategy, and ties to project management. Spewak was the Chief Architect for DHL Systems Inc. at the time of developing his "Enterprise Architecture Planning" (EAP) method. He was also the first person to prominently feature the term "enterprise" in his framework as a way to emphasize the need for architecture to move beyond individual systems planning. Spewak's definition of the term architecture is as follows:

"Since the aim of EAP is to enable an enterprise to share data, the term enterprise should include all areas that need to share substantial amounts of data. A good and proper scope for enterprise often equates to a business

unit, division, or subsidiary because such enterprise units include all of the business functions for providing products and services to customers. Also, with responsibility and control of the bottom line, the economic benefits and justification of EAP can more easily be established".

Spewak states that EAP is a method for developing the top two levels of Zachman's Framework. The seven phases of EAP are grouped into a four- layer "wedding cake" shaped model that crates an implementation sequence, as is shown in Figure 5-3 below.

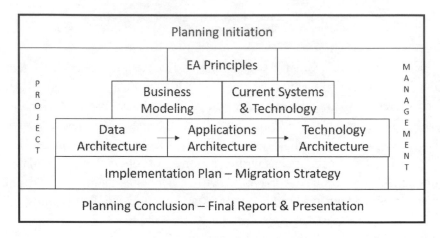

The EA3 and EA6 Frameworks (2004 and 2020)

This book introduces a generalized framework for EA analysis and design that can be used with any type of large, complex organization in the public, private, or non-profit sectors. Developed by Scott Bernard in 2003 and originally called the EA3 "Cube" Framework, various elements were drawn from the work of Talcott Parsons, James Thompson, John Zachman, Steven Spewak, the Federal EA Framework, and the Department of Defense Architecture Framework. The EA3 Framework used the generic shape and three visible faces of a cube to illustrate the close relationship between the structure, functional domains, and service areas of an organization. The framework was introduced as one of the six basic elements of a complete EA approach (see Chapter 1), and highlighted the hierarchical relationship of five sub-architecture domains (strategy, business, data, systems, and infrastructure) and three "threads" (security, standards, and skills) that touch each domain. The idea of consistent scaling was also introduced (cubes within cubes) to promote the documentation of organizational sub-units using the same methods, so that you can decompose EA views from overviews to individual systems, or you can aggregate consistently from systems, to programs, to lines of business, to the entire organization.

In 2017, Bernard began developing EA concepts to support organizational mergers and acquisitions (M&A) and for use in an EA professional certification curriculum that he has taught at Carnegie Mellon University since 2005. Bernard renamed the framework "EA6 Cube" and brought the other three faces into play (culture, value, and risk) to support the focus of pre-deal analytic due-diligence and post-deal design and restructuring. These concepts are presented in Chapter 14 and Appendix A.

Enterprises can implement the EA6 Framework directly or can use it as an initial baseline for the development of their own EA management and documentation approach. Many enterprises will most likely need to modify certain elements of the EA6 Framework to fit their particular needs, which is encouraged as it is recognized that business, government, military, non-profit, and academic enterprises have different cultures, economic drivers, and critical success factors. These differences may require adjustments in the framework in order to best implement an EA program that captures the current and future business and technology environment.

Common characteristics of most EA frameworks that the EA6 Framework also captures are that they address multiple, often hierarchical views of the enterprise and technology, and that they support integrated systems planning and implementation. The EA6 Framework serves primarily to organize IT resource planning and documentation activities. The framework is hierarchical to distinguish high-level views that are of value to executives and planners from the more detailed views that are of value to line managers and support staff. Figure 5-4 on the next page shows the design and key features of each of the six faces.

Six Faces of the EA6 Framework

The faces of the EA6 Framework are arranged in terms of the relationship to each other, the hierarchy of sub-architecture domains, and the grouping of lines of business, as shown in Figure 5-4 below and in Appendix A.

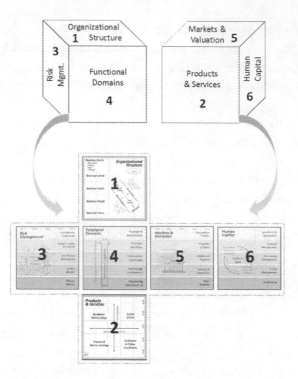

Hierarchical Levels of the EA6 Framework

The five levels of the framework are hierarchical and integrated so that separate sub-architectures are not needed, as shown in Figure 5-5 below.

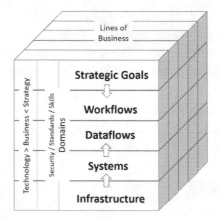

The sub-architectural areas covered at each level are arranged to position high-level strategic goals at the top, general business services and information flows in the middle, and specific support applications and the network infrastructure at the bottom. In this way alignment can be shown between strategy, information, and technology, which aids planning.

Goals and Initiatives. This is the driving force behind the architecture. The top level of the EA6 Framework identifies the strategic direction, goals, and initiatives of the enterprise and provides clear descriptions of the contribution that IT will make in achieving these goals. Strategic planning begins with a clear statement of the enterprise's purpose and/or mission, complimented by a succinct statement of the vision for success. This is followed by descriptions of the strategic direction the enterprise is taking, scenarios that could occur, as well as the competitive strategy that will ensure not only survivability, but success in terms that the enterprise must define. These overarching statements are then supported through the identification of goals and supporting initiatives that include measurable outcomes and performance measures.

Workflows. (Products and Services) This is the architecture's intended area of primary influence. The second level of the EA6 Framework identifies the business products service workflows of the enterprise and the contribution of technology to support those processes. The term 'business service' is used to mean processes and procedures that accomplish the mission and purpose of the enterprise, whether that is to compete in the private sector, provide public services, educate, provide medical services, or provide a defense capability. Strategic planning helps to direct and prioritize the various business services and product delivery activities in an enterprise to ensure that they are collectively moving the enterprise in the strategic direction that is set out in the Strategic Plan. Business services then need to be modeled in their current state and if change is anticipated, also modeled in the envisioned future state. Business services and product delivery processes should be eliminated if they are not adding sufficient value to the enterprise's strategic goals and initiatives. Business services and product delivery activities should be modified if change can increase value to the enterprise, be it a minor adjustment or a major shift in how that activity is accomplished. Technology is often a key enabling element in increasing value but should not be the driving factor in the reengineering or improvement of business services and product delivery processes. It is important to review and adjust the process before IT is applied to ensure that optimal value and efficiency are achieved.

Dataflows. Optimizing data and information exchanges is the secondary purpose of the architecture. The third level of the EA6 Framework is intended to document how information is currently being used by the enterprise and how future information flows would look. This level can be reflected through an IT Strategy document that ties into the enterprise's Strategic Plan and/or Business Plan. The purpose of the IT strategy is to establish a high-level approach for gathering, storing, transforming, and disseminating information throughout the enterprise. The use of concepts such as knowledge management, data mining, information warehouses, data marts, and web portals can be organized through the IT strategy. The design and functioning of databases throughout the enterprise are also documented at this level as are standards and formats for data, data dictionaries, and repositories for reusable information objects.

Systems and Applications. The fourth level of the EA6 Framework is intended to organize and document the current group of information systems, and applications that the enterprise uses to deliver IT capabilities. Depending on changes at the upper levels of the EA6 framework (Business services or Information Flows) there may be planned changes to systems/applications that must be reflected in the architecture's future views. This area of the EA6 framework is also where components are a prominent feature in service-oriented architectures, as increasingly interoperable commercial applications are available to enterprises (e.g., J2EE and .NET industry standards). Large, modular applications can handle entire lines of business and/or back office functions (i.e., financial systems, manufacturing control systems, and supply chain management systems). Often referred to as Enterprise Resource Planning (ERP) systems, these commercial applications may offer modules of functionality that can be customized to allow an enterprise to reduce the overall number of applications that they operate and maintain. While ERP systems rarely provide all of the functionality that an enterprise needs for business functions and administrative support, this modular approach is reflective of a "plug-and-play" strategy that enterprises can adopt at this level of the EA6 Framework to increase interoperability and reduce costs.

Networks and Infrastructure. This is the connectivity grid of the architecture, the host environment for applications and systems. The fifth and bottom level of the EA6 Framework is intended to organize and document current and future views of the voice, data, and video networks that the enterprise uses to host systems, applications, websites, and databases. This level also documents the infrastructure of the enterprise (e.g. buildings, server rooms, capital equipment). Local Area Networks (LANs), Wide Area Networks (WANs), System Application Networks (SANs), Intranets, Extranets, Wireless Networks, Mobile Networks, and Computing Clouds are documented at this level so that efficient designs can be implemented through the future architecture that reduce duplication, increase cost and performance efficiency, and promote availability and survivability. Often, an enterprise will determine that certain IT capabilities are critical to the success of the enterprise, and in these areas the architecture should reflect redundant resources in different locations such that these capabilities could continue to be available if the primary resource became unavailable.

Lines of Business within the EA6 Framework

A Line of Business (LoB) is a distinct area of activity within the enterprise. LoB can also be referred to as 'vertical' mission areas or a "segment", which may involve provision of services, product development/delivery, or internal administrative functions. Each LoB has a complete architecture that includes all five hierarchical levels of the EA6 Framework. The LoB therefore can in some ways stand alone architecturally within the enterprise, except that duplication in data, applications, and network functions would occur if each LOB were truly independent, and crosscutting activities that reduce this duplication would not be represented. There may be cases where an enterprise would want to incrementally develop their EA due to cost or other considerations, and architecting individual LOBs is one way to do this. The LoB architectures then must be tied together so that the EA correctly represents the entire enterprise, which is needed for the EA to be of maximum value to executives, management, and staff.

Crosscutting Components within the EA6 Framework

To avoid the inefficiencies of duplicative support within LoBs, crosscutting business and technology components are established to provide common service and product delivery capabilities, databases, application suites, and network infrastructures. Crosscutting services are aimed at reducing application hosting costs, increasing the sharing of information, and enabling enterprise-wide infrastructure solutions. Examples of crosscutting initiatives include email service, administrative services, telephone service, video teleconferencing facilities, and computer server rooms.

Planning Threads within the EA6 Framework

EA documentation includes "threads" of common activity that pervade all levels of the framework. These threads include security, standards, and workforce considerations.

Security. Security is most effective when it is an integral part of the EA management program and documentation methodology. A comprehensive security and privacy program have several focal areas including information, personnel, operations, and facilities. To be effective, IT security must work across all levels of the EA framework and within all of the EA components. Chapter 11 provides more.

Standards. One of the most important functions of the EA is that it provides technology-related standards at all levels of the EA framework. The EA should draw on accepted international, National, and industry standards in order to promote the use of non-proprietary commercial solutions in EA components. This in turn enhances the integration of EA components, as well as better supporting the switch-out of components when needed.

Skills. One of the greatest resources that an enterprise has is its people. It is therefore important to ensure that staffing, skill, and training requirements are identified at each level of the EA framework, and appropriate solutions are reflected in the future architecture. A Workforce Plan (Human Capital Plan) is perhaps the best way to articulate how human capital will be employed in enabling technology capabilities, which underlie business services and information flows.

Summary of Concepts

This chapter described how an EA framework is one of the foundational elements of an EA program and implementation methodology. The EA framework establishes the scope of the EA documentation effort and relates the areas of the architecture together. EA frameworks were first developed in the 1980's and have evolved in the public and private sectors, as well as internationally to provide support for particular approaches to EA. The EA6 Framework was described in detail, as part of an overall EA methodology. Chapters 6 and 7 provide information on how to develop current and future views of EA documentation using this framework.

Chapter 5 Questions and Exercises

1. Why does an EA implementation methodology begin with the selection of an EA framework?
2. What are some of the basic characteristics of an EA framework?
3. Why are hierarchical levels of an EA framework helpful in documenting an enterprise?
4. Why is it necessary to show current *and* future views of EA documentation?
5. How does the Spewak Enterprise Architecture Planning approach relate to the Zachman EA framework?
6. Would the Federal EA Framework be useable in private sector (business) enterprises? If so, how? If not, why?
7. Choose a medium or large size enterprise and provide the following regarding the areas of the EA6 Cube framework:
   a. List examples of documentation from the enterprise that would be appropriate at each of the five functional levels.
   b. List examples of documentation from the enterprise that would be appropriate for the three common planning threads.
   c. List examples of documentation from the enterprise that would illustrate Lines of Business.

Chapter 6

Components and Artifacts

Chapter Overview

Chapter 6 defines and describes EA components and artifacts within the context of an EA framework. Using the EA6 Framework as an example, EA components are replaceable elements within the framework that come and go with changes in strategy, business services, and new designs for resources involving information flows, applications, networks and other infrastructure. Descriptions are provided of example EA components at each level of the framework. Appendix E gives examples of each artifact.

Key Term: *EA Component*

EA components are those 'plug-and-play' changeable resources that provide capabilities at each level of the framework. Examples include strategic goals and initiatives; business services; information flows and databases; information systems, server farms, websites, and software applications; voice/data/video/mobile networks, cable plants, equipment, and buildings.

Key Term: *EA Artifact*

An EA artifact is a documentation product, such as a text document, diagram, spreadsheet, briefing slides, or video clip. EA artifacts document EA components in a consistent way across the entire architecture.

Learning Objectives

> ➢ Understand what EA components are and their role in an EA framework.
> ➢ Understand how EA artifacts describe EA components.
> ➢ See examples of EA components and artifacts throughout an EA framework.
> ➢ Understand how management views help executives understand EA components.

Introduction

While an EA framework provides an overall structure for modeling the enterprise's business and technology operating environment, components are the working elements of the framework at each level. In other words, EA components are "building blocks" that create discrete parts of the overall IT operational capability. EA artifacts describe EA components.

> *Home Architecture Analogy:* EA components are like the rooms of the house. Rooms can be added, remodeled, or taken away. EA documentation products are the description of each room, and can include statements, stories, pictures, and/or videos.

Discussion

EA components are the active elements of the enterprise's business and technology operating environment. EA components include IT-related strategic goals and initiatives, supply chains, information systems, software applications, knowledge warehouses, databases, websites, and voice/data/video networks, and the security solution. These EA components should function together to create a robust and seamless IT operating environment that effectively supports the enterprise's business needs. Availability, reliability, security, scalability, and cost effectiveness are key performance measurement areas for the general IT operating environment. These areas apply to each EA component, along with measures for integration and reuse. Examples are shown in Figure 6-1 below.

Strategic Goals	• Strategic Plan • Strategic Goals/Metrics • Strategic Initiatives	Vertical Components (1 LoB)
Workflows	• Production Processes • Administrative Services • Marketing & Sales	**Example Architecture Components**
Dataflows	• Knowledge Warehouse • Data Lakes/Marts • Object Library	
Systems	• Systems & Applications • Enterprise Service Bus • Websites & Portals	Crosscutting Components (Multiple LoBs)
Infrastructure	• Intranets/Extranets • Utilities & Backups • Facilities & Equipment	

Figure 6-1. Examples of EA Components

EA artifacts are types of documentation that describe components, including reports, diagrams, charts, spreadsheets, pictures, video files, and other types of recorded information. High-level artifacts are often text documents or diagrams that describe overall strategies, programs, and desired outcomes. Mid-level artifacts are documents, diagrams, charts, spreadsheets, and briefings that describe organizational processes, ongoing projects, supply chains, large systems, information flows, networks, and web sites. Low-level artifacts describe specific applications, data dictionaries, technical standards, interfaces, network components, and cable plants. When these artifacts are harmonized through the organizing taxonomy of the framework, new and more useful views of the functioning of components are generated. This is one of the greatest values of EA as a documentation process… creation of the ability to see a hierarchy of views that can be examined from several perspectives. For example, by recognizing that EA components are the building blocks of the an EA framework, and that most IT hardware and software is now commercially procured (versus being custom developed in-house), the stage has been set for a "plug-and-play" approach to IT support that must be reflected at all levels of the framework.

The following are detailed descriptions of EA components at each level of the EA6 Framework. A more detailed description of the current view of EA components and artifacts is provided in Chapter 8, and a description of the future view of these components/artifacts is provided in Chapter 9. Examples of each type of artifact are available at www. btmgllc.com.

EA Components & Artifacts at the Strategic Level

EA Components:
- *Strategic Plan*
- *E-Commerce/E-Government Plan*

EA Artifacts:
- *Strategic Plan (S-1)*
- *SWOT Analysis (S-2)*
- *Concept of Operations Scenario (S-3)*
- *Concept of Operations Diagram (S-4)*
- *Balanced Scorecard™ (S-5)*

Large, complex enterprises often require a formalized approach to planning that accounts for changing conditions, participants, and goals. An enterprise's purpose and direction, as well as its approach to leveraging resources, are documented at the strategic 'Goals and Initiatives' level of the framework. Strategic Plans should be viewed as "living documents" which are updated periodically, and which help an enterprise understand itself and adapt to changing conditions. Strategic Plans almost never are implemented without changes to the original version, because unforeseen internal and/or external events make elements of the plan unfeasible or sub-optimal for ensuring survival and maximizing success. The value of strategic planning is more in the process than in the product. By having a rational, repeatable process for dealing with the chaos and complexity of many operating environments, enterprises can better and more rapidly set a direction and goals in a formal plan that provides a common referent. The plan can be then be modified in response to changes in the environment.

The two key components at this level are (1) the Strategic Plan, and (2) Digital Transformation Plan. Supporting artifacts are mission and vision statements, scenarios, strategies, goals, and initiative measures that are developed through the strategic planning process. While the basic mission, purpose, and/or direction of an enterprise may change infrequently; the scenarios, goals, initiatives, and measures are the flexible components of the process that can be changed as needed to reflect new mission areas, market opportunities, competitor actions, laws and regulations, economic conditions, resource constraints, and management priorities.

Strategic Plan

Strategic planning produces a high-level view of the direction that an enterprise sets for itself. This direction is further articulated in long-range scenarios, strategies, goals, and initiatives that serve as the baseline for short-term tactical (operational) planning that is updated annually. Strategic Plans for enterprises in dynamic and/or highly competitive environments should look three to five years into the future and be updated annually. Strategic Plans for enterprises in more stable environments should look five to ten years into the future and be updated approximately every three years.

A Strategic Plan is a composite EA artifact that should guide the enterprise's direction over a 3-5 year period in the future by providing the following items, each of which are primitive (basic) EA artifacts. Full versions of abbreviated primitive artifacts are separate artifacts.

- Provide a Mission Statement and a Vision Statement that succinctly captures the purpose and direction of the enterprise.
- Develop a Statement of Strategic Direction that fits the enterprise's purpose, ensures survivability, allows for flexibility, and promotes competitive success. This statement is a detailed description of where the enterprise intends to go.
- Summarize the results of a SWOT Analysis that is based on the statement of strategic direction and which identifies the enterprise's strengths, weaknesses, opportunities, and threats. The full SWOT analysis is artifact S-2.

- Summarize the situation and planning assumptions for several 'Concept of Operations' <u>CONOPS Scenarios</u> that support the enterprise's strategic direction. This summary should include *one current scenario* that describes at a high-level the coordination of ongoing activities in each line of business, as well as *several future scenarios* that account for different combinations of internal and external drivers identified through the SWOT Analysis. The complete scenarios are artifact S-3.
- Develop a CONOPS Graphic that in a single picture captures the essence of and participants in the current operating scenario. This graphic is artifact S-4.
- Develop a <u>General Competitive Strategy</u> for the enterprise that incorporates the current and future CONOPS scenarios and moves the enterprise in the intended direction in a way that and address internal/external drivers such as culture, line of business requirements, market conditions, competitor strategies, and risk.
- Identify <u>Strategic Goals</u> that will accomplish the competitive strategy and specify the executive sponsors who are responsible for achieving each goal.
- Identify <u>Strategic Initiatives</u> and resource sponsors for the initiatives, which are the ongoing programs or development projects that will accomplish each Strategic Goal.
- Summarize <u>Outcome Measures</u> for each Strategic Goal and Initiative, using the Balanced Scorecard™ or similar approach. The full scorecard is artifact S-5.

Because some of these areas will contain sensitive information that the enterprise will want to protect from its competitors, the full Strategic Plan should be written for internal use by decision-makers. A generalized version can then be developed for external distribution.

By using proven approaches to develop the Strategic Plan, such as the Balanced Scorecard®, enterprises are able to identify IT-related goals for the enterprise that support overall strategic goals, as well as initiatives for achieving those goals and measures for tracking progress within each initiative. Figure 6-2 shows these relationships.

Mission Statement		
Vision Statement		
Strategic Plan		
Strategic Goal #1		
Intended Outcome (s)		
Initiative 1-1	IT Component	Performance Measure(s)
Initiative 1-2	IT Component	Performance Measure(s)
Initiative 1-3	IT Component	Performance Measure(s)
Strategic Goal #2		
Intended Outcome (s)		
Initiative 2-1	IT Component	Performance Measure(s)
Initiative 2-2	IT Component	Performance Measure(s)
Initiative 2-3	IT Component	Performance Measure(s)
IT Implementation and Support Strategy		

Figure 6-2: Relationship of Strategic-Level Artifacts

Mission Statement

An enterprise's Mission Statement succinctly describes the purpose and direction of the enterprise. This statement should be long enough to get the point across but provide no detail (1-2 sentences is recommended). The Mission Statement answers the "why does the organization exist" question. Examples are provided below:

Mission Statement Example – Business:
"The Acme Insurance Company provides high-quality, affordable business insurance to small business owners and farmers."

Mission Statement Example – Government:
"The Orange County Highway Department provides safe and efficient roadways and bridges for pedestrian and vehicle traffic."

Vision Statement

An enterprise's Vision Statement describes in abbreviated form the competitive strategy of the enterprise. This statement should be short and memorable. The Vision Statement answers the "how are we getting there?" question at the level of the entire enterprise. The following are examples of Vision Statements from business and government:

Vision Statement Example – Business:

"In offering unbeatable value and service, the Acme Insurance Company will be the insurance provider of choice for small business owners and farmers."

Vision Statement Example – Government:

"State-of-the art planning, execution, and responsiveness will make Orange County's roads and bridges the safest and most efficient in the State."

Vision statements are more than advertising slogans, they are meant to help members of the organization understand the direction being pursued and be able to communicate that inside and outside the enterprise.

Strategic Direction Statement

This statement establishes the strategic direction that the enterprise will pursue during the period covered by the Strategic Plan. It builds on the statements of purpose, mission, and vision, and identifies the character of the enterprise in its envisioned future state. While protecting sensitive competitive information, the statement of strategic direction should provide a guidepost for members of the enterprise to use in understanding general expectations for their contribution to survival and competitive success. It should also promote understanding among external stakeholders such that trust and perceptions of value are increased.

SWOT Analysis

One of the earliest activities the enterprise performs in developing a strategic plan is a Strength, Weakness, Opportunity, Threat (SWOT) analysis. This analysis looks at internal and external factors to determine areas that the enterprise should focus on to increase its survivability and success, as well as areas that the enterprise should avoid or decrease. The analysis should be summarized in the Strategic Plan, and details are archived in the EA Repository as a separate artifact (S-2). Figure 6-3 provides an example of how to present the results of a SWOT analysis.[16]

Time	Area	Internal		External	
Near-Term (1-3 Years)	Strengths	1. 2.	3. 4.	1. 2.	3. 4.
	Weaknesses	1. 2.	3. 4.	1. 2.	3. 4.
	Opportunities	1. 2.	3. 4.	1. 2.	3. 4.
	Threats	1. 2.	3. 4.	1. 2.	3. 4.
Long-Term (4-10 Years)	Strengths	1. 2.	3. 4.	1. 2.	3. 4.
	Weaknesses	1. 2.	3. 4.	1. 2.	3. 4.
	Opportunities	1. 2.	3. 4.	1. 2.	3. 4.
	Threats	1. 2.	3. 4.	1. 2.	3. 4.

Figure 6-3. SWOT Table Example

Concept of Operations Scenarios

Enterprises may find it helpful to develop detailed current and future Concept of Operations (CONOPS) scenarios that encompass several years of operating activity, and which considers different combinations of internal and external drivers that were identified in the SWOT Analysis. In so doing, the enterprise can evaluate the planning assumptions and expected outcomes in each scenario and evaluate the relative merit and danger of pursuing a particular course of action. Additionally, the enterprise can refine and maintain an ongoing file of information on several of the most plausible scenarios in order to be able to "bracket" a range of suitable strategies and goals for successful competition. The scenario development activity may be particularly valuable to enterprises in highly dynamic and turbulent operating environments. A summary of the scenarios and planning assumptions (matrix format) is included in the Strategic Plan, while the full version of the scenarios is a separate 'primitive' artifact (S-3). Chapter 8 provides more details.

Concept of Operations Graphic

The CONOPS Graphic is very important to the enterprise, as it describes in one picture all of the major activities in the current CONOPS, as well as the relationship of those activities. The CONOPS graphic becomes a touchstone to help the enterprise understand what it does at a basic level.

Competitive Strategy

This area of the Strategic Plan identifies how the enterprise will achieve success in pursuing its stated strategic direction. This is done at two levels: first, a general strategy related to growth, and second, a more specific strategy related to competition and/or differentiation.

First, at a general level the enterprise establishes that it intends to grow, shrink, or stabilize. Whether it is a turnaround strategy to recover lost ground, a growth strategy to enter new markets or provide new services, or a stabilization strategy to absorb and solidify recent growth or reduction, the competitive strategy must first and foremost be flexible enough to ensure survival in the face of unplanned internal and external events, and then promote success in the goals that the enterprise decides to pursue during the period of the Strategic Plan.

Second, the competitive strategy is detailed in a statement regarding service and/or product differentiation and delivery. This area identifies one or more methods that the enterprise will pursue to achieve success in what it produces. Examples include delivering the highest quality; delivering the lowest price; having the most flexibility and/or options; being first-to-market; being a niche player; dominating market share; and acquiring competitors. These statements involve sensitive information, which the enterprise may want to hold in a separate addendum to the Plan.

Strategic Goals

The enterprise's strategic goals are those objectives that when achieved together will ensure survival and attain success, as defined in the outcome measures and performance metrics that the enterprise develops for itself. Strategic goals also serve to logically divide enterprise activities into areas that will make a meaningful and valued impact on the enterprise to move it in the direction that the Strategic Plan sets forth.

Strategic Initiatives

The enterprise's strategic initiatives are those activities which are chartered by and support strategic goals. Not all of an enterprise's activities are strategic in nature, as some activities are support functions (i.e., payroll, accounting, IT infrastructure management, and human resources). Initiatives that are strategic in nature include those ongoing programs and specific projects that accomplish one or more strategic goals. One of the questions that executive decision makers often ask when funding decisions are made for an initiative is whether there is strategic value in the planned outcome(s). Investments that link to strategic goals are said to be "aligned".

Outcome Measures

Knowing that progress is being made on strategic goals and initiatives is imperative for an enterprise's success. By definition, these are the activities that are the most important to the enterprise and therefore require regular review and refinement. By identifying goals and initiatives that can be measured, the enterprise is able to manage these activities. Measures are the most detailed EA component at the strategic level of the EA framework, and are found at each of the other levels as well.

It is important to understand the difference between "outcome" measures and "output" measures. Outcome measures identify progress being made toward some new end-state, such as better product quality, increased customer satisfaction, or more efficient processes. Output measures provide data on activities and things, such as how many cars are produced in a day, how many new customers are gained or lost each month, or how closely an activity meets a quality checklist. Outcome measures often have both quantitative and qualitative elements to them, while output measures are usually quantitative. Output measures are important for indicating progress in an initiative area, but it is the attainment of outcomes that correlate to goal attainment, and an enterprise's strategic progress. Examples of outcome and output measures are provided below.

Outcome Measure #1:   Improve the factory safety environment by reducing injuries by 5 percent within one year.

Output Measure #1-1:   Increase the number of safety inspections by 10 percent.

Output Measure #1-2:   Require 100 percent use of safety helmets and eyewear.

Output Measure #1-3:   Require accident report completion within 24 hours.

Digital Transformation Plan

A Digital Transformation Plan (formerly called an eCommerce or eGovernment Plan) is often needed by large organizations in addition to the general Strategic Plan. This is because the general Strategic Plan usually does not address IT in sufficient detail to identify the various IT-related initiatives that may enable many of an enterprise's strategic goals. This is said in recognition that many enterprises are becoming "information centric", in that they depend on information and on IT resources to successfully accomplish key business, manufacturing, service, research, financial, human resources, and office automation functions. The Digital Transformation Plan is more like a tactical plan due to the dynamic nature of IT resources and the processes they support. The Plan should provide specific program, outcome, and performance information for a two or three-year timeframe. Beyond about three years, it is difficult to predict with accuracy what new capabilities IT will be able to provide. The Plan should be updated every 1-2 years.

EA Components & Artifacts at the Business Level

EA Components:
- ***Business Services***
- ***Business Products***
- ***IT Capital Planning Portfolio***

EA Artifacts:
- *Business Plan (B-1)*
- *Node Connectivity Diagram (B-2)*
- *Swim Lane Process Diagram (B-3)*
- *Business Process/Service Model (B-4)*
- *Business Process/Product Matrix (B-5)*
- *Use Case Narrative and Diagram (B-7)*
- *Investment Business Case (B-8)*

An enterprise's key business and support processes are documented at the "Business Process" level of the Framework. Components at this level include business process documentation and a capital planning portfolio that information on each investment in IT that meets operational and financial thresholds. Relationships between participants in eCommerce and eGovernment activities are often referred to as "B" for business, "G" for government, and "C" for citizen, resulting in acronyms such as B2B for business-to-business and G2C for government-to-citizen.

Business Services

Business services are those enterprise activities that directly contribute to mission accomplishment. This can be in the form of strategic initiatives to develop new or improved services or artifacts, ongoing manufacturing activities, public service delivery, and "back office" finance, accounting, administrative, and human resource functions. Business process documentation includes flow charts and modeling techniques that detail the inputs, outputs, enabling resources, and controls of an enterprise activity. It also includes the documentation of activities that completely reengineer an organizational process (called Business Process Reengineering - BPR), and activities that provide minor adjustments to a process (called Business Process Improvement - BPI).

Business Products

Business products are the tangible and intangible goods that the enterprise produces in pursuit of business and strategic goals. Examples include manufactured items, financial instruments, vehicles, structures, intellectual capital, art, music, and special events. Business product documentation is important to an enterprise as it captures and protects intellectual capital and various patent, trademark, and copyrights. Also, documentation of products is useful in BPR and BPI activities. EA artifacts that document business products contain sensitive information that should be protected.

IT Capital Planning Portfolio

Because resources are limited in most enterprises, the value of making a significant investment in IT should be shown in order to identify the costs, benefits, and rate of return on capital. It may be shown in a manner to justify not using those resources on other initiatives (opportunity cost). A 'business case' for any investment is a standardized format for developing and presenting the various aspects of alternatives, cost and benefit, and return that executives are interested in. A business case should include:

- Requirement Statement
- Alternatives Analysis
- Cost-Benefit Analysis
- Net Present Value Calculation
- Return on Investment Calculation

The IT Capital Planning and Investment Control (CPIC) process is a key management activity that is designed to plan, select, control, and evaluate the enterprise's major investments in IT. The CPIC process works in concert with the EA Management Plan to move an enterprise from the current architecture to the future architecture on an ongoing basis. The use of standardized IT Project Management Plans helps make the CPIC process more efficient and more useful to project managers (see Chapter 10).

EA Components & Artifacts at the Data Level

EA Components:
- *Knowledge Warehouses*
- *Information Systems*
- *Databases*

EA Artifacts:
- *Knowledge Management Plan (D-1)*
- *Information Exchange Matrix (D-2)*
- *Object State-Transition Diagram (D-3)*
- *Object Event Sequence Diagram (D-4)*
- *Logical Data Model (D-5)*
- *Physical Data Model (D-6)*
- *Activity/Entity (CRUD) Matrix (D-7)*
- *Data Dictionary/Object Library (D-8)*

How an enterprise uses data and information is documented at the "Data and Information" level of the EA6 Framework. EA components at this level include documentation on the design, function, and management of information systems, databases, knowledge warehouses, and data marts. It also includes detailed documentation on the structure and processing logic of data that the enterprise is interested in.

Knowledge Warehouses
Knowledge warehouses evolved from large mainframe databases that served multiple user groups across a number of systems and networks. A knowledge warehouse is a one-stop-shop for data and information about

various activities and processes in the enterprise. The more types of data and information in the knowledge warehouse, the more valuable it is for analysis activities that extend beyond simple queries and report generation, but enable 'data mining' wherein all levels of the enterprise can look for patterns or new information from otherwise disparate data. Typically, users interact with a warehouse through a portal-like interface that enables customized access to various elements such as databases, presentations, and data, audio, and video files. A knowledge warehouse may be developed for a specific use or bought as a customizable product.

Information System Content

IT system content is binary and comes in three forms: data, information, and knowledge. Aggregation, format, and context, are what primarily differentiate each form. Beyond this is wisdom that is usually not recorded in an IT system because this involves a person's situational insight, though the writings of someone's views on matters can be stored. Beyond wisdom is the great unknown... how does our universe really work? The figure below provides definitions and relationships between the levels of data, information, knowledge, wisdom, and beyond... there is less of each as you go up the hierarchy, as one level extracts from the others.

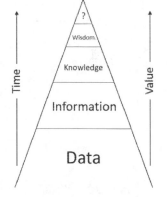

Data: Binary symbols, states, or signals that create bits/bytes representing pixels or alpha/numeric characters aggregated to form facts about things.

Information: Combinations of data arranged in a manner that provides meaning to users.

Knowledge: Data and information interpreted in the context of past use, norms, and environment.

Wisdom: *Insight* into the nature, value, and use of knowledge as part of a larger whole.

? Transcendental understanding of the universe.

Information systems consist of hardware and software that work together to efficiently collect and disseminate data, as well as to enable the development and analysis of information. Information systems serve many lines of business in enterprises including administrative and financial support, manufacturing, marketing and sales, government regulation, public services, and defense systems. Information systems originally were designed to support a particular need in an enterprise and connect to a single database. As enterprises developed more uses for information systems, greater efficiencies were achieved when several information systems shared one or more databases. This movement from "stovepipe" information system designs to more distributed and integrated designs, which span the entire enterprise, and which tie together via information warehouses, is one of the driving factors in the development of an EA.

Databases

Databases are software applications that are designed to support the storage, retrieval, updating, and deletion of data elements and/or data objects. Data elements are the fundamental facts and values that are stored in databases. Data elements and their identifying and characteristic attributes are usually stored in relational databases that consist of data tables which are logically related to create a speedy, efficient, and flexible query capability. Data objects are discrete 'blocks' of code that contain attribute information about a data element as well as behaviors that create an ability for objects to interact with each other in different ways, depending on the type of triggering event.

Object Library

A data object library is an online repository of reusable software code that has three characteristics: name, attributes, and methods/behaviors. Object-oriented development methods create data applications that contain "smart" objects that have built-in executable functions. An example is a template for invoicing that can be adjusted to work with several different applications.

EA Components & Artifacts at the Systems Level

EA Components:
- *Software Applications*
- *Web Services*
- *Service Bus and Middleware*
- *Enterprise Resource Planning (ERP) Solutions*
- *Converged/Hyper-Coverged Application Stacks*
- *Operating Systems*

EA Artifacts:
- *System Interface Diagram (SA-1)*
- *System Communication Diagram (SA-2)*
- *System Interface Matrix (SA-3)*
- *System Data Flow Diagram (SA-4)*
- *System/Operations Matrix (SA-5)*
- *Systems Data Exchange Matrix (SA06)*
- *System Performance Matrix (SA-7)*
- *System Evolution Diagram (SA-8)*
- *Web Application Diagram (SA-9)*

The systems and applications that an enterprise uses to support its business services, product delivery processes, and information flows are documented at the 'Systems and Applications' level of the EA6 Framework. One of the purposes of EA is to improve the integration and efficiency of the support systems and software applications across the enterprise. Duplication of functions and a lack of interoperability can be addressed through the establishment of technical and product standards for software. Components at this level range in size and complexity from large multi-function ERP solutions that extend throughout the enterprise to single-user desktop tools that enhance productivity.

Software Applications
Applications are software programs that provide a functional capability for "front-office" IT systems (e.g., manufacturing, sales, government services, logistics, and knowledge warehouses) or "back-office" IT systems (e.g., financial systems, human resources systems, e-mail, and office automation products such as word processors, spreadsheets, diagramming tools, photo editors, and web browsers). Enterprises often possess a myriad of applications from different vendors that are limited in their ability to function together. The selection of applications from a controlled number of vendors and/or which adhere to widely accepted standards is a method that can be used to promote the interoperability of software applications.

Web Services
Just as EA trends are emphasizing the use of plug-and-play software applications; the use of web-based IT services is significantly extending and accelerating this concept. These open standards-based web services

are replacing software applications that have unique hosting and access requirements. By using the TCP/IP, SOAP, REST, and UDDI protocols for application connectivity and internationally accepted formats for data/information retrieval/exchange (e.g., HTTP, HTML, J2EE, and XML), a common hosting and operating environment is created for web services. A web service is defined as any IT resource (e.g., application, program, database, or information portal) that functions through a web-based graphical user interface (GUI), such as a web browser. Web services include email, web- based ERP applications, websites, electronic commerce systems, web-based knowledge warehouses…. virtually any front or back-office function that is web-based and which operates within the enterprise on TCP/IP based compliant internal networks (Intranets). Service-Oriented Architecture (SOA) links processes to data to systems.

Enterprise Service Bus & Middleware

The "Service Bus" is a SOA term for a common operating environment for systems, applications, and web services that is characterized by non-proprietary open standards protocols and middleware for data exchange, software/hardware interfaces. The Service Bus is platform independent and allows any system/service to interoperate with any other system/service that is logically and physically linked to the Bus. SOA approaches promote the support of business functions through the use of shared, reusable services, which increasingly are web-based. The term that SOA approaches use for this capability is a "Virtual Enterprise Network", and the SOA term for the Service Bus is a Network Application Platform. Middleware is a software program that links other applications together which otherwise would not be able to exchange data and information. Examples include integrating older mainframe applications and databases to those which are web-based, or enabling the sharing of data between artifacts from different vendors that may have different application programming interfaces (APIs) that incorporate standards such as the Simple Object Access Protocol (SOAP) or the Representational State Transfer (REST).

Enterprise Resource Planning (ERP) Solutions

ERP solutions are marketed by vendors as one way to increase application interoperability and reduce the duplication of functions. Often based on "modules" of capability, ERPs are essentially a suite of applications offered by the Same vendor that are designed to work together to create an enterprise-wide capability. ERP solutions exist for finance, marketing, human resources, payroll and accounting, and supply chain management, all of which can be interconnected to create a relatively seamless environment for sharing information. While ERPs accomplish some of the goals of EA, they fall short of providing the holistic planning, documentation, and decision-making support that EA is intended to develop and maintain. Also, ERPs normally are not able to support all of the application requirements of the enterprise (i.e., office automation, finance and accounting, product line support, executive decision-making, e-mail). This wider yet incomplete coverage of application component requirements is one of the shortfalls of ERP solutions, which the EA program can address by establishing standards for the integration of ERP modules with other applications.

Converged / Hyper-Converged Application Stacks

A "stack" of applications is an integrated collection of hardware and software that brings together storage, computing, and networking capabilities to host a number of applications and user environments. In a "converged" configuration the storage array, computing blade servers/ load balancers, and network routers/switches are managed as separate but closely integrated entities. The stack's hardware and software products can come from different vendors. This converged stack becomes an easy-to-expand or contract (scalability), and is managed through virtualization middleware that allows for the creation of partititions at the operating system level which enables the establishment (spin-up) of "virtualized" (partitioned) computing environments (machines) and application sets (virtual modules)… to that on a single physical application stack (compute, storage, network) there can be dozens or hundreds of partitioned/virtualized user machines, application sets, and data sets. Virtualization software is the type of middleware that allows for the compute/storage/network stack convergence as well as the establishment of virtual modules and machines (VMs). Hyper-converged stacks have similar compute/storage/network functions, but the hardware and software products usually come from a single vendor and these functional areas and VMs are software defined and managed.

Operating Systems

Operating systems are applications that enable computers to provide basic networking and processing functions. Differences in operating systems are a large part of what distinguishes older centralized mainframe designs from newer decentralized client-server designs. Larger enterprises may operate computers that use several different types of operating systems, which may hinder the interoperability of these component resources. Commercial vendors traditionally have produced operating systems that are proprietary and are designed to limit integration to their own products; however, the proliferation of client-server network designs and the emergence of the Internet have forced vendors to offer operating systems that are increasingly interoperable.

EA Components & Artifacts at the Network Level

EA Components:
- *Data Networks*
- *Telecommunications Networks*
- *Video Networks*
- *Mobile Networks*
- *Cable and Wireless Backbones*
- *Security Solutions*
- *Buildings and Server Rooms*
- *Equipment*

EA Artifacts:
- *Network Connectivity Diagram (NI-1)*
- *Network Inventory (NI-2)*
- *Capital Equipment Inventory (NI-3)*
- *Building Blueprints (NI-4)*
- *Network Center Diagram (NI-5)*
- *Cable Plant Diagram (NI-6)*
- *Rack Elevation Diagram (NI-7)*

The Technology Infrastructure level of the EA6 Framework functions to integrate and connect the enterprise's IT resources at the application and information levels. Seamless integration of voice, data, video, and transport (cable/wireless) resources is one of the keys to creating an operationally effective and cost-efficient IT infrastructure.

Data Networks

Data networks are designed to transport data and information in coded digital form between various computers that support storage, retrieval, updates, and processing for end-users. These networks have a logical design that identifies how data and information will flow between systems, applications, databases, and websites. The network also has a physical design that consists of a data transmission "backbone", an information hosting environment, and external interface points (unless it is a stand- alone system). The network backbone often consists of commercially procured routers, switches, hubs, security equipment, backup power units, equipment racks, and cable. The hosted network environment includes commercially procured computers for storage, processing, and end-users, as well as commercial software for business and office automation requirements and custom-developed software that is designed to support unique requirements. Data networks within an enterprise, referred to as Local Area Networks (LANs) or Internal Networks (Intranets) normally interface with a telecommunications network to connect to the global Internet. Enterprise-specific External Networks (Extranets) are also known as Wide-Area Networks (WANS) or external public or private clouds.

Telecommunications Networks

Telecommunications networks are designed to transport voice signals in coded form (analog waves or digital electron/photon flows) between end- users. These networks also have a logical design that identifies how voice signals are transported between network components and a physical design that identifies the types of equipment involved in signal processing and transmission. This includes hardware, software, cable plants, cellular/wireless nodes, microwave repeaters, and relay satellites. Telecommunications networks exist at a local level to support parts of an enterprise or an entire enterprise. These are known as "Public Business Exchange" (PBX) systems which are commercially available from a number of vendors. Telecommunications systems are owned by government agencies or private companies (telcos) that are regional, national, or international in nature often involve multiple sub-networks that interface at numerous points to increase coverage, routing, and reliability. Because of the ubiquitous presence of telecommunications networks, the rapid development of the Internet on a global basis has been made possible in large part due to the conversion of voice transmission capacity to dedicated data transmission, as well as the addition of significant amounts of new capacity from existing and new commercial providers. The co-transmission of digital voice and data signals is now commonplace, and standards arose to support this on most telecommunications networks (e.g., ISDN and Voice-Over-IP). Yes, telcos own most of the Internet's global paths.

Video Networks

Video networks are designed to transport video image signals in coded form (analog waves or digital electron/photon flows) between production sites and viewing sites. Like the other types of networks, video networks have logical designs to show the flow of image signals and physical designs to identify production, transmission, and receiving equipment. National and international standards have emerged that promote the transmission and reception of video signals on a global basis. Video networks can be as small as peer-to-peer computer-based applications or video teleconferencing (VTC) equipment that operates internally and/or between several external users. Online learning platforms often incorporate VTC.

As with voice networks, digital coding of video signals supports the co-transmission of this information on the network backbone that transports voice and data. This seamless integration of voice, data, and video transmission capabilities brings new capabilities for information exchange within and between enterprises. Future architectures will often call for this type of integration, with applications and equipment that will support it.

Mobile Networks

Mobile networks are those which are specifically focused on providing telecommunications connectivity to users who are using compact devices to remotely connect to a voice, data, or video network from outside of the network. This includes the use of cellular telephones, portable laptop computers, tablets, and personal digital assistants. Connectivity to mobile (also called wireless) networks from a distance of up to 30 miles can be achieved through wireless radio frequency (RF) connections between telecommunications networks, cellular transmission towers and repeaters. Longer range RF connections to remote locations can be relayed by satellites in geostationary or low-earth orbit. Close proximity connectivity between mobile devices can be achieved through infra-red communications of up to 100 feet or low-power RF connections provided by technologies such as BluetoothTM.

Transmission Backbones

The transmission capability of an information network (voice, data, or video) has its foundation in connectivity between network equipment. This connectivity can be provided through various media including cables (copper or glass fiber), wireless cells (short-range radio waves), transmission towers (medium range microwaves), and/or satellite links (long-range up-link and down link of VHF, UHF, or EHF radio waves). These "backbones" of interconnectedness are what allow the electrons and/or photons to flow in a super fast stream of binary (on or off) code or in analog waves that are translated into data, voice signals, and/or video signals. Improvements in hardware, software, and cable media have allowed for the near instantaneous transmission of millions of binary elements called bits (one binary element) and bytes (a group of 8 binary elements). The ability to now transmit billions of bits and bytes of digital information has allowed for the development of sophisticated applications and databases that bring new capabilities for people and enterprises to communicate in robust ways that include information in the form of data, images, and sound. Low-Earth Orbiting Satellites (LEOS) constellations are growing significantly each year have become a robust part of the broadband global connectivity grid as they provide direct low-latency (signal delay) paths and also integrate with cellular and cable networks.

Management Views of EA Artifacts

EA management views are high-level composite graphics that depict multiple aspects of EA components in a simplified or more attractive big- picture format than that which is normally produced by EA tools. Without management views, the basic (primitive) EA artifacts may consist primarily of technical models that do not hold the interest of EA executive sponsors and users, therefore putting the EA program at risk. The purpose of management views is to lower this risk by:

- Gaining and maintaining EA executive sponsors and resources
- Communicating high-level management-friendly views of EA
- Showing the boundaries of the enterprise being documented
- Combining EA and other IRM artifacts into actionable information for managing and decision-making

EA management views can help various types of users to both understand and share EA artifacts. For example, members of the EA team who are modeling data in several information systems can develop a management view to show how information from those systems is used between various LoBs, and in so doing gain the support of managers in those business areas. In addition, management views can help to translate technical artifacts into views that are easier to understand by non-technical users. Examples of each type of artifact are available at www.btmgllc.com.

Summary of Concepts

This chapter described the purpose of EA components and artifacts within an EA framework. Using the EA6 Framework as an example, EA components were described as replaceable elements within the framework that come and go with changes in strategy, business services, and new designs for IT resources involving information flows, applications, and the technology infrastructure. Descriptions were provided of the types of EA components that exist at each level of the framework. Chapters 7 and 8 will focus on current and future views of the EA artifacts that describe EA components at all levels of the framework.

Chapter 6 Questions and Exercises

1. What are EA components and how do they relate to a framework?
2. What are EA artifacts and how do they relate to EA components?
3. What parts of a Strategic Plan can be viewed as EA components?
4. Why can an organization's business services, information flows, applications, and networks be viewed as EA components?
5. Are IT standards important to EA components?
6. Which elements of a security program can be EA components?
7. List several hypothetical EA components at each level of the EA6 Framework for a large automobile manufacturing company.
   a. Compare and contrast the use of the term "component" in the context of how it is used in this chapter with the use of the term in the software and application development industry.
   b. Obtain the Annual Report of a Fortune 500 corporation and list potential EA components at each level of the EA6 Framework.

Case Study:
Danforth Manufacturing Company
Scene 4: Developing Current and Future EA Views

CIO Roberta Washington and Chief Architect Raja Patil are leading an EA Working Group through the development of architecture segments that cover several lines of business at DMC. These segments of the overall DMC enterprise architecture will help COO Kate Jarvis and CFO Jose Cruz work together as they evaluate requirements and plan solutions for new information systems. Scene 3 had covered the need for a detailed implementation methodology, and this scene describes the approach the Working Group will take in documenting the current and future views of these segments of the DMC holistic architecture.

"Thank you for coming to today's meeting of the Enterprise Architecture Working Group" said Roberta. We are going to talk about the method for developing current and future views of the two segments of the company's enterprise architecture we are developing. These segments cover manufacturing and production, which are the lines of business identified by Kate and Jose that require more IT support. At the last meeting we developed the detailed implementation methodology that will guide our efforts and reduce the risk that we will not be successful. Raja Patil, our Chief Architect, will describe the documentation of current and future views."

"Thank you, Roberta" said Raja. "In accordance with our implementation methodology, we will be using the EA6 Framework to organize and guide the documentation of current and future views of these segments of the DMC architecture. Following the framework's structure, we will gather existing artifacts of information on the lines of business in the following order: strategic goals and initiatives, business services, information flows and data elements, systems and support services, and the network infrastructure. These documentation artifacts come in many forms including reports, policy memos, manuals, spreadsheets, briefing slides, diagrams, and video files. By organizing these artifacts in the online EA repository into categories that match the levels and areas of the framework, we can establish links between the information to produce robust new views of the lines of business. This also establishes a baseline of EA information for future planning and decision-making."

Raja continued. "As for documenting the future views, we will start by establishing several future operating scenarios with Jose, Kate and their staff members. These scenarios are short stories about possible future activities in a variety of friendly and hostile business climates. The scenarios help us to identify important planning assumptions about their future line of business activities, depending on the environment. Once the most probable scenario is selected, we will use the planning assumptions to guide discussions in our Working Group, and decisions by Jose and Kate on what they want to invest in to best position themselves for success in the future. Finally, we will identify how these decisions cause changes to the current EA at each level of the framework and will document those changes in new artifacts that are saved in the EA repository in a separate future EA section."

Over the next several weeks, the EA Working Group gathered existing or developed new documentation artifacts for the current views of the two EA segments at each level of the EA framework. The Group then developed several future operating scenarios from which future view artifacts were developed. Chapters 7 and 8 provide more details on the development of current and future EA views.

Buzzword Bingo

"Hello again most excellent leadership team!" says the CEO, "Are we ready to implement?" "Not quite" says the CIO. "We had some custom mods that the COO and CFO needed… and the vendor puked." "Wait, what?" says the CEO. "Well, even though we harmonized our requirements, some of them were not out-of-the box functionality for the vendor and they want six months and a half-million to meet our needs." "Whoa… hold on here, that's outside our time-to-market window and busts the budget right off the bat!" "I know, it freaked me out too" says the COO. "Ditto" says the CFO. "Double Ditto" says the CIO who pivots to: "let's pull out our crystal ball and see how we can virtualize and hyper-converge storage and compute across cloud platforms to transform and co-host SITS and WELLCO. Go get 'em! Says the CEO on his way back to the bus leaving for Abeline.

Chapter 7

Developing Current Architecture Views

Chapter Overview

Chapter 7 covers the development of current views of the EA in the context of a documentation framework and implementation methodology. The current architecture is actually a collection of EA artifacts that document existing EA components throughout the enterprise. Current EA views are important to an enterprise in that they establish or verify what resources are being used in lines of business to support the achievement of strategic goals. This becomes a reference baseline much like an inventory that then supports planning and decision-making for the future architecture.

Learning Objectives

> ➢ Understand how current views relate to the implementation method.
> ➢ Understand how current views relate to the EA framework.
> ➢ See examples of current views of EA components and artifacts.

Introduction

The current view of the architecture shows the processes and resources that are presently active in the enterprise's operating environment. This is also known as the "as-is" view of the EA. Depending on the amount of prior EA planning, these resources may or may not be aligned with the organization's strategic goals and business services. If little EA planning has occurred, a significant amount of duplication in function may be present.

As is shown in Figure 7-1 below, current views of the architecture provide an enterprise with documentation of existing strategic goals, business services, information flows, systems, infrastructure, and the common "thread" areas of security, standards, and workforce planning.

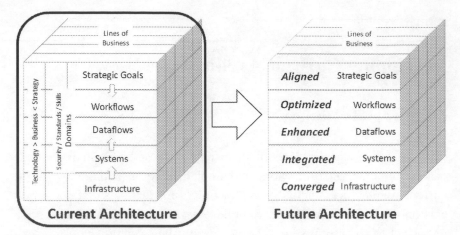

Figure 7-1: The Current Architecture

Discussion

Documentation of the current EA is important to an enterprise because it provides a set of baseline reference information/artifacts for planning and decision-making. Also, by completing the documentation of current EA components at all levels of the framework, a view of the enterprise emerges that reveals associations, dependencies, and performance gaps between the enterprise's business requirements and current capabilities.

Enterprise Architecture Artifacts

Various types of documentation are called "artifacts" and Figure 7-2 below provides list those that are recommended when documenting an enterprise. Examples of each type of artifact are available at www.btmgllc.com.

EA6 Cube Level/Thread	Artifact ID #	Artifact Name (* Composite Artifact)
Strategic Goals & Initiatives (I)	S-1	Strategic Plan*
	S-2	SWOT Analysis
	S-3	Concept of Operations Scenario
	S-4	Concept of Operations Diagram
	S-5	Environment Overview Diagram
	S-6	Balanced Scorecard™ *
Business Products & Services (B)	B-1	Business Plan*
	B-2	Swim Lane Process Diagram *
	B-3	Business Process/Service Model
	B-4	Business Process/ Product Matrix *
	B-5	Use Case Narrative & Diagram
	B-6	Investment Business Case*
Data & Information (D)	D-1	Knowledge Management Plan
	D-2	Information Exchange Matrix*
	D-3	Object State-Transition Diagram
	D-4	Object Event Sequence Diagram
	D-5	Logical Data Model
	D-6	Physical Data Model
	D-7	Activity/Entity (CRUD) Matrix *
	D-8	Data Dictionary / Object Library
Systems & Applications (SA)	SA-1	System Interface Diagram
	SA-2	System Communication Description
	SA-3	System Interface Matrix *
	SA-4	System Data Flow Diagram
	SA-5	System/Operations Matrix *
	SA-6	Systems Data Exchange Matrix *
	SA-7	System Performance Matrix *
	SA-8	System Evolution Diagram
	SA-9	Web Application Diagram
Networks & Infrastructure (NI)	NI-1	Network Connectivity Diagram
	NI-2	Network Inventory
	NI-3	Capital Equipment Inventory
	NI-4	Building Blueprints *
	NI-5	Network Center Diagram
	NI-6	Cable Plant Diagram
	NI-7	Rack Elevation Diagram
Security (SP)	SP-1	Security and Privacy Plan*
	SP-2	Security Solutions Description
	SP-3	System Accreditation Document*
	SP-4	Continuity Of Operations Plan*
	SP-5	Disaster Recovery Procedures *
Standards (ST)	ST-1	Technical Standards Profile
	ST-2	Technology Forecast
Workforce Skills (W)	W-1	Workforce Plan*
	W-2	Organization Chart
	W-3	Knowledge and Skills Profile

Strategic Level EA Artifacts – Current Views

EA Components:
- *Strategic Plan*
- *Environment Overview*

EA Artifacts:
- ***Strategic Plan (S-1)***
- ***SWOT Analysis (S-2)***
- ***Concept of Operations Scenario (S-3)***
- ***Concept of Operations Diagram (S-4)***
- ***Environment Overview Diagram (S-5)***
- ***Balanced Scorecard™ (S-6)***

Strategic planning produces a high-level view of the direction that an enterprise sets for itself. This is documented in the general Strategic Plan and accompanying eCommerce or eGovernment Plan where the role of IT is described in more detail. The enterprise's strategic direction is further articulated in EA artifacts that include long-range scenarios, goals, and initiatives that serve as the baseline for identifying short-term tactical (operational) goals. Strategic Plans should look five to ten years into the future and be published every two to three years. The current view of strategic level artifacts should be updated only as changes to the Strategic Plan and/or eCommerce/eGovernment Plan are formally published. This preserves the authoritative nature of the artifacts at this level and represents what is currently endorsed as policy by executive leadership.

Strategic Level Artifact – Current Strategic Scenario
Some enterprises choose to develop and maintain future scenarios of how the business and technology operating environment might function

under different sets of internal and external influences (see Chapter 8 for more details on future scenarios). In the current view of the EA, the desired artifact related to scenario planning is the scenario that has become the current planning context for the enterprise and contains the current planning assumptions. In other words, of the several future scenarios that are periodically developed through the strategic planning process, one eventually is selected as representing what the enterprise is going to do. When implemented, this selected future scenario becomes the current operating scenario. Periodically comparing the current strategic scenario to several potential scenarios that are maintained in the EA's future views can be a valuable strategic planning activity.

Strategic Goals

All of the enterprise's current strategic goals are artifacts that should be documented in the current EA. Of particular interest are IT-related strategic goals, which are those that rely on some element of IT to help to move the enterprise in the strategic direction described in each of several scenarios. These IT-related goals should be thoroughly documented in terms of related initiatives and outcome measures. These goals must meet several criteria to be of strategic value: (1) achieve some element of the enterprise's purpose, (2) result in an outcome within a scenario that is discernible and measurable, (3) not reduce the enterprise's flexibility so much that other scenarios cannot be pursued and/or threats to enterprise survival cannot be addressed, (4) have enterprise support for implementation. Examples of strategic goals that have an IT element are provided below:

"Improve global communications availability, quality, and cost."
(An example IT element are the voice, data, and video networks).

"Improve product quality and availability."
(An example IT element is the data related to quality control and inventory).

Strategic Initiatives

Each strategic goal that the organization identifies is pursued though strategic initiatives. Initiatives include such activities as mergers and acquisitions, research and development projects, system implementation or integration projects, process redesign and improvement, new market entries, product consolidation, business alliances, and service improvement to internal and external customers. Progress in achieving strategic initiatives must be measurable so that the enterprise can manage the resources given to that initiative and know whether success has been achieved. Strong executive support, sufficient resources, and program management skills are needed for an initiative to succeed.

IT-related strategic initiatives are those which relate to strategic goals in a way that enhances information flows, improves/integrates supporting systems, services, and/or applications, or optimizes the network infrastructure. An example of how strategic initiatives that are tied to example of a strategic goal and supporting initiatives are:

Strategic Goal #1: *Improve marketing and sales information.*

    - Strategic Initiative #1-1: *Begin sales data mart within six months.*
    - Strategic Initiative #1-2: *Consolidate marketing systems in two years.*
    - Strategic Initiative #1-3: *Increase customers by eight percent in a year.*

Performance Measures

Each strategic goal should be stated in a form that includes a measurable and meaningful outcome. Each supporting strategic initiative should include measurable and meaningful outcome and output measures. Outcome measures describe an intended future state. Output measures describe levels of activities/items that contribute to achieving an outcome.

    Example Outcome Measure: *"Improve competitiveness by being no lower than #3 in market share across all product lines in one year."*

    Example Output Measure: *"Increase the availability of products in retail outlets by ten percent within six months."*

Environment Overview

A visual depiction of the overall organizational environment is often helpful in understanding how goals relate to initiatives (programs and projects) as well as related data flows/collections and enabling IT systems/networks. An example of this type of diagram is provided in Figure 7-2 and btmgllc.com.

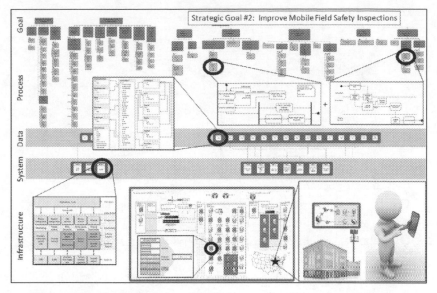

Figure 7-3. Organizational Environment Overview Diagram

Business Level EA Artifacts – Current View

EA Components:
- *Supply Chains*
- *Business Processes*
- *IT Capital Planning Portfolio*

EA Artifacts:
- ***Business Plan (B-1)***
- ***Swim Lane Process Diagram (B-2)***
- ***Business Process/Service Model (B-3)***
- ***Business Process/Product Matrix (B-4)***
- ***Use Case Narrative and Diagram (B-5)***
- ***Investment Business Case (B-5)***

Process Documentation

One method for modeling business processes is known as the Integration Definition for Function (IDEF) technique. Developed in the mid-1970's for modeling complex military projects, IDEF-0 uses Inputs, Controls, Outputs, and Mechanisms (ICOM) to show the parts of an activity within an enterprise, as is illustrated in Figure 7-2 below.

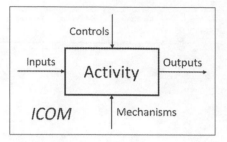

Inputs: Items that initiate/trigger the activity and are transformed, consumed, or become part.

Controls: Guide or regulate the activity; usually indicate when/ how a process will be performed.

Outputs: The results produced by the activity; the reason for which the process was performed.

Mechanisms: Systems, people, and equipment used in the activity.

IDEF-0 activity modeling is suitable for business process documentation in that it provides both high level context views, and more detailed views of each step in the activity in a format that can be further decomposed and interrelated with other processes to show linkages. IDEF-0 modeling is useful in showing linkages between steps in a process as well as internal external influences but does not indicate a particular time sequence for the overall set of activities.

Another method for showing business processes is a "swim lane" diagram that shows activities in horizontal rows, so as to identify areas of responsibility for those activities, as shown in Figure 7-4 below.

	Planning Phase		Selection Phase	
Chief Information Officer		Disapproval	Review ROI, Value & EA Alignment	Approval
Capital Planning Board		Schedule CPB Review	Review Project Plan	Assign Funding
Capital Planning Working Group		Review Business Case		Include in Investment Portfolio
Architecture Working Group		Review For EA Alignment		Put Project in Sequencing Plan
Program Manager	Initial Project Proposal	Develop Project Plan		Prepare for Project Implementation

A third method for showing business processes is a traditional flow diagram that includes events, decision-points, and sequenced flows of the activities and decision points in a business process. Figure 7-5 provides an example of a flow diagram of a simple business process.

The drawback of flow diagrams, in comparison to IDEF models is that the regulatory controls on inputs/outputs are not shown, nor are the mechanisms that are needed to perform the activity. The drawback of flow diagrams, in comparison to swim lane diagrams is that the roles of the various participants in the process are not identifiable.

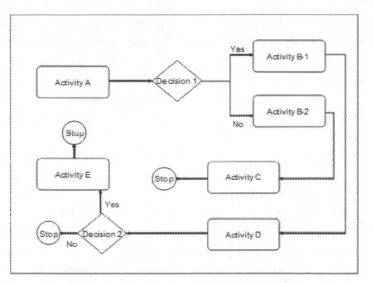

Figure 7-6: Process Flow Diagram

It is important for an enterprise to maintain descriptions and models of all of its key business services. This not only aids in reengineering and improvement activities, but also supports design and analysis work related to business process reengineering/improvement activities, as well as the development of future architecture views.

Business Level Artifact – Project Management Plans
The Project Management Plan (PMP) is a standard format document used by project managers, project sponsors, and the project team to improve the conceptualization, documentation, tracking, oversight, and execution of project work throughout the enterprise. The PMP should be used in

new IT system, application, database, or infrastructure projects, as well as upgrade efforts in the Same areas. In small-scale, quick-turnaround projects some of the elements of the PMP can be minimized, but none should be eliminated. By establishing project documentation in each area of the PMP, project managers will have more control over attaining cost, schedule, and performance goals. Also, the new IT resource is more likely to add value by being in alignment with strategic direction, investment policy, and the overall architecture.

The PMP should be tailored to identify the business need being addressed by the project as well as how the project will be accomplished. The amount of information and level of detail in the PMP should be determined by program characteristics such as size, complexity, and enterprise. It is important to include documentation in the appropriate sections of the PMP, such as the IT Strategic Plan, a Work Breakdown Structure, business case documentation, the Technical Standards Reference Model, training plans, and test plans.

The PMP documents the overall management concept and approach used to achieve program objectives. The project manager prepares and issues the PMP during the Planning Phase of the capital planning process (See Chapter 10). The PMP is the common link between the Project Manager and all others involved in the project. The Project Manager uses the PMP to schedule and direct the entire system development process, while higher levels of authority use the PMP as a baseline for planning activities. Many participants may see a project only via a PMP. The PMP should be updated at each project milestone as a prerequisite for proceeding to the next phase in the project life cycle. At a minimum, the PMP should cover the following areas:

Executive Summary	Project Requirements
Strategic Alignment	Architectural Alignment
Business Case	Project Controls
Project Enterprise	Security and Privacy

Business Cases

A business case is an analysis of the requirements and value of making a particular investment. In the context of EA, developing a business case for investments in IT helps to ensure that maximum value is generated from new development projects, as well as ongoing operations and maintenance activities. In addition, the routine development and review of business cases for IT investments helps to promote strategic alignment and architectural alignment such that the components and products of an EA are more integrated (Appendix B contains an example business case from the DMC Case Study).

There are six areas to a business case: (1) statement of the requirement, (2) an alternatives analysis, (3) a cost-benefit analysis, (4) a risk analysis, (5) a calculation of the return on the investment "ROI," and (6) selection of an alternative with recommendations on implementation.

Statement of the Requirement: This part of the business case clearly and succinctly establishes what the business requirement is, and should avoid making any recommendation on solutions, including technology. This part of the business case should describe the current situation and what need is not being met (a gap in performance).

Alternatives Analysis: This analysis looks at several (preferably three or more) alternatives to meeting a business requirement. The requirement may be to upgrade an existing component in the EA, develop a new component, or for the provision of support services such as help desk or systems administration functions. The alternatives can differ in the recommended process, technical solution, type of personnel to be employed, facilities to be used, etc. The chosen alternatives should represent the full scope of options that could be used to meet the requirement. One of the alternatives can be the "status quo" which recommends doing nothing different from what the current situation is.

Cost-Benefit Analysis: This analysis identifies and compares the costs and benefits of each alternative for meeting an IT requirement. Costs include the total of direct and indirect expenses incurred. Benefits include those that are tangible (measurable) and intangible (not directly measurable). The benefits must exceed costs for an alternative to be viable and should add significant value to the enterprise.

Risk Analysis: This analysis identifies the risk for each alternative. Risk is the identification of sources of uncertainty in a project and/or obstacles to success. Areas of risk for IT projects include being the first adopter of a new technology, budget reductions, loss of key personnel, insufficient testing or training, and schedule delays. "Mitigating" risk is the term commonly used to refer to the strategy identified to lower the probability that a particular risk will occur. Risk mitigation strategies should reduce uncertainty, prevent obstacles to success, or provide responses to overcome obstacles should they occur. An example of this is to have trained back-ups for key positions or using open standards products to avoid being locked into one vendor.

Return on Investment: This "ROI" calculation is done for each alternative and is calculated by dividing total quantified benefits (in dollars) by total quantified costs (in dollars). It is the percentage return on the originally invested capital. For multiple year calculations, the ROI should be discounted using Net Present Value (NPV) methods that discount future levels of funding in order to take into consideration inflation and other rising costs over the lifecycle of the alternative. ROI is calculated as a percentage by dividing quantified benefits in dollars by quantified costs in dollars over the total lifecycle of the alternative. ROI is one of the factors that executives use to determine the merit of investing in a proposed project and also to compare that merit to other investments/projects that cannot be done if that particular alternative is implemented (opportunity cost). Enterprises often establish a minimum acceptable ROI level in order to enforce evaluating the "opportunity cost" of the investment, which considers whether the amount equal to the cost of the IT investment would be better spent on another investment. Some IT investments can produce very high ROI levels if savings in personnel costs or cycle times are achieved.

Alternative Selection Statement: This statement documents the selection of the best alternative based on all aspects of the business case. This includes types of costs, types of benefits, the risk mitigation strategy, and ROI. The rationale for selecting an alternative and rejecting others should also be documented for future reference.

Data Level EA Artifacts – Current View

EA Components:
- *Knowledge Warehouses*
- *Information Systems*
- *Databases*

- **EA Artifacts:**
- *Knowledge Management Plan (D-1)*
- *Information Exchange Matrix (D-2)*
- *Object State-Transition Diagram (D-3)*
- *Object Event Sequence Diagram (D-4)*
- *Logical Data Model (D-5)*
- *Physical Data Model (D-6)*
- *Activity/Entity (CRUD) Matrix (D-7)*
- *Data Dictionary/Object Library (D-8)*

Documenting information flows involves the development of data models that show the structure and flow of data in the enterprise's business services and supporting IT systems/services. Data can be modeled and analyzed using "traditional" and/or "object-oriented" methods, depending on how the resulting documentation is intended to be used. For example, if the intended use is with relational databases and/or third-generation procedural programming languages (i.e., C, FORTRAN, or COBOL) then the use of traditional methods (i.e., Entity-Relationship Diagrams and Data Flow Diagrams) is called for. If the intended use of data is with object-oriented databases, fourth generation object-oriented (OO) programming languages and associated object-oriented diagrams that use the Universal Modeling Language (UML) are called for (e.g.., Java, C++, ADA, and Smalltalk). This OO approach also uses what is called the Common Object Reuse Brokered Architecture (CORBA).

Data Structure and Data Flow Diagrams

The "traditional" approach to information systems development is based on the modeling technique called Entity Relationship Diagramming (ERD). ERDs are used by IT systems analysts and programmers to identify the "things" (data entities) that an enterprise wants IT systems to capture, as well at those external entities that a system interfaces with. ERDs also provide data entity descriptions, attributes, relationships, and the rules for the frequency of those relationships. In that enterprise architecture seeks to provide an enterprise-wide view of all IT resources, it is important that ERDs show not only what is in each system, but also how systems interface with each other. ERDs are not decomposed per se, but they can serve to show several systems, or parts of large complex systems. Figure 7-6 below shows an example ERD diagram.

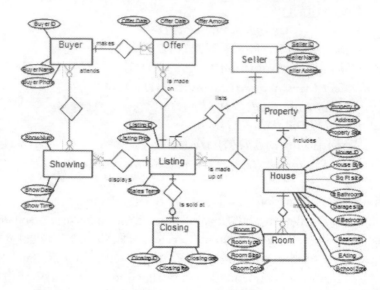

Modeling Information Flows. Data and information flows are documented in traditional and object-oriented methods, depending on how the resulting documentation is intended to be used. The traditional method of documenting data flows was developed in the early 1970's and centers on the use of Data Flow Diagrams (DFDs). DFDs should reflect the processes that transform data within an information system. Transformation can involve the creation, update, deletion, or reading of data. An Entity/ Activity Matrix (also known as a CRUD matrix) can help analysts and programmers to move from ERDs to DFDs as they design how an information system will function in support of enterprise requirements. DFDs can be decomposed from a "context" level, to a basic process level, to several sub-levels that examine each process in greater detail, as is shown in Figure 7-7 below.

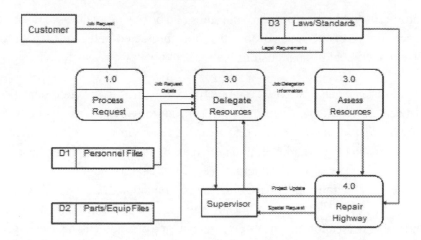

Object-Oriented (OO) approaches to modeling data structure and process together were developed in the mid-1980's by Ivar Jacobson, Grady Booch, and James Rumbaugh. Their combined efforts produced what is now known as the Uniform Modeling Language (UML). Objects are specific sequences of code in fourth generation programming languages that represent something in the business requirements domain that an IT system must create, use, or interact with. Objects are like entities in that they have a name and attributes, and link to other objects according to rules for frequency. One might say that objects "know things about themselves." Objects are unlike entities in that the code for objects also contains behaviors (also known as methods), which are triggered by events that are also identified in the code... one might say that objects also "know how to do things." Beyond knowing things about themselves and knowing how to do things, there are three defining characteristics of an object:

- Polymorphism: Multiple object behaviors invoked by triggering events.
- Inheritance: Attributes that carry over between parent and child objects.
- Encapsulation: Hidden code that protects object attributes and behaviors.

The concept of objects allows analysts and programmers to take a more intuitive approach to designing information systems, applications, databases, and websites. Also, because objects are specific sequences of code they can be reused, which saves programming time and increases quality and performance. For example, an "invoice" object developed for a sales system might be reused across several lines of business in an enterprise that has multiple product lines and billing procedures. The basic functionality of the invoice object is both protected and inherited in all systems, with additional custom features and behaviors as needed.

Object-oriented analysis and design activities begin with the documentation of business requirements in the form of a narrative Use Case. Four basic types of diagrams are then used to describe the Use Case, each of which is an EA artifact that should be maintained at the Information level of the EA framework: (1) Use-Case Diagram; (2) Class/Object Diagram; (3) Object Sequence Diagram; and (4) Object State-Transition Diagram. Use Case Diagrams show a static (snapshot) overall view of the activities (use cases) and actors in an information system, and how information will be exchanged. Class/Object Diagrams show a static view of the things that interact in each Use Case in the information system, and how the object's behaviors will perform those interactions. Object Sequence Diagrams show how groups of objects exhibit behaviors in response to a specific event called a trigger. Note that the Same Object can exhibit different behaviors in response to different events. The State-Transition Diagram shows the entire lifecycle of a particular Object, in terms of how event triggers can invoke different behaviors.

Data Dictionary / Object Library

Data Dictionaries are repositories for the data entities and attributes that an enterprise collects and stores in databases. Standards for the format of data are documented in the Data Dictionary, as are dependencies and rules for relationships and dependencies among data entities that are identified in Entity Relationship Diagrams.

Object Libraries are repositories for reusable objects. From a technical perspective, it is the discrete pieces of programming code that actually make up an object, and that are being stored in the Object Library as a complete reusable unit. Object-oriented programming languages (i.e., JAVA, ADA, Smalltalk, C++) develop code segments that are distinct in their identity and function, and which are reusable in that the object can be integrated into other applications with little customization. Commercial software developers increasingly create applications using an object-oriented approach so that they can maintain the application more efficiently by adjusting or adding/deleting individual objects. Vendors also are increasingly selling objects that are common to financial, manufacturing, and administrative applications. These commercial objects and those custom developed by the enterprise should be archived in the Object Library. Other information products developed in platform independent languages should also be included in the Object Library. These include EA artifacts such as web pages and web service components that are developed in object-oriented languages and saved in compatible formats such as HTML, XML, XHTML, J2EE, and ebXML.

System Level EA Artifacts – Current View

EA Components:
- *Software Applications*
- *Web Services*
- *Service Bus and Middleware*
- *Enterprise Resource Planning (ERP) Solutions*
- *Operating Systems*

EA Artifacts:
- ***System Interface Diagram (SA-1)***
- ***System Communication Diagram (SA-2)***
- ***System Interface Matrix (SA-3)***
- ***System Data Flow Diagram (SA-4)***
- ***System/Operations Matrix (SA-5)***
- ***Systems Data Exchange Matrix (SA-6)***
- ***System Performance Matrix (SA-7)***
- ***System Evolution Diagram (SA-8)***
- ***Web Application Diagram (SA-9)***

The current view of IT systems and applications should function to show an accurate picture of the software applications, front/back office services, and operating systems that the enterprise currently has active in its IT operating environment. In that many of these IT resources were developed in an independent manner, the completed current view of the support applications level of the framework may show (1) a lack of integration in areas with requirements for exchanges of information, (2) duplications of function, (3) little or lots of vendor diversity, and/or (4) where business requirements are not being met.

System Level EA Artifact – Application Programs

The various types of software applications that an enterprise uses to support business, office automation, and other functions are often varied in their design, programming languages, interface points, and source vendors. It is sometimes helpful to develop a graphical view of these support applications to show what is present, and the general types of functions being supported. Figure 7-8 below is an example of the type of diagram that can show an overview of the enterprise's current "suite" of systems, applications, and supporting network protocols.

E-Commerce Service	Supply-Chain Management Service	Public Web Portal	E-Government Service	Web Services
HR Module	Payroll Module	Inventory Module	Sales Module	Enterprise Resource Planning System/Applications
CAD Drawing Application	Data Mining Application		Scheduling Application	Back-Office Business and Office Automation Systems/Applications
Project Tracking Application	Graphics Application	Photo Editing Application	Document Tracking Application	
Office Automation Application Suite	Web Browsers & Applications		Database Application	
Load Balancers & Hypervisors	Enterprise Service Bus & Open APIs		Partitions & Virtual Modules	Middleware
Desktop - PC Operating System	File Server Operating System		Storage Area Network	Desktop & Server Operating Systems
Print Server Operating System	Web Server Operating System		Security Firewall Operating System	
Ethernet	Frame Relay VPN, ATM	TCP/IP	VOIP / ISDN	Network Transport Protocols (voice, data, video)

Additional descriptions and views can focus on specific types of support applications to show specific functions and interfaces. It may be beneficial to show a "hierarchy" to the applications such that operating systems are at the base, office automation and business applications are in the middle, and web applications are on top.

An Application Programming Interface (API) is a series of functions that software applications use to make other applications and operating systems perform supporting actions. In other words, APIs define how applications will interact at the Systems/Services level of the EA. For example, an API for a program can be used to open windows, files, and message boxes and perform more complicated tasks, just by passing a single instruction. API descriptions should describe both internal function and external connectivity so that a picture of activity and interrelationships is created.

System and Service Interface Diagrams

IT systems are distinct collections of applications, databases, operating systems, and hardware that meet specific business or technology requirements of the enterprise. These systems increasingly are required to directly and indirectly interface with other IT systems to enable information sharing across the enterprise. The use of non-proprietary industry and international standards for software and hardware solutions enables these interfaces. System Interface Diagrams (also called Node Connectivity Diagrams) are physical and logical depictions of how and where these interfaces occur. Additional documentation on the type of supporting standards and protocols is needed to complete the documentation of system and service interfaces.

As described in Chapter 6, a Service-Oriented Architecture (SOA) approach is used to describe and document IT systems and web services at the Systems level of the framework and can be considered to be a sub-architecture of the EA6 framework. Web services are based on the TCP/IP (HTTP) information exchange protocol and open standards information formats such as HTML, XML, and J2EE (.NET is a proprietary protocol owned by Microsoft ®). Web services are therefore platform independent and can exchange information with any other web services in the common operating environment, which is referred to as the Network Application Platform (NAP) Service Bus, or an Enterprise Service Bus (ESB).

Web service interfaces within the NAP/ESB Service Bus are defined by two major industry standards, the first being Simple Object Access Protocol (SOAP), which is an extensible XML messaging format and the World Wide Web Consortium (W3C) adopted as an international standard. SOAP interfaces consist of an envelope, EAder and body, and utilize a transport binding framework to define HTTP bindings, and a serialization framework for XML encoding. The other standard is the Representational State Transfer (REST) or "RESTful" interface which promotes communication between ESB-discoverable applications by transferring a representation of that resource in a format that matches a standard data type that that is determined dynamically to match the capabilities of a sender and recipient.

Universal Description, Discovery, and Integration (UDDI) is a standard format and method for registering and discovering web services. UDDI is a web "meta-service" that functions as a registry by using SOAP messages to find web services. The UDDI registry organizes web service information into four categories: business entity, business service, binding template, and service type. Additionally, a Web Services Description Language (WDSL) is used to describe the web service found by the UDDI registry. Figure 7-9 below shows a general view of an ESB and the roles of SOAP, the UDDI Registry, and WDSL.

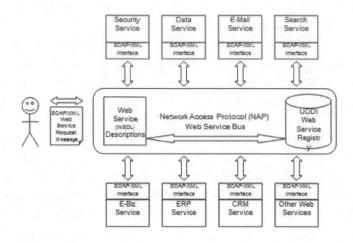

Technical Standards

IT applications should be selected based on technical standards and protocols from industry, national, or international bodies which have no bias toward particular vendors or products. Standards for APIs, service functionality, and software/hardware integratability should be documented to assist in decision-making regarding the selection of new applications and the operations and maintenance of existing applications. The WSDL web service descriptions and NAP Web Service Bus interface documentation are some of the additional artifacts that need to be gathered.

Infrastructure Level EA Artifacts – Current View

EA Components:
- *Data Networks*
- *Computing Clouds*

- *Telecommunications Networks*
- *Video Networks*
- *Cable Plants*
- *Security Solution*

EA Artifacts:
- ***Network Connectivity Diagram (NI-1)***
- ***Network Inventory (NI-2)***
- ***Capital Equipment Inventory (NI-3)***
- ***Building Blueprints (NI-4)***
- ***Network Center Diagram (NI-5)***
- ***Cable Plant Diagram (NI-6)***
- ***Rack Elevation Diagram (NI-7)***

Network Documentation

At the infrastructure level of the EA, networks, backbone routers/ switches/hubs, equipment rooms, wiring closets, and cable plants should be described in detail using both text documents and diagrams to show logical and physical designs. Each of the enterprise's voice, data, and video networks should be documented such that analysis and decision-making regarding current operations and maintenance is supported. Figure 7-10 below provides an example of this type of diagram.

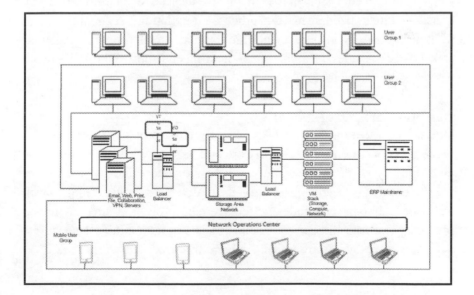

Technical Standards

Technical standards for voice, data, and video networks should be identified to provide a reference for the analysis and support of current infrastructure resources as well as the planning for future resources. Standards from national and international bodies should be used to encourage the selection of vendor products that will better integrate with other existing and future products. Network technical standards are also provided in the form of policies, technical specifications, and standard procedures.

Security Documentation

Each network, computing cloud, and IT system that is supported by the technology backbone must be tested and certified for security vulnerabilities. This is done so that an effective level of business support is maintained, and that an overall IT security solution is established for hosted applications, services, databases, and websites. The related EA artifacts include the development of system/network security plans, vulnerability test reports, disaster recovery and continuity of operations plans, and certification/accreditation review results (see Chapter 12).

Configuration Change Requests

There should be a standard method for requesting changes to the EA artifacts, so that configuration control over the current and future EA views can be maintained. Using an EA Change Request (EACR) form is one way to have a standardized format and process for updating EA documentation. Making the EACR form an electronic template helps promote use by all stakeholders, as does the archiving of pending and approved EACRs in the EA repository's database.

Hardware/Software Inventories

One of the functions of the EA is to provide a repository for periodic inventories of the enterprise's software and hardware assets. Maintaining an inventory of these IT resources helps to determine what levels of investment will be needed for operations, maintenance, and training as well as major technology upgrade and replacement projects. Using automated inventory systems and bar code labels assists in maintaining an accurate inventory as resources are implemented and retired.

Summary of Concepts

This chapter provided descriptions and examples of EA artifacts that document the current state of components at all levels of the EA framework. The collection of current artifacts represents the "as-is" view of the EA. This is important to the enterprise because it serves as an integrated inventory of reference information for resource planning and decision-making. The current views of EA components also show how strategic goals, business services, and technology resources are effectively aligned, and performance gaps can also be revealed. Chapter 8 will discuss the development of future views of the architecture, and Chapter 9 will describe the concept of an EA Management Plan that serves to manage the ongoing transition between current and future states of the enterprise's EA.

Chapter 7 Questions and Exercises

1. What is the purpose of current views of EA components?
2. How do artifacts relate to EA components?
3. Provide some examples of artifacts at the Goals & Initiatives level of the EA6 Framework.
4. What is IDEF-0 modeling and how can it be used to document EA components at the Products & Services level of the EA6 Framework?
5. What are the differences between traditional (ERD/DFD) data modeling techniques and object-oriented modeling (UML)?
6. Provide some examples of artifacts at the Applications & Services level of the EA6 Framework.

Chapter 8

Developing Future Architecture Views

Chapter Overview

Chapter 8 covers the development of future views of the EA, within the context of a documentation framework and implementation methodology. The future views of the EA are important to the enterprise because they capture one or more possible business and technology operating scenarios, which supports planning and decision-making. These future operating scenarios are based on assumptions of capability and strategies for successful performance in response to internal and external influences. The creation of future view artifacts is accomplished by using the planning assumptions in the scenarios and the Same documentation and modeling techniques as were used to develop the current view artifacts. This allows future view artifacts to be directly related to current view artifacts at each level of the framework, so that potential and planned changes are evident, and various types or combinations of changes can be modeled.

Learning Objectives

- ➢ Understand how future views relate to the EA documentation framework.
- ➢ Understand how future views relate to the EA implementation methodology.
- ➢ Understand how scenario planning helps the development of future views.
- ➢ See examples of future views of EA components and artifacts.

Introduction

The future view of the EA documents the IT resources that will be active in the operating environment several years in the future. This is also known as the "to-be" view of the EA, as opposed to the "as-is" view that documents current IT resources and was described in Chapter 7. Depending on the amount of EA planning that has occurred previously in the enterprise, future IT resources may or may not be aligned with the organization's strategic goals and business services. If little EA planning has occurred, then a significant amount of duplication in function may be present and the future view of the EA should show how that duplication will be eliminated.

> *Home Architecture Analogy:* Having future EA views is like having a full set of blueprints for the modification of an existing home or for building a new home. It provides an authoritative reference for the architect and homeowner to use in discussing options and changes during development.

As is shown in Figure 8-1, future views of the EA provide an enterprise with documentation of identified changes to strategic goals, business services, information flows, support applications, and network resources.

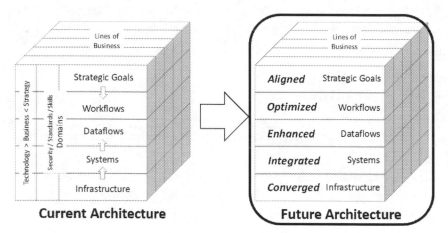

Figure 8-1: Future Architecture Views

Discussion

The development of future EA views is important to an enterprise because it supports resource planning and decision-making. Also, by completing the documentation of the future EA at all levels of the framework, a view of the potential future enterprise emerges that reveals changes in priorities, processes, and resources. This serves to promote communication about these potential changes throughout the enterprise.

In developing the future EA, each level of the framework is documented with artifacts to show components that are approved for implementation or are in the idea/planning stages. The potential changes to existing EA components include new or updated strategic goals and initiatives, business services, information flows, systems, support applications, and networks. Initiatives that are in the very early stages of consideration can be left out of future views until they have firm backing from sponsors, strong business cases, and viable technical solutions. This avoids cluttering future EA views with initiatives and updates that have little chance of being implemented, and which over time will detract from the perceived value of the EA as an authoritative reference for planning and decision-making. Candidate initiatives are better documented in a special section of the EA Management Plan (see Chapter 9).

Developing Future CONOPS Scenarios

Concept of Operations (CONOPS) scenarios looking into the future have been used as a military planning tool for millennia. Similarly, the ability to envision several potential courses of action is key to winning many types of recreational games. Using chess as an example, anticipating how an opponent might react to your moves is part of what makes for a chess master. Top levels of play involve being able to think through several alternative scenarios of moves and countermoves that create a dynamic balance between acting and reacting. Similarly, an enterprise should continuously monitor the internal and external operating environment and make tactical and strategic moves so as to simultaneously avoid catastrophic situations and pursue opportunities to maximize mission success. Large enterprises in the public and private sector have used future scenarios for a number of years, including Royal Dutch Shell and the World Bank.

One of the most effective formats for developing a shortened version of a CONOPS Scenario that is easy to share and use in the enterprise was developed by Dr. Robert Neilson.[17] This type of scenario takes the form of a short story which is told through the eyes of a central character who is involved in future events that reveal the internal and external drivers of the business and technology operating environment at that time. These drivers are then related to specific planning assumptions in three areas of change: process, people, and technology. Neilson states that stories are easy to remember, and the highlighting of planning assumptions reveals the resources and capabilities that will be needed if that scenario is implemented.

The role that future scenarios can play in the development of EA future views is that of identifying a range of operating options and planning assumptions for the enterprise. Developing several scenarios that capture a variety of good and bad operating environments helps the enterprise to think through its probable responses (defensive moves) and initiatives (offensive moves) in advance. It also helps to identify the resources and capabilities that will be needed for those responses/initiatives.

CONOPS Scenarios can be quite detailed and are used to document both the current operating environment, and a number of plausible future operating environments. Enterprises should identify a range of internal and external factors from the SWOT Analysis in deciding which future CONOPS scenarios to document. Having a number of future scenarios is helpful to an enterprise because it is impossible to predict which particular internal/external factors will come into play to create either a helpful or hostile operating environment. Figure 8-2 on the next two pages provide an example CONOPS scenario.

Making a Sale in 2020
Future Challenges for DMC

Planning Assumptions

1. Global converged voice, data, and video remote capability.

2. Do product rollouts at industry conferences.

3. Need to hold detailed product discussions on short notice, globally.

4. 24x7 work availability.

5. Increased suburban commuting.

6. Auto-tracking of Government reports to anticipate product needs.

7. Changing population demographics that drive new products and features.

8. Increased output and cost-efficiency of solar-powered lighting.

Jeff Linder, Vice President of Industrial Sales for Danforth Manufacturing Company (DMC) had just finished a presentation at the 2020 National Highway Safety Conference along with Richard Danforth, DMC's CEO, who had teleconferenced in on the stage-wide display screen behind the podium.[1] As Jeff was leaving the main conference room, Andrea Newman, Director of Safety and Transportation for the State of Tennessee, asked Jeff if they could talk for a few minutes about the new line of solar- powered highway and street lights that they had just given a presentation on. [2,3]

"Thanks for taking a minute to talk Jeff. I want to tell you about a situation we have in Tennessee and see if your new product line can help" said Andrea as they found a table in the refreshment area.[4] "No problem, thanks for asking" Jeff said. Andrea pulled up a document on her tablet computer and said "Jeff, here is a report that shows an increasing number of serious accidents in rural areas of Tennessee involving passenger cars and agricultural equipment or commercial trucks. We've attributed it to the growth of suburban communities further out in the countryside that then depend on two-lane country roads for commuting into the city.[5] When you put slow tractors and trucks together with cars that are in a hurry at all hours to get somewhere, you have a recipe for disaster." "Isn't this problem being seen in other places around the country?" asked Jeff. "Yes, and one of the contributing factors that is consistently coming out of investigations of the night-time accidents is the lack of good lighting on these country roads.[6] I am thinking that your highway solar lighting can help us provide more nighttime visibility on high- risk rural roads without having to invest in the supporting electrical infrastructure." [7,8]

DMC Future Scenario (continued)

Planning Assumptions	Jeff thought for a minute before responding. "You know, the new line of highway lights has options to incorporate 911 emergency call boxes and Global Positioning System (GPS) equipment that can connect to both State and local level first responders.[9]
8. Continued Incorporation of additional product features to expand customer base.	
	This might be useful in also improving response times should an accident occur in spite of the improved lighting." Andrea nodded and said, "Yes, I doubt that better lighting will solve the entire problem, but it will help people see each other better, and these other options can improve accident response times, which will also save lives. What is the pricing like on these units?"
9. Global use of smart phones for employee communication.	
10. Integration of sales, marketing, and production information.	
11. Accurate customer quotes on the fly.	Jeff pulled his smart phone[10] out of his pocket and connected to DMC's marketing and sales database at headquarters via a satellite Internet link.[11] "Andrea, these units are $6,830 each, including shipping and the GPS/911 features." Andrea took notes and responded, "If I can get permission to conduct a pilot test in a couple of months can you provide the lights?" Jeff asked, "How many miles of road?" "About four miles in the particular area I'm thinking of" said Andrea.
12. Open-source customer collaboration tool	

Ok, the suggested density for the new unit is 18 per mile, so that would be 72 units total. I can give you our 10 percent early-adopter discount, so the total would be $491,760. Let me check what the shipping time would be." Jeff sent a high priority email to Bob Green, Vice President of Manufacturing. Bob was in the factory when he received Jeff's email on his phone and after checking the DMC Production Scheduling System, responded two minutes later that a special order for 72 units could be completed and shipped 35 days from when the order is received. Jose relayed this information to Andrea, who said, "Wow, that was fast. I have all the information I need to propose the pilot project. I will get back to you in the next week."[12]

Updating Future EA Views – Version Control

At some point the new components and artifacts in the future view of the EA become implemented and therefore should be documented as part of the current view of the EA. These ongoing changes to the EA represent a challenge in terms of how best to show at any given time what is current and what is planned. Perhaps the simplest and most effective way to approach this is to 'freeze' the current and future views of the EA at regular periods (e.g., twice each year). This promotes clarity and supports EA version control. Using this example, changes to current and future views are collected for four to five months and then are published in the sixth month as a new release of the enterprise's EA. EA stakeholders come to expect the new releases and know that they can then rely on the information not changing in the EA repository for the next few months. Special releases can be made if a there is an important change in the middle of the normally static period. Without this type of version control, the EA repository where no-one is sure when and where changes will appear detract from the perceived value of EA information. The following are examples of how new or upgraded EA artifacts would be documented in the future view of related EA components at each level of the EA6 framework. Examples of each type of artifact are available at btmgllc.com.

Strategic Level EA Artifacts – Future View

EA Components:
* *Strategic Plan*
* *Environment Overview*

EA Artifacts:
* *Strategic Plan (S-1)*
* *SWOT Analysis (S-2)*
* *Concept of Operations Scenario (S-3)*
* *Concept of Operations Diagram (S-4)*
* *Environment Overview Diagram (S-5)*
* *Balanced Scorecard™ (S-6)*

EA components and artifacts at the Strategic Level of the EA6 Framework serve to articulate the general direction and priorities that the enterprise intends to take along with the goals, initiatives, and measures that define success. The eBusiness or eGovernment Plan then serves to provide more detailed descriptions of how IT initiatives will support the enterprise's Strategic Plan, with a focus on strategic goals and key business services. Updated plans should be published every few years to reflect the changes in direction and priorities that the enterprise intends to take. The future view of these plans can be draft documents where changes that have executive sponsorship are recorded until publication of the new plans.

Strategic Scenarios
Strategic scenarios can be added or deleted from the Strategic Plan's future view in response to changes in the internal and external operating environment. To promote comparison and analysis, potential future scenarios should be documented in the Same way that the current scenario is documented: as an integrated narrative and set of planning assumptions regarding enterprise priorities, performance, resources, and risks.

Strategic Goals
While the current view of IT-related strategic goals represents high-level EA artifacts that are documented in the enterprise's current Strategic Plan, the future view of these EA artifacts represents changes to those goals, or new goals that are not yet formally adopted and published as part of the Plan. New strategic goals also serve to direct the development of future operating scenarios, which should capture the priorities and direction of those new goals.

Strategic Initiatives
The current view of IT-related strategic initiatives serves to create an awareness and appreciation for the role that IT plays in supporting key business and administrative processes throughout the enterprise. It also supports high-level resource planning, also known as "capital planning and investment control (CPIC) process (see Chapter 9 for additional details). The future view of IT-related strategic initiatives is intended to show the changes that are being planned to existing initiatives as well as new initiatives that will be introduced in coming years. This is valuable to enterprises that have highly structured planning and budget processes.

Performance Measures

Changes to strategic goals and initiatives in the future views will require new or modified outcome and output measures of success.

Business Level EA Artifacts – Future View

EA Components:
- *Supply Chains*
- *Business services*
- *IT Capital Planning Portfolio*

EA Artifacts:
- ***Business Plan (B-1)***
- ***Swim Lane Process Diagram (B-2)***
- ***Business Process/Service Model (B-3)***
- ***Business Process/Product Matrix (B-4)***
- ***Use Case Narrative and Diagram (B-5)***
- ***Investment Business Case (B-6)***

Enterprises continually change their business services in response to a number of influencing factors including new customer requirements, different competitive strategies, new technologies, and changes in resource availability. These factors (also known as drivers) are documented at both the Strategic Level and the Business Level of the EA6 framework. The documentation of drivers at the Strategic Level often centers on those influencing factors that originate in the external operating environment, while the documentation of Business Level drivers often focuses on influencing factors that originate in the internal operating environment. EA components at the Business Level may extend beyond the internal operating environment (i.e., supply chains involving external suppliers), but they are fundamentally internal management processes. Future views of related EA artifacts primarily reflect approved changes to these business services and associated implementation activities.

There are four general types of changes to business services that occur: (1) the introduction of a completely new process, (2) elimination of an existing process, (3) major reengineering of an existing process, and (4) minor improvement of an existing process. Effective management at the Business Level requires that these changes be coordinated so that the performance of the enterprise does not decline. Therefore, reviews of existing business services should be performed periodically by line-of-business managers to identify those which may be obsolete, duplicative, or not adding sufficient value to the achievement of strategic goals. Resulting decisions to eliminate or change processes are what get documented in the future view of Business Level EA components and artifacts.

Process Documentation

Similar to the approach to documenting future views at the Strategic Level of the EA6 Framework, only those potential changes to business services that have executive sponsorship should be documented at the Business Level. This maintains value in the future view and promotes the use of this information for planning and decision-making.

Documenting approved changes to business services helps to maintain "upward alignment" in the EA6 Framework with strategic goals and initiatives. It also promotes "downward alignment" in the EA6 Framework to ensure that EA components and artifacts at the lower three levels are properly adjusted to best support the anticipated process changes. The enterprise should be consistent in how current and future business process are documented (e.g., IDEF-0 models, swim lane diagrams, and/or flow-charts) so that analysis and planning is best supported.

Project Plans

The Project Management Plan (PMP) is a living document that promotes proven, standardized approaches to implementing new or upgraded IT resources. The current view of the PMP is developed in the requirements planning stage of the project lifecycle, with updates being made as changes in requirements, solutions, or resources occur. A future view of a PMP may not be needed with certain EA component development approaches, also known as Systems Analysis and Design Methods (SADMs) that promote the development of the entire system capability in one effort (e.g., the "waterfall" or "rapid application development" methods). However, those SADM approaches that promote the incremental (phased), or evolutionary (spiral) development of EA components may benefit from having a future view of the PMP to show the implementation of system modules that are envisioned at some future time. The phased implementation of large ERP projects with several modules would be an example of where having both a current and future view of the PMP would be beneficial. PMPs are maintained on systems throughout the lifecycle.

Business Cases

The investment business case is the part of the PMP that documents the value of the investment to the enterprise. The business case is unique in that it ties directly to the enterprise's budget and financial planning process, and as such usually requires a review at least annually. The initial approval of the business case centers on an identification of benefits that exceed costs (both quantitative and qualitative). Approval also focuses on a determination that the rate of return on the capital invested (ROI) meets meaningful, measurable targets established by the enterprise, such that another use of those funds is not warranted (opportunity cost). The business case should then be reviewed annually to determine if sufficient benefits continue to be generated to merit continued investment. If they are not, the investment should be cancelled or modified such that sufficient ongoing value is created. Chapter 9 provides additional details on business case development and evaluation as part of the IT capital planning process.

Data Level EA Artifacts – Future View

EA Components:
- *Knowledge Warehouses*
- *Information Systems*
- *Databases*

EA Artifacts:
- ***Knowledge Management Plan (D-1)***
- ***Information Exchange Matrix (D-2)***
- ***Object State-Transition Diagram (D-3)***
- ***Object Event Sequence Diagram (D-4)***
- ***Logical Data Model (D-5)***
- ***Physical Data Model (D-6)***
- ***Activity/Entity (CRUD) Matrix (D-7)***
- ***Data Dictionary/Object Library (D-8)***

Future views of EA components and artifacts at the Information Level of the framework reflect changes that are anticipated in the collection and flows of information that are needed to support changes in business services (upward alignment) or changes at the Systems/Services or Technology Infrastructure levels of the framework.

Data Models

Traditional views of data models that show structure (Entity-Relationship Diagrams) and process (Data Flow Diagrams) can be developed to show future changes either as separate documents or through the use of special notation that can be integrated into current views (e.g., the use of dashed lines and symbols to show future data entities, flows, stores). Whichever approach is taken, the important idea is to provide a future view of data structure and process in a way that is directly comparable to the current view so that areas of change can be easily identified.

Another "traditional" data modeling artifact that merits the development of a future view is the Activity/Entity Matrix (also called a CRUD Matrix). This matrix maps activities occurring at the IT system boundary to the data entities that are affected. This mapping enables the data analyst and enterprise architect to see where and how data is Created, Read, Updated, or Deleted (CRUD). By identifying who in the enterprise is responsible for (owns) the activity, the logical owner of the data and the processes that transform the data can also be identified. Having current views of the CRUD Matrix and knowledge of future changes in business services enables the development of a future view of the CRUD Matrix, which identities potential changes in the ownership of data and which may lead to discussions of changes in data standards and formats. IT system consolidation, upgrade, or replacement activities that seek to improve the efficiency of data handling or increase the cost-effectiveness of the new system will benefit from a detailed analysis of current/future views of the CRUD Matrix.

Object-Oriented Data and System Models

Object-Oriented (OO) views of future system activities (Use Cases), data process/structure (Class and Object Diagrams), data transformation (State Transition Diagrams), and information flows (Sequence Diagrams) should be developed in the Same way that the current views of these Same EA artifacts were developed so that easy identification of changes is made.

One of the most powerful reasons for adopting an OO approach to data modeling and IT system analysis and design is that objects can be modified with minimal effort to reflect changes in requirements or use in different scenarios. Object reuse lowers the cost of systems upgrade projects and supports the use of modular applications that are object-based (e.g., Java applications). Developing future views of how information in the form of objects will be stored differently helps analysts, programmers, and architects to produce better logical and physical data models, promotes application interoperability, and supports plug-and-play EA components that are based on open standards or a particular vendor product line.

Data Dictionaries / Object Libraries

Data Dictionaries provide taxonomies and standard formats for the data entities that are used in the enterprise's various IT systems. Data Dictionaries do not store actual data, they just provide a list of entities, attributes, data field formats, and standards. These standards help to promote system interoperability and the consolidation of databases. The future view of a Data Dictionary would show the changes in data standards and formats that are anticipated to be needed as a result of system changes.

Object Libraries are similar in concept, except that they store both the formats/standards and the actual modules of code that constitute an object. Since one of the basic features of objects is encapsulation (protection of parts of the code module from alteration) the object library can store distinct objects just as a book rests independently on the shelf among other books until pulled off the shelf and checked out of the library. Various versions of an object can be separately stored for use in different systems and applications (e.g., an invoice object that provides different types of invoices that are custom tailored for different product lines).

Systems/Services Level EA Artifacts – Future View

EA Components:
- *Software Applications*
- *Web Services*
- *Service Bus and Middleware*

- *Enterprise Resource Planning (ERP) Solutions*
- *Operating Systems*

EA Artifacts:
- ***System Interface Diagram (SA-1)***
- ***System Communication Diagram (SA-2)***
- ***System Interface Matrix (SA-3)***
- ***System Data Flow Diagram (SA-4)***
- ***System/Operations Matrix (SA-5)***
- ***Systems Data Exchange Matrix (SA06)***
- ***System Performance Matrix (SA-7)***
- ***System Evolution Diagram (SA-8)***
- ***Web Application Diagram (SA-9)***

The Systems/Services level of the EA6 Framework is organized around integrated "plug-and-play" components that are based on open standards, and reusable objects of code that underlie and enable a component-based and service-oriented approach to EA. Various artifacts are used to document the future components at the Systems/Services level, including program code and technical documentation on releases and upgrades; interface diagrams; and standards.

Application Interface Descriptions

Descriptions of application software programs and their interfaces in the future view provide an understanding of what will change from what is currently in operation as well as what new functional capabilities will have to be integrated. Application Program Interfaces (APIs) are a feature of most commercial software programs and are where the designed interface points in the programming code are located. These APIs define the extent of interoperability and may include open standards if maximum integration with a wide variety of other products is desired by the vendor. Conversely, APIs may be proprietary and limit interoperability to products from a specific vendor (e.g., interfaces between modules of an ERP product). The artifacts at this level are technical descriptionof APIs and standards lists.

Application Interface Diagrams

Interface diagrams in the future view show the changes to existing system, service, and application interface points. These interface points are where information exchanges occur, and infer connectivity which is shown in more detail at the Technology Infrastructure Level of the EA. Interface diagrams are also important to show how component applications will interact the enterprise's common operating environment, including how web-based services exchange information through the NAP/ESB Web Service Platform. In the case where these applications are commercial products from different vendors, these interfaces can identify where compatibility must be present and with future requirements for integration.

Systems Integration

IT systems have evolved from single-vendor compute/storage/networking mainframes to client-server components from different vendors, to "converged" hardware/software configurations from different vendors, to hyper-converged hardware/software configurations from the same vendor... somewhat of a circular evolutionary path. The converged and hyper-converged "stacks" of storage arrays, computing clusters (CPU blades), and networking devices are all managed by software that "virtualizes" some of the integration and load-balancing/failover-failback functionality.

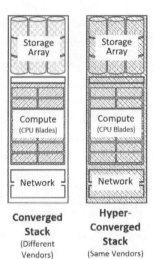

Standards

Technical standards documentation in the future view shows the international, national, local, and industry standards that changes to commercial and custom-developed services, systems, and applications must meet. This includes APIs and other interoperability or performance requirements, virtualization software, application stack management software, WSDL descriptions of web services in the UDDI Registry are an example of the technical standards that need to be identified for future implementation if a Service-Oriented Approach to this level of the framework has not yet been adopted by the enterprise.

Infrastructure Level EA Artifacts – Future View

<u>EA Components</u>:
- *Data Networks*
- *Telecommunications Networks*
- *Video Networks*
- *Cable Plants*
- *Security Solutions*

<u>EA Artifacts</u>:
- ***Network Connectivity Diagram (NI-1)***
- ***Network Inventory (NI-2)***
- ***Capital Equipment Inventory (NI-3)***
- ***Building Blueprints (NI-4)***
- ***Network Center Diagram (NI-5)***
- ***Cable Plant Diagram (NI-6)***
- ***Rack Elevation Diagram (NI-7)***

The Technology Infrastructure level of the EA6 Framework documents components such as the enterprise's voice, data, and video networks, as well as the security solution that protects them. In that one of the goals of EA is to promote the integration of these networks into one seamless technology backbone, the future view of EA artifacts at this level documents changes to this infrastructure.

Network Documentation

Documentation of the enterprise's IT networks in the future view show changes to the integrated voice, data, and video infrastructure components. The enterprise's LAN, WAN, and other networks are shown mainly in diagrams and technical specification documents. These EA artifacts should focus on changes to cable plant(s), wireless, telephone and data wiring closets, network backbone hardware and software, servers, desktop and portable computers, peripherals, and remote access resources.

Technical Standards

IT network technical standards documentation in the future view shows changes to national, international, and commercial standards that are being used to guide changes to the enterprise's technology backbone.

This includes changes to standards that are reflected in models of networks, including the OSI model and TCP/IP model. It also includes standards for telephony, wireless communications, and remote video conferencing.

Security Documentation

Future views of security documentation show the expected changes and updates to security standards, plans, testing, and certification of each IT system and network component of the EA, as well as related security documentation for applications and databases, and the COOP Plan.

Configuration Changes

The future view of EACRs consists of an archive of approved, but yet to be implemented EA Change Requests. These EACRs document the technical and operational impact of changes to EA components at all levels of the EA. See Chapter 9 for more information on EACRs.

Hardware/Software List

The EA artifact in this area of future views is a list that documents anticipated changes in the quantity and type of IT hardware and software products that will be used in EA components at each framework level.

Summary of Concepts

This chapter provided examples of EA artifacts that document future views of EA components at all levels of the EA6 Framework. The use of future scenarios is one way to identify possible future operating environments and planning assumptions which the future EA views can then be based on. The Same documentation techniques should be used in developing both current and future views of EA components so that changes are easier to highlight and compare. Chapter 9 describes the purpose and composition of an EA Management Plan, which provides a description of the ongoing transition between current and future views of the EA.

Chapter 8 Questions and Exercises

1. How far into the future should the EA future views attempt to provide documentation?
2. Why is the Same documentation technique used in the current and future view of an EA component?
3. What is the relationship between the enterprise's Strategic Plan and EA future views?
4. How can the transition between current/future views be managed?
5. How can Business Process Improvement (BPI) and Business Process Reengineering (BPR) activities be reflected in future views at the Products & Services level of the EA6 Framework?
6. How can changes in information flows and data structures be reflected in future views at the Data & Information level of the framework?
7. How can changes in applications and functionality be reflected in future views at the Applications & Systems level of the framework?
8. How can changes in voice, data, and video networks be reflected in future views at the Networks & Infrastructure level of the framework?
9. Develop a scenario that describes changes in processes, people, and technology. Identify planning assumptions that underlie these changes.

Chapter 9

Developing an Architecture
Transition Roadmap

Chapter Overview

Chapter 9 discusses the development of an Architecture Transition Roadmap (Roadmap), which is the document that describes how an enterprise will manage the transition of its current processes and resources to those which will be needed in the future. This transition from the current to the future architecture is an ongoing activity, as new resources are implemented and therefore become part of the current architecture. The purpose of configuration management and version control are also discussed, along with the need to provide a sequence for implementation projects.

Learning Objectives

> ➢ Understand the purpose of a Roadmap.
> ➢ See an example format for a Roadmap.
> ➢ Understand the types of content that go into a Roadmap.
> ➢ Understand the purpose of summaries of the current and future architecture.

Introduction

The Roadmap documents the enterprise's performance gaps, resource requirements, planned solutions, a sequencing plan, and a summary of the current and future architecture. The Roadmap also describes the architecture oversight (governance) process, the implementation methodology, and the documentation framework. It is a living document that is updated at regular intervals (e.g., annually) to provide clear version control for changes in current and future views of components and artifacts throughout the framework. The Roadmap should be archived in the on-line repository to support easy access to the information and to promote the linkage of the architecture to other IT management processes.

The enterprise's architecture is in continual transition as IT implementation and upgrade projects are completed. Large and mid-size enterprises often have many IT projects underway at any given time, which requires an overarching level of coordination, prioritization, and oversight. As is shown in Figure 9-1, the Architecture Transition Roadmap provides this coordination and supports oversight for changes to the enterprise's architecture between the current and future views.

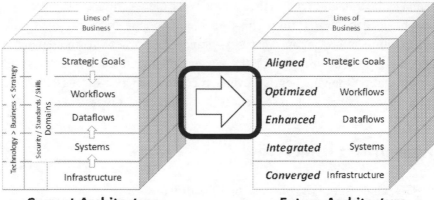

Current Architecture   **Future Architecture**

Figure 9-1: The Role of the Architecture Transition Roadmap

> *Home Architecture Analogy:* The Transition Roadmap is like the architect's project plan, which summarizes the work and shows the design, approach, timeframe, and sequencing of work for the remodeling of a home.

Architectural transition and the management thereof are documented in a Transition Roadmap, which has several sections as shown in this example:

Architecture Transition Roadmap

Part 1. EA Program Management

- Governance and Principles
- Support for Strategy and Business
- EA Roles and Responsibilities
- EA Program Budget
- EA Program Performance Measures

Part 2. EA Current Architecture Summary

- Strategic Goals and Initiatives
- Business Services and Information Flows
- Systems and Applications
- Technology Infrastructure
- IT Security
- EA Standards
- Workforce Requirements

Part 3. EA Future Architecture Summary

- Future Operating Scenarios
- Planning Assumptions
- Updating Current & Future Views
- Sequencing Plan
- Configuration Management

Part 4. EA Glossary and References

Figure 9-2: Example Format for an Architecture Transition Roadmap

Part 1. EA Program Management

EA as a management program supports policy development, decision-making, and the effective/efficient use of resources. The EA Program Management section documents the activities associated with administering EA as an ongoing program.

1.1. Governance and Principles: This section documents the way that policy and decision-making will occur within the EA program. It is also where the underlying principles of the EA program are articulated. EA governance is perhaps best described through a narrative that provides EA program policy and an accompanying flow chart that shows how and when decisions are made on EA issues such as IT investment proposals, project reviews, document approvals, and standards adoption and/or waivers. EA principles articulate the enterprise's values as they relate to the EA. These principles then guide the EA program's establishment and management.

The concept of EA principles was first proposed by Steven Spewak in his 1992 foundational book on "Enterprise Architecture Planning: A Blueprint for Data, Applications, and Technology".

Examples of EA principle are (1) the degree to which the enterprise promotes the open sharing of information, (2) an emphasis on stakeholder participation, (3) the recognition that IT is normally a means and not an end in itself, (4) an emphasis on using commercial products that are based on open standards, and (5) a recognition that EA adds value for planning, decision-making, and communication.

1.2. Support for Strategy and Business: This section emphasizes that one of the main purposes of the EA program is to support and improve the enterprise's strategic and business planning, as well as to identify performance gaps that EA components can help close. By showing how EA components are being currently used and identifying useful new processes and technologies at each level of the framework, improvements in performance can occur that are captured in the future EA views. For EA components to be viewed as a strategic asset and EA be viewed as part of the strategic planning process, business executives must see the value of the EA program in supporting the outcomes that matter to them. It is therefore important to show the linkage of the EA program to the accomplishment of the enterprise's strategic goals, as well as to clearly show how EA components support line of business activities.

1.3. EA Roles and Responsibilities: This section documents the roles that stakeholders in the EA program will play, and what the responsibilities associated with those roles will be. This is where the players on the EA team are also identified. A table format is an effective way to show roles and responsibilities, as is exemplified in Figure 9-3 on the next page.

Role Title	EA Team Role	Responsibilities
Sponsor	Executive Leadership	Be the champion of the EA program. Provide resources. Assist in resolving high-level EA issues.
Chief Information Officer	Executive Leadership and Decision-Making	Facilitate the establishment and ongoing operation of the EA Program. Lead the resolution of high-level EA issues. Integrate EA and other areas of IT and business governance.
Chief Architect	Team Leader, Program Manager	Manage the EA program and documentation process. Select and implement the EA framework and documentation methodology. Identify EA standards and manage EA configuration management sub-process.
Line of Business Managers	Requirements Identification	Participate in EA program decision- making. Promote the identification of IT- related requirements and EA solutions for each LOB.
Solutions Architect	Problem Solving	Collaboratively identify solutions for IT-related problems within LOBs. Support EA documentation.
Applications Architect	Analysis and Design	Provide technical analysis and design support for full lifecycle software development/ operation in various configurations (stand-alone, client-server, converged, virtualized).
Systems Architect	Analysis and Design	Provide technical analysis and design support for systems-related EA component selection and implementation. Ensure that IT systems meet integration and interoperability requirements. Support EA documentation.
Data Architect	Analysis and Design	Provide technical analysis and design support for database-related EA component selection and implementation. Ensure that databases meet integration and interoperability requirements. Support EA documentation.
EA Tool Expert	Application and Database Support	Maintenance of EA Software Application. Maintenance of EA repository and information.

End-User Rep.	Requirements Identification And QA	Identify end-user requirements for EA components. Provide feedback on the effectiveness of solutions.
Repository Manager	Website Content Support	Maintenance of EA website, associated content, and links to other websites as needed.
Research Analyst	Requirements Analysis	Document and verify LOB and end-user requirements. Assist in EA component design and documentation activities

Figure 9-3: Example EA Roles and Responsibilities Matrix

1.4. EA Program Budget: This section documents the budget for the EA program by fiscal year and over the total lifecycle, so that the total cost of ownership (TCO) is identified. While EA program is ongoing, a lifecycle period of five years is recommended to be able to calculate TCO. In general, the costs to be included are those for EA program start-up and operation, salaries and work facilities for the EA team, the initial documentation of the EA, periodic updates to the EA, development of the Roadmap, EA tool purchase and support, and EA repository development and maintenance. The initial estimate of these costs represents the "baseline" for EA program funding. Spending during the lifecycle should be tracked against this baseline to promote effective management of the EA program. If changes in the scope of the EA program occur, a corresponding change in the funding baseline should also be made.

1.5. EA Program Performance Measures: This section documents how the effectiveness and efficiency of the EA program will be measured. As was described in previous chapters, there are two types of measures: outcome and output. Outcome measures identify progress being made toward some new end-state, such as better component integration, increased application end-user satisfaction, or more effective IT investment decision- making. Output measures provide data on activities and things, such as how many databases exist, how many e-mail are sent each day, or how closely an IT project is meeting baseline estimates for cost/schedule/performance. Outcome measures often have both quantitative and qualitative elements to them, while output measures are usually quantitative in nature. While output measures are important for indicating progress in an initiative area, it is the attainment of outcomes that correlate to goal attainment, which is the most important thing to an enterprise. It is important to be able to measure the attainment of outcomes, so that the positive effects (added value) of the program can be identified. Example outcome and output measures are provided below:

EA Outcome Measure #1: Reduce planning costs 10% in one year.
EA Output Measure #1-1: Number of IT projects planned that year.
EA Output Measure #1-2: Prior three year's average cost of IT project planning.
EA Output Measure #1-3: Prior three year's average # of project scope changes.
EA Output Measure #1-4: Current year's average cost of IT project planning.
EA Output Measure #1-5: Current year's average # of project scope changes.

Part 2. Summary of the Current Architecture

One of the purposes of the Roadmap is to show an overview of the linkages between components at various framework levels. In this way, the present role of IT in the enterprise is better understood and can be further analyzed from either a top-down, or bottom-up perspective. The objective of this part of the Roadmap is not to duplicate the extensive documentation that is described in Chapters 4 and 5, but to provide an integrated view of how the components and artifacts work in support of each other. This also sets the stage for Part 3 of the Roadmap, which discusses future changes in components and artifacts to achieve improved performance and/or efficiency. The following are examples of how current components and artifacts can be described at each level of the framework.

1.1. Strategic Goals and Initiatives: This section identifies how the EA program and specific components support the attainment of the enterprise's strategic goals and initiatives. This section builds upon comments provided in the Strategic Plan and is included to more clearly show which components and strategic initiatives are involved in each strategic goal area. A general description is then provided of how IT components support each goal and initiative at the strategic level of the framework. Figure 9-4 provides an example format for an artifact that maps components to strategic goals and initiatives.

Strategic Goal	Strategic Initiative	Supporting EA Component(s)
Be #1 in Product Service	New Customer Service Website	New Service Website, Service Database, Product Parts Database, Customer Database, PCs and Laptops, Sales Database
	Upgrade of Customer Service Database	Service Database, Customer Database, e-Billing Application, Sales Database
Increase Safety	New Assembly Line Safety Features	Robotics Controllers, Production Scheduler, Safety Database

Figure 9-4: Mapping EA Components to
Strategic Goals/Initiatives

1.2. Business services and Information Flows: This section identifies and emphasizes the role that EA plays in supporting business process analysis and improvement, as well as identifying and optimizing information flows within and between these processes. It also re-affirms the EA principle that components are a means to enable effective business services and should not be procured unless there is a strong business case that supports investment. Within this section, the enterprise's main LOBs should be listed along with the key business services and associated information flows in each LOB. A general description is then provided of how IT components support processes at the business level of the framework.

Detailed diagrams of information flows and data structure are also provided using the various types of artifacts that populate the data level of the framework (e.g., Entity Relationship Diagrams, Data Flow Diagrams, and OO Diagrams). As shown in Figure 9-5 on the next page, a table format can be effective in creating an artifact that maps the relationships between LoBs, key business services, information flows, and supporting components.

LoB	Key Processes	Information Flows	Supporting Components
Sales	Marketing	Daily marketing and sales data pushed to data mart. Periodic summaries.	Sales Data Mart Web Site, Sales & Inventory Database, Laptops, Remote Access Extranet
	Invoicing	Receipt and processing of customer orders. Customer invoicing.	Customer Database, e-Billing System, Sales Database
	Commissions	Recording and payment of sales commissions, in conjunction with base salary payments.	Sales Force Tracking Database, ERP-Payroll Module and Database
Mfg.	Production Runs	Tracking of product manufacturing and inventory levels.	Robotics Controllers, Scheduling Application, Inventory Database
	Supplier Parts Orders	End-to-end supply chain management with internal and external customers.	Supplier's Extranet Web Portal, Parts Inventory Database 3D-Printers
Admin	Payroll	Recording of work hours data, salary data, and payment information for bi-monthly payroll and Mo/Qtr/Yr Summaries.	ERP - Payroll Module and Database, Benefits, Deductions
	Accounting	Integrated management of data for the General Ledger, Working Capital Fund, Accounts Payable, and Accounts Receivable	ERP – Accounting Module, Customer Database, e-Billing Application, Sales Database g Module.
	Human Resources	Employee benefit participation and claims information.	ERP – HR & Benefits Module and Database, External Supplier of 401K Plan's Database

		Email transmission and archiving, document and file management and archiving, print, copy, and fax transmissions.	Bundled COTS Application for Word Processing, Spreadsheets, Web Page Creation, and Presentations
	Office Automation		

Figure 9-5: Mapping Components, LoBs, and Activities

1.3. Systems and Applications: This section identifies how current components and artifacts at the systems and applications level of the framework support the information flows that are required for LOBs throughout the enterprise. The discussion should summarize how well this "suite" of commercial and custom developed IT systems and front/ back office services provide the functionality the enterprise needs for LOB operations and office automation. This can range from large scale, multi- module ERP solutions, to commercial applications and databases, to small custom-developed websites. Comments should focus on degree of integration, potential scalability, user satisfaction, and any reliance on proprietary solutions.

1.4. Technology Infrastructure: This section discusses the voice, data, and video components and artifacts that make up the Technology Infrastructure level of the framework. The discussion should focus on how well these internal and external networks, systems, and cable plants integrate to create a "seamless" infrastructure. Comment should also be made on how well the infrastructure currently handles the transport of voice, data, video, and mobile information, in terms of reliability, scalability, and cost-efficiency.

1.5. IT Security. This section discusses the general approach to IT security at all levels of the EA framework. IT security should be part of any strategic goal or initiative that depends on accurate, properly authenticated information. High-level descriptions are provided on how security is built into business services and the control of information flows, as well as the design and operation of systems, services, and networks. Specific IT security information should not be part of the Roadmap because it could reveal vulnerabilities. This type of information should be documented in a separate IT Security Plan that only certain people in the enterprise have access to (see Chapter 11).

1.6. EA Standards. Standards should be documented in an authoritative list (see Figure 9-6 on the next page). This includes standards for voice, data, video, mobile, satellite, security, facility, and other relevant areas that are used during EA component development. The TSRM can also provide a list of preferred vendors and products that meet the technical standards that an enterprise adopts. EA standards are a key element of the configuration management (CM) process and come from international, national, local, government, industry, and enterprise sources. Selected standards should include standards for voice, data, and video technologies from leading standards bodies throughout the world, including the Institute of Electrical and Electronics Engineers (IEEE), the National Institute of Science and Technology (NIST), and the European Committee on Standardization (CEN), with EA examples as follows:

- ISO 14258 (1998): Concepts and Rules for Enterprise Models

- ISO 15704 (2000): Requirements for Enterprise Reference Architectures

- CEN ENV 40003 (1991): CIM Systems Architecture Framework

- CEN ENV 12204 (1996): Constructs for Enterprise Modeling

Standards Area	ISO/CEN Standard	IEEE Standard	NIST Standard	Local Standard	Approved Products
Voice					
Data					
Video					
Mobile					
Satcom					
Security					
Facility					

Figure 9.6: Example Technical Standards Reference Matrix

1.7. Workforce Skill Requirements. This section describes the approach to IT workforce planning and training that the enterprise uses in human capital management. People are often the most valuable resource an enterprise has, and IT workforce plans should detail training requirements for component operations support and new development projects at all levels of the framework.

Part 3. Summary of Future Architecture

1.1. Future Operating Scenarios. In this section, the future operating scenarios are presented along with a narrative description of the purpose of the scenarios and the spectrum of operating environments that the scenarios respond to. For example, three scenarios are presented with an opening narrative that explains that they represent:

- Scenario 1: Continuing with the status quo.

- Scenario 2: An aggressive business strategy in a good market.

- Scenario 3: A defensive business strategy during a market down-turn.

Each scenario has planning assumptions built into it, as was described in Chapter 8, that highlight changes that will need to occur in processes, people, and technology. Lastly, in this section, a description is provided of the selected course of action for the enterprise (e.g., Future Scenario 2 will be pursued because a good business environment is forecast).

1.2. Planning Assumptions. The planning assumptions from the scenarios are further discussed in terms of what they mean to the priorities of the enterprise as it implements the future architecture. The assumptions identify new capabilities and resources that will be needed if the enterprise is to be successful in each scenario. This section then focuses on the selected scenario and the planning assumptions that will underlie that course of action. Continuing the example from above, if Future Scenario 2 is being pursued, then several new e-commerce systems may need to be built and new manufacturing capacity supported. The planning assumptions that were identified in Future Scenario 2 become the guideposts for decisions about how to change the current architecture, which needs to be described.

1.3. Updating Current and Future Views of the EA. Documentation of planned changes in processes and resources is what creates the future views of the EA at all levels of the framework. Using the EA6 Framework as an example, these updates should be accomplished in a "top-down" manner, to preserve the emphasis on strategy and business, and to maintain the logic of the documentation's relationships. Therefore, these updates would begin with to the enterprise's strategic goals and initiatives.

Changes to the enterprise's strategic plan are made periodically or in response to a significant new internal or external business or technology driver. Most strategic plans are intended to last several years, with associated goals, initiatives, and measures changing very little. Changes in the framework at this level therefore may be minimal if it is not time to update the strategic plan. Goals, initiatives, and measures should be considered as exchangeable components. This means that a goal or measure can be added, dropped, or modified without nullifying the entire plan.

A similar approach is used to review and update the enterprise's business services at the second level of the framework. It is important to ensure that the current views of business services are complete and can show how they support the accomplishment of current strategic goals. The changes in business services then can be made considering any changes in strategic goals, initiatives, and measures that may be planned and documented at the top level of the framework. Also, documentation at the business level of the framework should show future planning for more effective, cost-efficient, and technically integrated processes.

At the third level of the framework (data), the development of future views enables proactive planning to improve information exchange within the enterprise and promotes the establishment of standards for the format of commonly used data entities/objects which further promotes component interoperability. Planning at this level of the framework first considers the information-related requirements of the level above, business services. Once these are identified, cross-cutting information flows between processes, as well as flows within single processes can be identified and documented using whatever methodology is selected for use in the framework (traditional structured or object-oriented methods).

Documenting changes to the flow of information within and between business services (and new data standards) will enable EA planners to select components at these two lowest levels of the framework that best support the information flows and data standards. A focal point for the discussion in this section is to identify any current performance gaps that exist at the higher levels of the framework and map them to current components and products. The future view of the systems level should show which components will be changing and in what timeframe. Components should be interoperable and scalabile whenever possible.

At the infrastructure level of the framework, future changes will reflect components (hardware and software) that will provide a more robust, reliable, and secure voice, data, and video backbone transport capability. Interoperability, cost-effectiveness and open standards are additional factors to be considered.

EA Sequencing Plan: The Sequencing Plan section of the Architecture Transition Roadmap documents the tasks, milestones, and timeframe for implementing new components and artifacts. Large and mid-size enterprises often have many new development, upgrade, retirement, or migration projects underway at any given time and these require coordination to establish the optimal sequencing of activities. Sometimes there are dependencies between projects that also require proper sequencing. For example, an improvement to the capacity of the data infrastructure may be required before additional systems and/or databases can be effectively hosted so that maximum performance can be attained.

Another common example is the consolidation of components to improve both performance and overall cost effectiveness. Figure 9-7 provides an example sequencing diagram to show component consolidation activities.

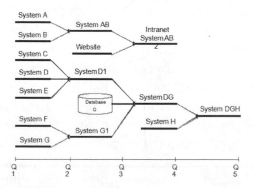

Figure 9-7: Example EA Sequencing Diagram

1.4. EA Configuration Management: The EA Configuration Management (CM) section of the Roadmap serves to support the sub- process by which changes to the EA are managed and the standards in the TSRM are applied. Changes to the EA include the addition, upgrade, retirement of components or artifacts. CM ensures that (1) a standardized process is used in reviewing proposed changes, (2) technical standards for voice, data, and video are followed or waived, (3) there is a documented waiver process, (4) waivers have specific time limits, so that EA standards are eventually realized, (5) there is enforcement for EA documentation version control. The CM process should be overseen by the Chief Architect and be supported by an Architecture Working Group that includes stakeholders from throughout the enterprise. The CM process works through the submission, review and approval/rejection of an EA Change Request (EACR), an example of which is shown in Figure 9-8.

Date Submitted: ______
EACR Control#: ______

Enterprise Architecture
Change Request Form

Submitted By: ______________________________

EAF Level: *Strategic Business Information Application Technology*
Description Of Requested Change

____

Justification:

____

Group(s) Affected:

____

Description of Supporting Documentation (attach to EACR):

EACR Action (Completed By Chief Architect)

Approved Not Approved Waiver Granted Until (date: ______)

Include in EA Version ______ Publication Date: ______

EAF Standard Area: *Documentation Voice Data Video Security*
EAF Standard(s) Affected: ______________________________

Reason for Non-Approval or Waiver:

____

Chief Architect:
____

Figure 9-8: Example EA Change Request Form

Part 4. Glossary and References

This part of the Roadmap is where a glossary of key EA terms is provided along with an Acronym List. There should also be a bibliographical list of reference books and articles that might provide additional background or that help the reader's understanding of the EA Management Plan. Because the EA is still an emerging area of professional practice, the Acronym List and Glossary are important to include as they help to implement a common set of terms and definitions for use throughout the enterprise.

Summary of Concepts

This chapter provided a description of the purpose, format, and content of an EA Transition Roadmap, which describes the EA management process, implementation methodology, and documentation framework, as well as summaries of current and future views of the EA. It is a living document that is updated at regular intervals to provide clear version control for changes in current and future views of EA components and artifacts at each level of the framework. The Roadmap should be archived in the on-line EA repository to support easy access to the information and promote linkage of the EA program to other IT processes.

Chapter 9 Questions and Exercises

1. What is the purpose of an Architecture Transition Roadmap?
2. What is an EA Change Request and how is it used within the Configuration Management process?
3. What is the purpose of the Sequencing Plan?
4. What is the role of a Chief Information Officer in the EA program?
5. What is the role of a Chief Architect in the EA program?
6. How do standards contribute to the EA program?
7. Why are standardized terms important to an EA program?
8. How can an EA Management Plan show "gaps" in enterprise performance?
9. Develop a flow chart for EA governance in a public or private sector enterprise. Show where policy development and decision-making

occur, as well as interfaces to other management processes, including capital planning, project management, and security.

10. Develop a Sequencing Plan for the implementation of a major commercial Enterprise Resource Planning (ERP) product.
11. Develop an EA Roles and Responsibility Matrix for a public or private sector enterprise of your choice.

Section III

Using an Enterprise Architecture

This section discusses how to use and maintain EA information within the enterprise, how related governance processes can be integrated, and examples of how to apply EA methods when designing business and technology solutions as well as when organizations are undergoing major structural and functional changes.

Case Study (Scene 5) - Linking EA to Other Processes
The Case Study continues the scenario at Danforth Manufacturing Company (DMC) that was presented in Sections I and II. This scene describes how the EA information will be used in the company's capital planning process to support investment decision-making. It also talks about how the EA information supports project management and security planning.

Chapter 10 - The Role of Investment Planning and Project Management
Chapter 10 introduces the concepts of the capital planning and investment control (CPIC) process and its relationship to enterprise architecture and project management. The four phases of the CPIC process are described (plan, select, control, and evaluate). The chapter also introduces the concepts of project management and how they relate to enterprise architecture.

Chapter 11 - The Role of Security and Privacy

Chapter 11 introduces the concepts of security and privacy and how they relate to enterprise architecture. Four elements of an IT Security Program are described: information security, personnel security, operational security, and physical security. Additionally, EA artifacts related to IT security are discussed, including security plans, risk assessments, test and evaluation reports, continuity of operations plans, disaster recovery plans, and system certification and accreditations.

Chapter 12 - Repository and Support Tools

Chapter 12 discusses the purpose and functionality of the on-line EA repository. The design of an example repository (Living Enterprise) is described, as well as the relationship of a repository to the underlying EA documentation framework. The chapter also provides a mapping of EA component documentation techniques to the areas of the EA repository, and discusses the role of architecture support softward (tools).

Chapter 13 – Solution Architecture Methods

Chapter 13 introduces the concept of solution architecture, which is where EA concepts and methods are used in projects to develop or improve business and technology components throughout the organization. The chapter defines terms and gives examples of the types of solution architecture projects that can occur at each level of the framework (strategy, business, data, systems, networks) as well as in the thread areas (security, skills, and standards).

Chapter 14 – Enterprise Architecture for Mergers & Acquisitions

Chapter 14 discusses how EA concepts and methods can be helpful to organizational mergers and acquisitions (M&A). This includes the use of EA in the pre-deal due diligence phase and in the post-deal organizational restructuring phase. The use of a holistic EA frameowork to enable the "likewise" comparison of two different organizations is a highlighted example, as is the use of EA artifacts to support planning and decision-making as the organizations are being merged.

Chapter 15 – The Future of Holistic Enterprise Architecture

Chapter 15 provides the author's thoughts on future trends in the profession and practice of holiostic enterprise architecture, based on readings and observations during work on EA projects. This is done to give the reader a sense of the issues that are currently of interest to enterprise architects and organizations considering EA programs. These comments are also intended to help promote discussion in each topic area as well as to encourage the adoption of a common language for EA greater collaboration among those in the profession.

Case Study:
Danforth Manufacturing Company
Scene 5: Linking EA to Other Management Processes

This is the final scene of the Case Study, which continues the scenario at Danforth Manufacturing Company (DMC) that was presented in Sections I and II. The CIO and Chief Architect have now completed a project with the sponsors of two lines of business who currently have requirements for IT systems. The sponsors, CFO Jose Cruz, and COO Kate Jarvis, had their teams work with the EA Working Group to develop EA segment documentation for the financial and production lines of business. These segments represent the first parts of the company's architecture. This scene describes how the EA segment documentation will be used in the company's new capital planning process that will support IT investment decision-making. This scene also includes a discussion about how the EA artifacts support project management and security planning activities. Upon Roberta's recommendation, Jose agreed to lead a new Capital Planning Working Group, and DMC's CEO Rick Danforth acknowledged that the Executive Committee's would serve as the company's Capital Planning Board with final investment decision approval.

CIO Roberta Washington opened a day-long workshop for DMC's EA Working Group, which included members of the newly formed Capital Planning Working Group. "Today's workshop will be a bit different because we are going to use the EA documentation that we have developed during the past few weeks to help Kate and Jose make decisions about solutions to their IT requirements. Raja Patil, our Chief Architect, will lead the morning session and will start by describing the documentation of current and future views of the production and financial segments and how that will support the analysis and decision-making process. Then, Jose Cruz, our CFO, will lead the afternoon session, which is also the first meeting of the Capital Planning Working Group, who will work with us to develop a combined recommendation on the solution to Jose and Kate's requirements for new IT systems. Raja, what have we learned from the EA documentation activities?"

"Thanks Roberta" said Raja. "The EA Working Group did a great job with Jose's and Kate's staff teams over the past two weeks in developing EA artifacts for the EA components in the production segment and the financial segment of the DMC architecture. We now have EA artifacts that describe the components in these two segments at each level of the framework. This includes strategic goals/initiatives/outcome metrics, the flow diagrams for processes in these two lines of business, the data structure and flow diagrams for the IT systems, application/web service lists and interface diagrams, and network diagrams. Further, we were able to develop a future operating scenario together that looks three years in the future and highlights both the unique and common IT requirements in the two lines of business that these segments represent. From this scenario, several planning assumptions were revealed, which may help us determine a common solution to several IT requirements. The other aspect of the EA framework that we addressed was a set of EA components that represent IT security resources that serve these two segments, as well as an initial set of standards for voice, data, and video infrastructure resources that serve the segments. Finally, we identified workforce and training requirements related to these lines of business but are waiting on developing the future requirements until the groups determine the recommended solution."

Raja then led the two working groups in a more detailed review of the EA documentation that had been developed, and Jose then opened the afternoon working group session. "Thanks again Roberta and Raja for providing the approach and oversight for the documentation of the EA segments for production and finance. Kate and I are now going to review the requirements that we have for additional IT support within our lines of business. We would like the Enterprise Architecture and Capital Planning Working Groups and our staff members to help us this afternoon to determine what the most effective way is to meet those requirements, be it separate systems or a combined solution. DMC is always interested in maximizing the return on any investment in resources we make, and it already is apparent that by looking across the entire enterprise of DMC, that our planning and decision-making will be enhanced."

Jose and Kate discussed their previous proposals for IT systems in their respective lines of business. Jose had initially identified a commercial ERP solution (WELLCO) which had the service modules that he needed. Kate had initially identified a custom-built Sales and Inventory System (SITS) as the solution for new requirements in those areas. The working groups and line of business staff members reviewed the information from the initial requests, and then used the EA documentation of these lines of business to establish what the most operationally efficient and cost- effective solution would be. They were able to determine that the WELLCO commercial ERP application suite had a module available for sales and inventory functions. By contacting the vendor, they were also able to determine that this module could support the addition of some custom functionality, which would then allow it to fully meet Kate's requirements. The cost of this additional WELLCO module would be approximately $1,675,000, as opposed to the $3,000,000 that was estimated to create SITS. Further, the use of the WELLCO ERP product within both lines of business promoted additional information exchanges through the use of common data formats.

Jose addressed the group in the late afternoon after the analysis work and discussions had been completed. "Thank you all for taking the time today to help us review the creation of the first two segments of our company's architecture and use that information to evaluate two requests for new IT support. Originally, these two requests were submitted by Kate and me separately at our annual planning conference several months ago. The estimated cost of the two separate solutions was $3,600,000. By looking at our business areas from an enterprise-wide architecture perspective, we have been able to find a combined solution that will save the company $1,325,000 and promotes higher levels of information sharing than we otherwise would have achieved. Roberta, this is a win-win for Kate and me. I believe it is a win for you and Raja, because you have just shown why the EA program is needed, and how it will more than pay for itself. Roberta and I will now take the combined recommendation of the EA Working Group and the Capital Planning Working Group to the Executive Committee for final approval. If approved, we will be calling on the two groups to assist in conducting the control reviews and evaluation review of the project that are part of our new capital planning and investment control process. This will lower the risk of failure and help us to mature our EA and capital planning processes. I look forward to seeing you all at those reviews."

The DMC Executive Board approved the recommendation of the working groups, and CEO Rick Danforth commended Kate, Roberta, and Jose for working together to identify a more cost-efficient solution for their needs. The EA program was then approved for funding to complete the remaining segments of the DMC architecture over the following 18 months, as well as annual operations funding for the next two years, at which time the value of the EA program would be reviewed by the Executive Committee.

Buzzword Bingo

The COO looked at the CIO and said, "Wait, what? Did the leadership team just get on the Same page here?" The CIO said "Yup". The CFO said, "This is a shared enterprise solution – who would have thunk that we'd embrace that – I admit that I was always promoting my own silo of excellence." The CEO smiled and said, "This morphed from a bare-knuckle brawl to a no-brainer slam-dunk win-win! Thank goodness for Enterprise Architecture – it will be the secret sauce in all of our digital transformation initiatives from now on." The room was filled with high-fives, DMC became world-class, and everyone lived happily ever after in their social media clics. The End.

PS: This Case Study does not incorporate the many changes in how we work and play due to global conditions… telework, social distancing and virtual organizations are new elements that EA can and will include in designs.

Chapter 10

The Roles of Investment Planning and Project Management

Chapter Overview

Chapter 10 introduces the concepts of the capital planning and investment control (CPIC) process and its relationship to enterprise architecture and project management. The four phases of the CPIC process are described (plan, select, control, and evaluate). The role of Project Management is also discussed in the context of using EA and artifacts as a reference baseline.

Key Term: *Capital Planning*

The management and decision-making process associated with the planning, selection, control, and evaluation of investments in resources, including EA components such as systems, networks, knowledge warehouses, and support services for the enterprise.

Learning Objectives

- ➢ Understand how capital planning relates to EA.
- ➢ Understand the basic phases of capital planning.
- ➢ Understand how project management relates to EA.
- ➢ Understand the format and role of a Project Management Plan.

Introduction

The EA program is only effective if the enterprise's resources are effectively applied to gaps in operational performance. It takes people, money, facilities, software, hardware, training, and other resources to do this through the investment in an ongoing series of development and improvement projects. If there were no gaps in operational performance, there would be no requirement for new or upgraded components. However, this is rarely the case, and so capital planning and project management processes are needed to manage the projects that enable the ongoing transition from the current architecture to the future architecture. These processes also help to ensure that strategic, business, and architectural alignment are maintained as the enterprise plans, selects, controls, and evaluates investments in components.

> *Home Architecture Analogy:* For an architect's design to be approved by the owner, their requirements must be met within budget. The architect must then work with a builder to ensure that the design is properly constructed, the schedule is met, and budget is not exceeded.

Discussion

Capital Planning and Investment Control (CPIC) process supports EA by planning, selecting, controlling, and evaluating investments in new or upgraded components. This cyclic process promotes the following:

- Identification of operational performance gaps in the enterprise
- Identification of new or upgraded EA components to close performance gaps
- Development of business cases that consider alternatives, alignment, and value
- Development and management of an overall portfolio of investments in the EA
- Maximizing the value of individual investments in EA components
- Encouraging a culture of learning by evaluating each completed investment

The CPIC process operates in four distinct phases that serve to (1) standardize how requirements for technology are identified within a strategic and business context; (2) associate the technology requirement with an EA component; (3) make an investment decision; and (4) implement a solution through standardized project management practices. The process is coordinated by a Project Management Plan (PMP), which serves as the authoritative documentation source for all phases. Figure 10-1 shows the four phases of the CPIC process.

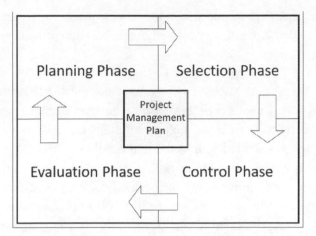

Figure 10-1. The CPIC Process

CPIC Planning Phase

The CPIC Planning Phase is where business and technology requirements that emerge throughout the enterprise are reviewed at a preliminary level for merit, need, and identification of an association with an EA component.

Those requirements that are determined to have sufficient value to enterprise are then associated with an EA component and formalized in a PMP using standard templates for large and small projects. The PMP contains detailed information about the proposed investment/project including the requirement, the business case, a work breakdown structure, a schedule, a budget, roles and responsibilities, measures for success, and a communications plan. The PMP is intended to be a living document that is updated throughout the lifecycle of a project from conception to completion. When the PMP is completed and all project and investment information are present, the potential investment/project moves to the CPIC Selection Phase. Here is also where a cost-benefit analysis is done.

CPIC Selection Phase

The CPIC Selection Phase is where a funding decision is made for a proposed investment in an EA component. The funding proposal, as documented in the PMP, is reviewed for value, alignment, strength of business case, strength of technical solution, security, risk, and return. Based on this review of the PMP, the enterprise's management determines if the investment should be made in light of available resources. Some enterprises review proposed investments as a group on a periodic basis (e.g., quarterly or annually) so as to align the selection process with budget and business cycles.

Return on Investment (ROI) can be one of the most difficult aspects of a proposed investment's business case to develop because many of the benefits of enterprise-wide technology solutions are qualitative in nature. For example, in calculating benefits attributable to the EA component that contains enterprise-wide e-mail, there will be an estimate of the dollar values for improvements in productivity, communication, record keeping, and morale; all of which are difficult to precisely measure. For that reason, enterprises should use ROI as only one of a number of factors in selecting investments in EA components. Once a proposed investment in an EA component is selected for funding, the investment becomes an active project and the PMP is refined to reflect any updates to the implementation schedule and funding plan that may be needed for that project to be activated within the Sequencing Plan of the Architecture Transition Roadmap. The project then moves to the CPIC Control Phase.

CPIC Control Phase
The CPIC Control Phase is where ongoing development and upgrade projects are evaluated for how closely cost, schedule, and EA component performance milestones are being met, and how well areas of risk are being managed. Cost, schedule, and performance milestones are tracked by establishing baseline estimates and then managing to that baseline. This is the basis of "Earned Value Management" (EVM) which is a project management technique that looks at planned versus actual cost, schedule, and performance data throughout the life of the project.

One of the key concepts in EVM is that projects that significantly diverge from planned (baseline) estimates are more difficult to return to the baseline the further along that the project is. EVM emphasizes identifying significant divergence within the first third of the project's schedule in order to have the best chance to recover to baseline values, or to reset the baseline if new requirements have been added which increase cost and/or time estimates. Project planning and tracking documentation is maintained as part of the PMP and includes a Work Breakdown Structure (WBS), project task list and schedule (Gantt Chart), critical path information

(PERT Chart), EVM information, and performance metrics. Performance metrics are those which measure the capability of the EA component that is being created. This could include database query speed, application or web page refresh rate, usability, navigability, peak network bandwidth, and interoperability.

Risk is related to uncertainty and any potential obstacle to success in the project. It is important to have identified risk areas before the start of the project and implemented proactive and reactive strategies for limiting (mitigating) those risks. Sources of risk include the use of new technologies, loss of key personnel, loss of funding, adding new requirements without adding time/money (called "scope creep"), insufficient testing prior to acceptance, lack of stakeholder buy-in, and insufficient training for end-users and maintenance personnel.

CPIC Evaluation Phase
The CPIC Evaluation Phase is where (1) completed IT projects receive a Post-Implementation Review (PIR), and (2) where operational systems are periodically reviewed for continuing value. PIRs help an enterprise to review the "lessons learned" from each project and in so doing, to mature in their ability to implement similar projects in the future. For example, if an enterprise completes several website projects a year and no PIR is held, the problems, successes, approaches to risk, etc. will not be shared and an opportunity to improve in this area is lost. PIRs help to reduce cost, cycle time, and risk for IT projects, and they help to create a culture of sharing and learning in the enterprise.

Once a system is accepted into the IT operating environment, it becomes what is referred to as a "legacy" system. It is important to not only conduct PIRs just after systems are brought into the IT operating environment, but also to review these legacy systems at regular intervals to determine if each one is continuing to add sufficient value to the enterprise to merit additional spending for operations, maintenance, and upgrades. If it is found that a legacy system is not performing to the level that the enterprise needs, or it is duplicating capabilities, then that system is identified for phase-out and disposal. Disposing of legacy systems (after needed data and functionality are transferred) is important to maintaining an efficient IT operating environment.

Governance and Capital Planning

Governance processes, including CPIC, are those that provide policy and decision-making, and they should be overseen by some form of Executive Steering Committee that is comprised of the enterprise's top executives. The CPIC process should be managed by the enterprise's Chief Financial Officer (CFO) in collaboration with the Chief Information Officer (CIO) and LOB managers. Because CPIC is primarily a financial investment decision-making process, the CFO should lead it, but it is very important in information-centric enterprises that the CIO be a partner in the process and that these two executives effectively integrate CPIC and the EA Management process. CPIC decisions in each phase of the process should be made by an executive level Capital Planning Board (CPB) that is supported by a Capital Planning Working Group (CPWG) and an Enterprise Architecture Working Group (EAWG). In this way, CPIC decision-making has senior stakeholder involvement and the documentation and analysis activities are accomplished by subordinate groups of experts in business and technology. Figure 10-2 shows this.

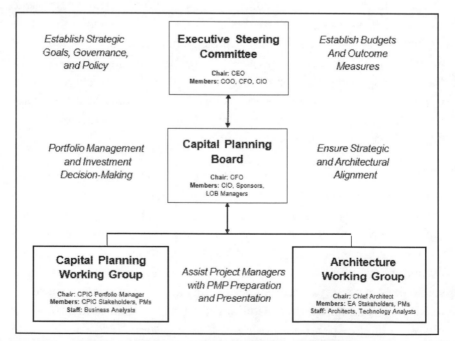

Figure 10-2: The CPIC Governance Process

The Executive Steering Committee

The ESC is a top-level policy making and decision review committee. Its purpose is to establish the enterprise's strategic goals and initiatives, governance processes, and policies to implement and integrate those processes. Enterprise-wide governance regarding the use of information technologies primarily involves six processes, which must work together to promote effective policy and decision-making: strategic planning, enterprise architecture, capital planning, project management, security, and workforce planning. The ESC provides the CPB with policy and guidance regarding strategic goals and governance. The ESC also reviews the decisions of the CPB to ensure that they best promote the achievement of the enterprise's strategic goals.

The Capital Planning Board

The CPB is an executive-level decision-making board. The CPB decides which projects are selected for funding, determines if active projects involving capital assets (including components) are effectively implemented, evaluates completed projects for lessons learned, and determines if ongoing programs are continuing to add value to the enterprise.

To establish a baseline for investment decision-making, the CPB develops a portfolio to aggregate, categorize, and manage individual investments in capital assets, including EA components. This "Investment Portfolio" reveals total spending on capital assets, supports portfolio-level management, and allows for the shifting of resources away from categories with low ROI. Alternatively, general business categories can be used such as Operations, Sales and Marketing, Finance and Accounting, Human Resources, Research and Development, and Office Automation. The goal of portfolio level investment management for the CPB is to identify the right balance of capital spending between categories, and to weed out weak investments in each category. The CPB also does cost-benefit analyses.

The CPB should establish a regular schedule for reviewing investment proposals, current projects, and ongoing programs. Each investment (and investment is a new project or legacy program) in the portfolio should be reviewed at key schedule milestones or at least once a year. The CPB should be chaired by the CFO, and the members should include the CIO, program sponsors, and program managers.

<u>The Capital Planning Working Group</u>
The CPWG supports the CPB by (1) helping Project Managers to prepare and update PMPs, especially the business cases, (2) providing documentation and business analysis support for CPB reviews, (3) coordinating their analyses with the EAWG, and (4) maintaining an archive of CPB documents. The CPWG should be chaired by a CPIC Portfolio Manager and the members include project managers and CPIC stakeholders. Support staff for the CPWG should include experts on strategic planning, business analysis, project management, and workforce planning. The CPWG also performs Cost-Benefit Analyses.

<u>The Enterprise Architecture Working Group</u>
The EAWG supports the CPB by (1) helping Project Managers to prepare and update PMPs, especially EA information, (2) providing documentation and technical analysis support for CPB reviews, and (3) coordinating their analyses with the CPWG. The EAWG should be chaired by the Chief Architect and the members should include project managers and EA stakeholders. Support staff for the EAWG should include the EA team and experts on information technology analysis at all levels of the EA6 Framework, security, project management, and configuration management.

The Role of Project Management

Project (and program) management is a professional discipline that focuses on developing, implementing, operating, improving, and/or retiring enterprise resources. Project and Program Managers (PMs) are responsible for meeting the goals of the project or program. Controlling successful outcomes involves the management of five primary aspects of a project/program: managing scope; controlling costs, maintaining the schedule, improving product performance, and lowering risk.

Projects and Programs are terms that encompass the work that an enterprise does. Projects are different from programs in that projects create new or updated resources/capabilities. Programs include projects as well as the ongoing governance and business services that constitute most of the activities of an enterprise. Programs are oriented toward the management of existing (legacy) resources/capabilities, whereas projects build new or upgrade existing resources/capabilities.

Key Term: *Project*

A *temporary* activity that creates a product, service, or result.

Key Term: *Program*

An *ongoing* activity that manages existing processes/resources or oversees the development of new processes/resources via projects.

PMs manage both projects and programs by establishing a detailed plan for accomplishing the strategic and/or tactical goals that are supported. Project Management Plan (PMP) and adjusting it to meet changes in requirements or resources. The PMP is a living document that provides information for PMs and others in all phases of the CPIC process. When the project involves the development, upgrade, or retirement of EA components, the development of the PMP also provides some of the EA artifacts needed for that component. Figure 10-3 on the next page provides an example outline of a PMP. PMs should develop PMP as follows:

PMP - Executive Summary
Provide a one or two-paragraph summary of the purpose of the project, its value to mission accomplishment, the technical approach, alternatives considered, the total lifecycle cost, funding availability, the proposed schedule, and potential implementation risks.

Project Management Plan

Executive Summary

Introduction
Project Requirements
Project Description
Project Sponsorship and Stakeholders

Strategic Alignment
Alignment to Strategic Goals
Value to Strategic Initiatives

Architectural Alignment
Alignment with Enterprise Architecture
Integration With Existing Resources
Standards and Product Selection Strategy
System Development Lifecycle Method
System Performance Metrics
System Standard Operating Procedures

Business Case
Alternatives Analysis
Cost-Benefit Analysis
Return on Investment Analysis

Project Controls
- Cost Controls and Project Budget
- Project Performance Goals and Metrics
- Schedule & Work Breakdown Structure
- Agile Scrums & Sprints
- Minimum Viable Product & Iteration
- Risk Management

Project Management
- Project Sponsor, Manager, Team
- Roles and Responsibilities
- Testing and Quality Assurance
- Workforce Training

Security and Privacy
- Security Plan
- Data Privacy Procedures
- System/Solutions Accreditation
- Records Management Procedures

Appendix A   Business Case Worksheets
Appendix B   Reference Documents
Appendix C   Glossary of Terms

Figure 10-3: Example Contents of a Project Management Plan

PMP - Project Requirements: *Documentation and Analysis*

Provide a general description of the background and context of the project, as well as the EA-related requirement(s) that this project meets. Determine the outcomes that the project must achieve, and how the successful attainment of those outcomes will be measured. Describe the type of EA component(s) that this project develops, upgrades, or retires (system, application, database, website, cable plant, hardware platform, etc.). Determine if this project creates a new IT capability or upgrades an existing capability. Also determine if there is any duplication of existing capability and if so, describe why it is beneficial to create this duplication. For project sponsorship and stakeholders, identify who the funding and implementation sponsor is at the executive level; this is the person with budget approval and operational approval authority. Finally, identify who the stakeholders are in this project (i.e., users, developers, and managers).

PMP - Strategic Alignment: *Value and Impact*
For strategic alignment, describe how this project supports the enterprise's strategic goals. Describe if this project responds to a directive or a

government mandate or initiative, and how this project will meet all aspects of these requirements. For value and impact, describe the value of this project in terms of improving internal and/or external business services and optimizing the utilization of resources. Determine if re-engineering or improvement of those processes is needed before (or as part of) project implementation and operations. Describe the impact if this project is not implemented.

PMP - Architectural Alignment: *Integration, Standards, and Approach*
For EA alignment, discuss and then document the project's proposed technical approach with the enterprise's EAWG for design and operational alignment at the various levels of the EA6 Framework: strategy, business, information, applications, and technology infrastructure. Determine the costs associated with documenting the project throughout its lifecycle in the on-line EA repository, including views of EA components at all levels of the EA6 Framework in both the current and future architectures, as well as the EA Management Plan. Include these costs in the total lifecycle cost of the project. For integration, determine if there are data or telecommunication interfaces to other EA components and describe how integration, interface, and information exchange issues will be handled.

For standards, determine if approved data, telecommunications, and video technical standards at all levels of the EA6 Framework are being followed. If there are new standards being introduced, explain the effect of adopting those new standards on other IT system(s), application(s), database(s), and/or website(s). Describe the approach to configuration management that will be taken in terms of using EACRs at all levels of the EA6 Framework. Determine and describe the System Development Lifecycle Methodology (SDLC) method that will be used to organize IT system implementation efforts (e.g., waterfall, rapid application development, evolutionary, incremental/phased). For performance measures, determine the performance metrics that will be used to measure proper system design performance, to be evaluated as part of acceptance criteria, and during the operations and maintenance phase of the delivered EA component(s). Determine the Standard Operating Procedures (SOPs) that will have to be written for the operations and maintenance phase of the lifecycle and utilize draft SOPs as part of acceptance testing.

<u>PMP - Business Case</u>: *Value and Results*
Perform an Alternatives Analysis to determine if there are several viable alternatives for meeting the stated EA-related requirement(s). Identify how each alternative meets or does not meet the requirement(s). Perform a Cost-Benefit Analysis for each alternative and then determine what the Return on Investment will be (using a Net Present Value discount factor) during the lifecycle. Perform a risk analysis to identify areas of risk and mitigation strategies. Select the best alternative based on (1) strategic alignment, (2) architecture alignment, (3) ROI, (4) security solution, (5) level of risk, (7) total cost of ownership, and (7) available resources. Ensure that the rest of the PMP documentation focuses only on the selected alternative. (See Appendix A for additional details on the business case).

<u>PMP - Project Controls</u>: Cost, Schedule, Performance, and Risk
For cost controls, describe the total lifecycle cost of this project, including planning, design, development, operations, and maintenance. Describe the source of funding for the project during the total lifecycle including operations and maintenance. Describe the method for acquiring key project resources (i.e., funding, hardware, software, operating facilities, trained personnel). Use an Earned Value Management approach to track planned versus actual costs, as well as the baseline schedule and actual progress. For additional schedule controls, document the baseline schedule with both task (Gantt Chart) and critical path (PERT Chart) views that identify major milestones, in-progress, reviews, testing, and post- implementation events. For project performance oversight, establish what the performance metrics are for the EA components that are being created and/or upgraded in this project, especially what the acceptance criteria are prior to going operational. In the area of risk mitigation, describe what the potential obstacles to success in implementing this project are and how will this risk be mitigated. Examples include technological risk if the enterprise is an "early adopter", cost risk imposed by budget cuts, schedule risk imposed by losses of key personnel, late shipment of hardware or software components, and implementation risk if all stakeholders were not involved in all aspects of project development.

<u>PMP - Project Enterprise</u>: *Structure and Responsibilities*
Identify the Project Sponsor, PM, and the project team. Determine and describe the roles and responsibilities of the Project Sponsor, PM, and other

key team members. Document this in a project "Roles and Responsibilities Matrix." Determine a project Work Breakdown Structure (WBS) that identifies all of the major work areas and then decomposes each significant activity in terms of time and budget goals. Use these cost and schedule goals in the Gantt Chart and business case. For testing and quality assurance, describe the approach to testing during development and acceptance. Determine if third-party integration or verification testing is also required, and if so, describe the approach and key participants. Describe the training, user guide, operations, maintenance, and other reference materials that will have to be written for the project's delivered system(s), application(s), database(s), and website(s). Identify the technical, business process, or other training that users will be required to have in order to operate and maintain the delivered system(s), application(s), database(s), or website(s). Identify sources and cost estimates for all required training and schedule accomplishment prior to acceptance and operations. Identify back-up personnel for key positions to receive training.

PMP - Security and Privacy: *Protecting and Assuring Information*
In the area of physical security, determine and describe the facilities and other direct access protection that will be required to achieve an acceptable level of risk to prevent unauthorized access to these EA components. In the area of information security, determine how the information created/used by the EA component will be protected and authenticated. In the area of personnel security, determine how access control will be provided for system administrators, database administrators, webmasters, security personnel, and end-users. In the area of operational security, determine and document (via a SOP) the procedures for handling end-user agreements, login and access control, incident response (i.e. virus attacks, denial of service attacks, hackers), password issuance and control, and employee termination. For testing and accreditation, determine and describe the method that will be used to test certify that the delivered EA components(s) meet the risk-adjusted goals in the areas of physical, information, personnel, and operational security. For data privacy, determine the sensitivity and classification of information on delivered EA component(s). Determine the issues related to data privacy and describe how they will be handled (e.g., access to employee's personal information). For records management, determine the issues related to records management and describe how they will be handled. Determine if information exchange and records

management issues exist with other IT resources and describe how they will be handled.

<u>PMP – Appendices</u>.
Appendices to the PMP should provide amplifying documentation. This can include the detailed worksheets used in the business case (alternatives analysis, cost-benefit analysis, and NPV/ROI calculations), EA Artifacts, and a project glossary and list of terms.

Summary of Concepts

This chapter discussed the role of capital planning and project management processes in the EA Management Program and the implementation of EA components. The four phases of the Capital Planning and Investment Control process were described, as was an investment governance process that centers on the decision-making of the Capital Planning Board and its supporting working groups. These are the groups that perform both business case and EA alignment analyses and help PM prepare and update their Project Management Plans in all phases of the Capital Planning and Investment Control process. The role of project and program management was also discussed in the chapter and an example Project Management Plan was provided.

Chapter 10 Review Questions

1. Why is it important to integrate the EA Management Program with the enterprise's capital planning process and project management practices?
2. Describe the four basic phases of the capital planning process.
3. How can the capital planning process help support decisions on investing in future EA component upgrades or new capabilities?
4. What is a business case for investment in EA components? What are the roles of an Alternatives Analysis, Cost Benefit Analysis, and Return on Investment calculation in the business case?
5. Describe roles and responsibilities in the capital planning governance process.

6. Why is it important to have a standardized format for a Project Management Plan?
7. How are security and privacy issues described in the Project Management Plan?
8. What kinds of updates to a Project Management Plan occur in each of the four phases of the capital planning process?
9. What is meant by "architectural alignment" in developing a Project Management Plan?
10. Describe how an enterprise's Chief Information Officer, Chief Financial Officer, and Chief Operating Officer should cooperate and coordinate in developing and managing an integrated approach to enterprise architecture, capital planning, and project management.
11. Describe how cost, schedule, performance, and risk managed would be managed in a project to implement an email system in a new location.
12. Develop a business case for the hypothetical outsourcing of an enterprise's IT Help Desk. The elements of the business case are (1) an Alternatives Analysis that compares in-house operation of the Help Desk and outsourcing to an external service provider, (2) a Cost-benefit Analysis for each of the two alternatives and (3) a Return on Investment calculation for each of the two alternatives.

Chapter 11

The Role of Security and Privacy

Chapter Overview

Chapter 11 discusses the role of security and privacy as part of an EA program and architecture. Security is one of the vertical "threads" that has an impact at all levels of the EA framework. The enterprise's Security and Privacy Program is described in four basic parts: information security, personnel security, operational security, and physical security. The chapter also covers discusses the role of security and privacy as part of risk management and the elements of an example Security and Privacy Plan.

Learning Objectives

> Understand the role of security and privacy in the EA program
> Understand the role of security and privacy in managing risk
> Understand balance between information sharing and protection
> Understand the eight basic elements of a security framework
> Understand the parts of an example Security and Privacy Plan

Introduction

The role of security and privacy within an EA program is best described as a comprehensive set of controls that pervade all architectural domains and are a key part of an organization's risk management strategy. One can think of this as a vertical thread that weaves through all levels of the architecture. The thread metaphor is used (as opposed to a separate dedicated level) because security and privacy are most effective when they are integral to the enterprise's strategic initiatives, business services, information flows, applications, and technology infrastructure.

> *Home Architecture Analogy:* The set of security controls are like a home's intruder detection and response service that monitors entry points, and internal spaces, provides an alarm system, notifies occupants of a problem, and can generate a response from a security service.

Discussion

Effective security and privacy controls should operate throughout the architecture and reflect a comprehensive and integrated risk management solution for the enterprise. This is implemented through a Security and Privacy Program comprised of eight areas that are implemented and maintained in the context of an enterprise-wide EA and risk management strategy. Those areas are Governance, Operations, Personnel, Workflow, Information, Applications, Infrastructure, and Physical, as is shown in Figure 11-1.

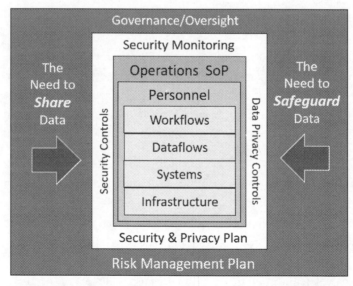

Figure 11-1: Risk Management and Security / Privacy

Drivers and Threats

Drivers for managing risk come primarily from an enterprise's need to integrate processes/systems and share information, with a concurrent need to protect those resources from unauthorized access and use. Finding the right balance point in each area of an enterprise is the purpose of the Risk Management Strategy.

Threats to the security of an enterprise's business and technology operating environments come in many forms. This includes fires, floods, earthquakes, accidents, terrorism, hackers, disgruntled employees, runaway technologies, and unintentional mistakes. Additionally, as the global use of IT continues to accelerate, fueled by the ubiquitous Internet, enterprises are increasingly exposed to daily threats from both the outside and the inside. How seriously the enterprise addresses these threats is often related on how aware the enterprise is of its dependency on IT to support key business services, and the probability of a threat affecting the enterprise. Without an awareness of threats, or an appreciation of their relevance, enterprises will not invest in a robust security/privacy program.

One fundamental aspect of security and privacy is the realization that there isn't a 100% foolproof solution for any enterprise. The reason for this is that the security and privacy program and risk management strategy are created by members of that enterprise or by contracted service providers, The employees and contractors who are in security and system administration positions can decide to disable, evade, or sabotage the security and privacy solutions. This type of "insider threat" is the Achilles Heel of all IT security and privacy programs and is what underlies what are referred to as "risk-adjusted" solutions. This means that a security or privacy solution is selected based on several considerations, including the cost, the level of protection needed, the effect on end-users and system administrators, and the effectiveness of available technologies.

The best way to address security and privacy solutions throughout the enterprise is to a set of controls/solutions within and around key business and technology resources and services. Using a "defense in depth" approach, these controls provide an integrated set of risk-adjusted security solutions in response to physical, personnel, and operational threats to the proper functioning of EA components.

Creating an Integrated Set of Controls

An integrated set security and privacy controls for the enterprise is created by including these considerations security in the planning, design, implementation, and operation of all EA components and artifacts. For information-centric enterprises, including IT security and data privacy as required design elements of EA components, and having leadership support at the strategic and line of business operations levels can provide a strong and meaningful statement about the importance of protecting the business and technology operating environment. These controls should also be a consideration in business process reengineering and improvement activities and should be a requirement for the design of workflows, dataflows, applications, systems, and networks. An example of an integrated set of control types from NIST SP800-53A is provide in Figure 11-2 below.

Access Control	Audit and Accountability
Awareness and Training	Configuration Management
Contingency Planning	Identification and Authentication
Incident Response	Maintenance
Media Protection	Personnel Security
Physical/Enviro Protection	Planning
Program Management	Risk Assessment
Security Assessment/Auth.	Authorization
System/Comm Protection	System/Information Integrity
System/Services Acquisition	

Security and privacy controls should function to reduce or eliminate external and internal threats – doing so through a combination of perimeter defense and internal configuration management. Controls should also support rapid bounce-back capabilities (resilience) when incidents occur from minor to major in scope. Controls detect and deter unauthorized access attempts, denial of service attacks, malware insertion attempts, spoofing, phishing, and virus attacks, and code manipulation attempts.

In 2018, the American Institute of CPAs (AICPA) developed criteria and certification processes for security and privacy controls in three business areas. Their SOC-1 report looks at controls over financial reporting, while a SOC 2 report looks at controls relevant to operations and compliance.

The Security and Privacy Program / Plan

The Security and Privacy Program is intended to provide expertise, processes, and solutions for the protection of IT resources active in the business and technology operating environment. The Security and Privacy Program supports the EA by providing requirements for standards and procedures that are used in the planning and implementation of EA components and artifacts. Each EA component and artifact should be assessed to determine if the proper level of protection is provided, and if not, that solutions are identified on a risk-adjusted basis. Risk-adjustment refers to the trade-off between sharing and protection, as well as how much security is desired versus the cost and effort required to implement it.

The Security and Privacy Program looks at all possible sources of threat, including threats to the source and validity of information, control of access to the information, and threats to the physical environment where IT resources are located. The Security and Privacy Program also provides Standard Operating Procedures (SOPs) that help to organize and improve the development and certification of new systems, the operation of legacy systems, and the response to security incidents.

The Security and Privacy Program should be managed by a specialist in this field, and increasingly enterprises are establishing positions for a Chief Information Security Officer (CISO). The CISO should have business and IT operating experience in addition to training in the various elements of IT security. The CISO should report to the CIO and work collaboratively with the Chief Architect to ensure that EA component and artifact design, implementation, and operational activities have effective security as a requirement. The ISSM should also be responsible for the development, implementation, and maintenance of the enterprise's Security and Privacy Plan, in alignment with the Risk Management Plan and the EA. The Security and Privacy Plan should provide the security- related controls, policies, and procedures for the documentation, testing, certification, accreditation, operation, and disposal of EA components and artifacts at all levels of the framework, shown in Figure 11-2 on the next page.

Security & Privacy Plan

1.Introduction
- Purpose of the Security & Privacy Program/Plan
- Principles of Risk Management
- Critical Success Factors
- Intended Outcomes
- Performance Measures

2.Policy
- Executive Guidance
- Technical Guidance
- Applicable Law and Regulations
- Standards

3.Reporting Requirements
- Roles and Responsibilities
- Schedule and Milestones
- Incident Reporting

4.Concept of Operations
- Threat Summary Risk Mitigation
- Integration with Enterprise Architecture
- Component/System Level Accreditation

5.Security Program Elements
- Information Security
- Personnel Security
- Operational Security
- Physical Security

6.Standard Operating Procedures
- Test and Evaluation Risk Assessment
- Certification and Accreditation
- Disaster Recovery
- Continuity of Operations
- Records Protection and Archiving
- IT Security Training and Awareness

Appendix A   Inventory of IT Components
Appendix B   Terms and Definitions
Appendix C   References

Figure 11-2: Example Security & Privacy Plan Contents

There are four key elements of the Security and Privacy Program that will be discussed in more detail: information security, personnel, operations, and physical protection.

Program Key Element #1: Information Security

In the area of information security, the Security and Privacy Program should promote security and privacy-conscious designs, information content assurance, source authentication, and data access control. Additional information on this area is as follows:

Design: These are the physical and logical systems analysis and design activities that look at data structure, relationships, and flows. Whether traditional structured methods are used or the newer object-oriented methods are used (see Chapter 4 for additional details), security and privacy controls should be one of the requirements that must be met for the design to be approved. Security and privacy issues in this area affect the Business Process and the Information Flow levels of the architecture.

Assurance: This is the protection of information content from being altered unintentionally or by an unauthorized source. Enterprises rely on the quality of data and information, regardless of subject matter. The quality is important, whether the data takes the form of financials, employee benefits, manufacturing, research, or government services. Controlling the access to information significantly contributes to assuring the integrity of that information. Also, configuration management activities such file naming conventions, automated document archiving (full and incremental saves), and version control of information all maximize information assurance. Security and privacy issues in this area mainly affect the Business Process and the Information Flow levels of the architecture.

Authentication: This refers to being able to verify the source of information. It is often important to know, without a doubt, who it was that created or manipulated information. Software applications often automatically create a log entry or attach a "stamp" to information/documents created by that application. Computer machine addresses, Internet Protocol (IP) addresses, instant messaging names, and e-mail addresses that are automatically generated in on-line transactions provide a basic level of authentication, however, "spoofing" of these is possible. Some enterprises are using digital signatures and a Public Key Infrastructure (PKI) to be able to authenticate someone's handling of information (e.g., banking transactions, e-commerce, cryptocurrency blockchains, and executive correspondence). Security and privacy issues in this area affect all levels of the architecture.

Access: This focuses on who can access information within the enterprise and how that access is managed. Software applications often provide some form of access control through the use of login identifications and passwords. Some applications use what is called "user rights and permissions" to limit the extent of access that a particular user has. There are often several levels of rights and permissions, including: normal user; super user; and system administrator. The system administrator level of access often enables unrestricted use of a system, application, or database and as such, has a high level of security interest and should be monitored closely. Security and privacy issues in this area mainly affect the Information Flow, Systems/Services, and Technology Infrastructure levels of the architecture.

Program Key Element #2: Personnel

In the area of personnel security, the Security and Privacy Program should promote user authentication, security awareness, and training as follows:

User Authentication: The verification of the identity of employees, contractors, and others who use the enterprise's facilities and systems, and other resources. With regard to IT this includes all end-users and system administrators before they gain access to an EA component. Technologies that can help in this area include personal passwords, smart cards, identification badges, and biometrics. Security and privacy issues in this area mainly affect the Systems/Services and Technology Infrastructure levels of the architecture.

Awareness Training: Security and privacy awareness training should be provided to all of the enterprise's end-users and system administrators. It includes having all end-users and administrators read and sign an IT Awareness Agreement before they have access to any EA component, which acknowledge that the enterprise owns these resources and hosted information. The IT Awareness Agreement should also state that access to these resources is contingent upon following the enterprise's operational and security SOPs and that monitoring of end-user and system administrator on-line activity is to be expected. IT awareness training should be repeated annually to reinforce compliance. Security and privacy issues in this area affect all levels of the architecture.

Procedures Training: Security and privacy procedures training should be provided to end-users and system administrators to build proficiency in avoiding security breaches, recognizing threats, and reacting to security incidents. This training is very important because the timely response to a security incident (such as a virus attack) can mean the difference between a minor inconvenience and a total disruption of IT operations. Procedures training should be repeated annually or as follow-up to significant security upgrade actions or incidents. Security and privacy issues in this area mainly affect the Systems/Services and Technology Infrastructure levels of the architecture.

Program Key Element #3: Operations

In the area of operational security, the Security and Privacy Program should promote the development of SOPs for EA component security, risk assessment, testing and evaluation, remediation, certification, operation, and disposal. SOPs should also be developed for extreme events such as recovery from major outages or natural disasters and enabling the continuity of operations if all or part of the enterprise becomes disabled. Additional information on this area is as follows:

Risk Assessment: An overall evaluation of risk at all levels of the architecture. EA components at different levels of the architecture have different security risks. Strategic risks include not promoting IT security if the enterprise is information-centric, not identifying desired outcomes and enabling initiatives, and not providing sufficient resources for the IT Security Program. Business process risks include activities that expose information, applications, and/or the technology infrastructure to unauthorized access and manipulation. Information risks center on the protection of the source and integrity of data. Support application and infrastructure risks include corruption and/or disablement. Security and privacy issues in this area affect all levels of the architecture.

Component Security Testing and Evaluation: This is the testing of EA components or integrated groups of EA components in order to identify security or privacy vulnerabilities. Testing is followed by an evaluation of the nature of each vulnerability and the potential effect on the enterprise's business and operating environment if the vulnerability is left uncorrected. Testing is performed on the hardware, software, and procedures of each EA component as well as auditing security-related documentation (system and firewall logs, administrator files, reports, etc.). Security and privacy issues in this area affect all levels of the architecture.

Vulnerability Remediation: This is the act of correcting any security or privacy vulnerabilities found during EA component Testing and Evaluation. Remediation actions are based on an evaluation of the effect of the vulnerability if it is left uncorrected. This involves the selection of a security or privacy solution based on the determination of an acceptable level of risk. Level of risk determinations take into consideration various alternatives for corrective action and the cost and operational affect of each alternative. Higher levels of protection often cost more and have a more intrusive affect on business services. Security and privacy issues in this area affect all levels of the architecture.

Component Certification and Accreditation: This is the certification that all remediation actions have been properly implemented for an EA component or integrated group of EA components. Accreditation is the acceptance of component certification actions by the appropriate executive (usually the CIO or CISO) and the issuance of a formal letter to operate that EA component in the configuration in which it was tested and evaluated. If the configuration changes, the process of risk assessment, test and evaluation, and remediation should be repeated to ensure that the IT security solution remains effective and has the identical corresponding risk level that is accepted by the enterprise. Security and privacy issues in this area affect all levels of the architecture.

Standard Operating Procedures: The documentation of security and privacy SOPs is important to ensuring that timely and effective action is taken by end-users and system administrators when faced with an IT security incident. SOPs also help in the training of new personnel. SOPs are normally required for items such as password management, biometrics/

access control, loss of sensitive data, virus incident response, denial of service attacks, hackers and other unauthorized users, spam, inappropriate material, user agreements, periodic backups, training requirements, disaster recovery, and submission of EA Change Requests. Security and privacy issues in this area affect all levels of the architecture.

Disaster Recovery: The assessment and recovery procedures for responding to a man-made or natural event that significantly disrupts or eliminates business and technology operations yet does not threaten the existence of the enterprise. This includes sabotage, theft or corruption of resources, successful large-scale hacker/virus attacks, building damage, fire, flood, and electrical outages. Two time-related aspects of disaster recovery need to be immediately and continually evaluated: (1) the method for recovery, and (2) the affect on mission accomplishment. Both of these may change as the amount of time increases from the moment the disaster occurred (e.g., facilities considerations, system and data restore procedures and the affect on business services will probably be different for 2-minute, 2-hour, 2-day, and 2-week outages). Security and privacy issues in this area affect all levels of the architecture.

Continuity of Operations: This refers to procedures that are invoked if all or part of the enterprise are unexpectedly destroyed or forced to disband. In this scenario, the enterprise is unable to conduct any business or IT operations for a period of time. The recovery response is scripted in a Continuity of Operations Plan (COOP) that identifies where, how, and when business and IT functions would be restored. Security and privacy issues in this area affect all levels of the architecture.

Program Key Element #4: Physical Protection

The aspects of physical protection that should be captured in the EA include controls for the facilities that support IT processing, control of access to buildings, equipment, networks, and telecommunications rooms, as well as fire protection, media storage, and disaster recovery systems.

Building Security: This focuses on the control of personnel access to the enterprise's buildings where IT resources are used. Depending on the level of building security that is desired, a perimeter around the building can be established with barriers and/or monitoring. This is augmented by limited entry points to the building, elevators, and workspaces with doors that open only with an authorized and current employee badge, appropriate lock combinations or biometric scan. Security and privacy issues in this area mainly affect the Business Process and the Technology Infrastructure levels of the architecture.

Network Operation Centers, Server Rooms, and Wiring Closets: This refers to the control of personnel access to those places where EA components are physically located. This includes network operation centers, remote server rooms, and wiring closets where voice, data, and video cables and patch panels are located. Doors to these areas should be locked and entry should be controlled by badge swipe and/or biometric devices. Access to the power and air-conditioning units that support these rooms should also be controlled and monitored. Security and privacy issues in this area affect the Business and Infrastructure levels.

Cable Plants: This refers to the control of logical, physical, and personnel access to the various types of fiber and copper cable that connect the technology infrastructure together. Unauthorized tapping is possible, so some level of protection is recommended. If highly sensitive information is being carried by the cable plant, the enterprise may consider enclosing the cables in hard-to-cut metal pipes or cable run boxes along the upper wall/ceiling edges. Security and privacy issues in this area mainly affect the Business Process level and the Technology Infrastructure.

Summary of Concepts

This chapter provided an overview the relationship of security and privacy considerations to the EA program and the documentation of EA components. The chapter also described the four key areas that should be included in a Security and Privacy Program and Plan that articulates and guides the design, implementation, and use of protective controls for every EA component. In this way, an effective, risk-appropriate set of security and privacy controls are created that encompasses the entire architecture and that penetrates each level of the architecture. Only by addressing all of the relevant aspects of security and privacy drivers and threats can effective solutions be identified for individual EA components, or groups of EA components that function together. Finally, there should be awareness that foolproof security is not possible because EA components are designed and managed by humans, and "insider" access is the ultimate threat which cannot completely be overcome.

Chapter 11 Questions and Exercises

1. Why is it important to include security and privacy in an EA program and the documentation of EA components?
2. What are the key elements of a Security and Privacy Program?
3. Why are there no 100 percent fool-proof IT Security solutions?
4. How can the EA Management Program help to promote effective security and privacy solutions?
5. What is the difference between a Disaster Recovery Plan and a Continuity of Operations Plan?
6. What are the differences between perimeter defense and core configuration controls?

Chapter 12

The Enterprise Architecture Repository and Support Tools

Chapter Overview

Chapter 12 describes the role of an on-line EA repository and support tools in the EA program and the documentation of EA components. The design and structure of an EA repository is discussed, and the relationship to an underlying EA documentation framework. The example of the EA³ Cube Framework and the Living Enterprise™ repository design is used in this discussion. Additionally, different types of EA documentation and support tools are discussed in the context of developing EA component documentation and populating the on-line EA repository.

Learning Objectives

> Understand the role of an on-line EA repository in the EA program.
> Understand how the EA repository supports documentation of EA components.
> Understand how the design of the EA repository relates to an EA framework.
> Understand the role of EA support tools in documenting EA components.

Introduction

The EA repository is intended to provide a single place for the storage and retrieval of EA artifacts that are created using EA software applications (tools). A repository works best if it is easy to access and use. For this reason, an on-line, web-based EA repository is recommended. This type of web "portal" for EA should be located on the enterprise's internal Local Area Network to promote security of the information while still supporting access by executives, managers, and support staff.

> *Home Architecture Analogy:* The EA repository is like having an electronic copy of the home's current blueprints and future remodeling plans. This electronic information is stored on a home PC in a web format to allow for easy navigation with a web browser.

Discussion

Providing easy access to EA information and artifacts is essential for their use in planning, management, and decision-making. The EA repository is intended to provide this type of easy access by being a "one-stop-shop" for all of the documents that populate the various levels of an EA framework as is shown in Figure 12-1.

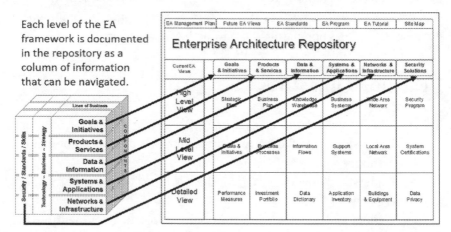

Figure 12-1: Relating the EA Framework and Repository

EA Repository

The approach to the design of the example EA repository (and the underlying EA6 Framework) provided in Figure 12-1 is based on the work of John Zachman who in 1987 first introduced a very intuitive schema for visually organizing EA information. He did this by using hierarchical rows and functional columns to create cells that contain "primitive" EA artifacts which answer basic questions about information systems (who, what, why, where, when, and how).

The design of the "Living Enterprise" EA repository is similar in that it uses hierarchical rows and functional columns. However, it is different in that (1) it is based on a separate meta-framework (the EA6 Framework); (2) it uses three hierarchical levels; (3) the functional columns are not based on basic interrogative questions; (4) the cells of the matrix are changeable and are often populated with EA documentation that represents composite views of several types of primitive products; (5) it has areas for additional information on the EA program; and (6) it is designed to be implemented as a website and therefore has navigation and version control features. As is shown in Figure 12-2 on the next page, this overall design for an EA repository is referred to as the Living Enterprise, which is shown on the next page in Figure 12-3. This EA repository is linked to EA software tools and a database to store EA data and artifacts.

Current Architecture	EA Program	EA Standards	EA Tutorial	Site Map	Search		EA Tools
Future Architecture	Enterprise Architecture Repository						
Transition Plan	Goals & Initiatives	Products & Services	Data & Information	Systems & Apps	Networks & Infra.	Security Solutions	Web Tools
			Domains				
High Level View	Strategic Plan	Business Plan	Knowledge Warehouse	Business Systems	Wide-Area Network	Security Program	Graphics Tools
Mid Level View	Goals & Initiatives	Business Processes	Data/Info Flows	Support Systems	Local Area Network	System Approvals	Analysis Tools
Detailed View	Key Perf Measures	Investment Portfolio	Data Dictionary	Application Inventory	Buildings & Equip.	System Controls	EA Repository Database

Figure 12-2: The Living Enterprise EA Repository

The word "primitive" in Zachman's work refers to EA documentation that is singular in its method of development and use. For example, using traditional methods, diagramming data structure yields an Entity-Relationship Diagram and diagramming data process yields a Data Flow Diagram that are Zachman primitives in that they are fundamentally different in both symbology and use. If one were to find a way to combine them into one diagram, this would yield what Zachman calls a "composite" EA documentation product.

Current Architecture	EA Program	EA Standards	EA Tutorial	Site Map	Search

Enterprise Architecture Repository

Future Architecture					

Transition Plan	Goals & Initiatives	Products & Services	Data & Information	Systems & Apps	Networks & Infra.	Security Solutions
			Domains			
High Level View	Strategic Plan	Business Plan	Knowledge Warehouse	Business Systems	Wide-Area Network	Security Program
Mid Level View	Goals & Initiatives	Business Processes	Data/Info Flows	Support Systems	Local Area Network	System Approvals
Detailed View	Key Perf. Measures	Investment Portfolio	Data Dictionary	Application Inventory	Buildings & Equip.	System Controls

Figure 12-3: Example EA Repository Design – Living Enterprise

In implementing the Living Enterprise approach to a web-based EA repository, it is recommended that enterprises stay with the six columns, because they directly relate to the levels of the EA6 Framework, which also guides the type of EA artifacts that go in each column and cell. If another framework is needed, the number of rows and columns can be changed, along with the names of the cells. It should be noted that the amount of time, money, and effort to complete additional perspectives (rows) of EA component documentation will be significant, which is one reason that only three perspective rows were chosen for this format. Three rows provide distinct perspectives that are analogous to executive, manager, and support staff views.

One of the valuable aspects of having this approach to an EA repository is that the different levels of the enterprise can view complete perspectives of business and technology, which they otherwise might not be able to see. If limits to access are desired, then particular cells or groups of cells can be password protected.

One of the flexible features of Living Enterprise is that the purpose and names of the cells in each framework column can be changed to fit the particular needs of the enterprise. For example, the middle cell in the Business Process column can be changed from Investment Portfolio to "Customer Relationship Management" if that is more important and/ or appropriate. In this way, a customized version of Living Enterprise can be created for each enterprise. Drawing from the descriptions of EA components and artifacts in Chapters 4 and 5, comments on potential content for each cell is provided as follows.

Strategic Goals and Initiatives Column

Mission and Vision Cell: Here is where the enterprise's mission and vision statements are located. These are the highest-level policy statements that the enterprise has, reflecting why the enterprise exists and in general what it strives to be.

Goals and Initiatives Cell: Here is where a list of the enterprise's strategic goals and initiatives is presented. For each strategic goal the desired outcome should be identified. For each strategic initiative, mapping to the goal(s) should be provided, as well as identification of the performance gaps that the initiative will correct. If there is an IT component in the initiative, that should be clearly identified. Each strategic initiative should then be hyperlinked to amplifying metrics information in the Performance Measures Cell, as well as related investments in the Business services column.

Performance Measures Cell: Here is where the IT performance gaps are again identified for each strategic initiative. Then the outcome and output measures are provided that will measure the success of each initiative. Tracking information on the measures should also be provided, beginning with the original levels of achievement in each measurement area (called the "baseline"), and subsequent levels of achievement, which will form a trend line that tracks toward a goal level of improved level of performance.

Business Products and Services Column

<u>Lines of Business Cell</u>: Here is where the basic areas of activity (lines of business) for the enterprise are identified. The lines of business should support the enterprise's strategic goals and initiatives, or there is no reason to be doing those activities... they are not adding value. To better show this, the lines of business should be hyperlinked to the strategic goals and initiatives that they support in the Strategic Initiatives column.

<u>Investment Portfolio Cell</u>: Here is where the enterprise's investments in IT are shown. When aggregated, these investments form an "investment portfolio". This portfolio should be documented along with categories for investments in IT (e.g., IT operations, office automation, IT research and development, IT infrastructure). Information on the business case for each particular investment should be shown, to include how the investment supports a particular strategic initiative and/or LoB. Investment performance information on the overall portfolio and individual investments should also be provided in this cell.

<u>IT Projects Cell</u>: Here is where information on all of the active IT projects throughout the enterprise is shown. Project Management Plans and other associated documentation are the types of EA artifacts that should be archived in this area. Summaries of Earned Value Management information regarding project status are also helpful (e.g., planned vs. actual cost, schedule, and performance graphs).

Data and Information Column

<u>Knowledge Management Cell</u>: Here is where the enterprise's approach to Knowledge Management (KM) is provided. Items to be covered include the overall concept for sharing knowledge, information, and data, as well as whether there is an acknowledged commitment to be a learning enterprise. A learning enterprise is one which has a process for evaluating LoB processes and the management of programs and projects, and continually incorporating the lessons learned into the improvement of those processes, programs, and projects. In this way a culture of learning is created which can lead to increased levels of performance for the enterprise. Documentation of this can

be effectively accomplished through a combination of diagrams and text descriptions of the EA components that are active in aggregating data into information and then into knowledge, as well as how that knowledge is shared (e.g., knowledge warehouses, data marts, storage area networks, and databases).

Data Flows Cell: Here is where the sharing and transformation of information and data is documented for all processes in the enterprise's LoBs. Documentation should also reveal how the information and data is used within each LoB, in the form of requirements. Documentation methods should provide the structure of basic data entities/objects, the rules for relationships between these data entities/objects, and the flow of the data entities/objects through the various EA components at the Information Level of the EA6 Framework. This includes Entity-Relationship Diagrams and Data Flow Diagrams that document relational databases and are used in procedural programming languages such as COBOL, FORTRAN, and C. It also includes object-oriented documentation using the Unified Modeling Language, which documents object-based databases that are created using event-driven programming languages such as JAVA, C++, Ruby on Rails, Python, and .Net.

Data Dictionary Cell: Here is where standards and the format for the enterprise's data entities/objects are documented, and where a link is provided to a library (database repository) of those entities and objects. The library promotes the reuse of data entities and objects throughout the EA components, increasing interoperability and lowering costs.

Systems and Applications Column

Support Services Cell: Here is where the overall view of business-related support services is presented in a format which promotes an understanding of how these resources are supporting the information sharing requirements of each LOB. There is a focus on supporting business operations in this cell. As was presented in Figure 7-7, an effective presentation format is a high-level diagram that shows the applications being used within each LOB and across the enterprise and shows this as distinct areas of support (e.g., databases, operating systems, websites, and middleware).

Front Office Systems Cell: Here is where the overall suite of front office support systems and applications are presented in a format that promotes an understanding of how they support the enterprise's information sharing requirements across all LoBs. This includes ERP solutions, supply chain management systems, customer relationship management systems, sales and marketing support, manufacturing support, and on-line e-commerce transactions.

Back Office Systems Cell: Here is where the overall suite of back office (administrative) systems and applications are presented in a format that promotes an understanding of how they support the enterprise's administrative support requirements across all LoBs. This includes financial and accounting systems, human resource systems, a common e- mail system, telephone, video-teleconferencing, fax, print, and copying systems. Also located here are the standard desktop, laptop, and personal digital assistant applications. Enterprises increasingly are distributed across multiple geographical locations, have individuals who are telecommuting, and have individuals in the field doing remote-site work and/or meeting with customers. This creates requirements for portable computing that should be documented in this cell, along with a clear picture of how information is being shared between these computing platforms to support LoB processes.

Networks and Infrastructure Column

Common Operating Environment Cell: Here is where information about the enterprise's Common Operating Environment (COE) is presented. The COE is the integrated business and technology operating environment, wherein a seamless voice, data, mobile, and video network infrastructure hosts front office and back office services and systems.

Wide Area Network Cell: Here is where information about the enterprise's Wide Area Network (WAN) is presented. An effective way to present information about the WAN is a map with WAN symbols for hardware and communication links that are hyperlinks, that when clicked- on lead to a new level of detail about that part of the WAN (e.g., dedicated voice and data lines, wireless links, mobile solutions, and interfaces with service providers). Also appropriate for documentation in this cell is the connectivity for Supply Chains and/or information transfer via Extranets that connect to specific external business partners and/or remote office locations. Standards for voice, data, mobile, and video WAN components should also be available in this cell.

Local Area Network Cell: Here is where information about the enterprise's Local Area Network(s) is provided. There may be several LANs (also called Intranets) in the enterprise… perhaps in particular LoBs or at EAdquarters and several remote offices. In this case, the relationship of these LANs and their external linkage via the WAN needs to be shown. An effective way to present information about the LAN is a map with LAN symbols for hardware and communication links that are hyperlinks, that when clicked-on lead to a new level of detail about that part of the LAN (e.g., location of segments, interface points, and hosted applications, databases, and websites). The local and LAN aspects of mobile solutions should also be covered in this cell.

Security Solution Column

Policy and Procedures Cell: Here is where a high-level view is presented of the enterprise's policies regarding IT security. Key extracts from the enterprise's IT Security Plan are appropriate that link to specific Standard Operating Procedures (SoPs) to handle various security and privacy activities and the response to incidents (e.g., password policies, access procedures, user agreements, virus protection, inappropriate material, and incident handling). The full text of the Security and Privacy Plan and the SOPs should be available in this cell, and links to additional educational information on IT security should be available in this cell and links to additional educational information on IT security should be provided. IT Security on particular vulnerabilities should not be part of the documentation available in this cell, as it should be protected from all but those with a need-to-know. This protected information includes EA component security plans, risk analysis reports, security test and evaluation results, disaster recovery procedures, and technical diagrams of security hardware and software.

Data Privacy Cell: Here is where the enterprise's policy on information privacy is presented. How information and data are collected, archived, and disseminated should be covered for each EA component at the Business Process Level and the Information Flows Level of the framework, with comments on how privacy requirements are being met. For example, in on-line financial transactions credit card information must be protected. For general sales and marketing databases, customer contact information must be protected.

IT Inventory Cell: Here is where an inventory of all IT resources (hardware and software) in each EA component throughout the enterprise is maintained. This inventory not only promotes effective IT security, but also enables EA planners to obtain information on the "as-is" business and technology operating environment. For example, to support a decision on purchasing an upgrade to a COTS product, it is important to know how many licenses are currently owned, and when the expiration date is. In another example, knowing how many desktop PCs of a particular type exist can help procurement decisions that accompany "technology refreshments" across the enterprise that need to occur every 2-3 years.

Tabular Information

EA Management Plan Tab: Here is where the Architeture Transition Roadmap is archived. The Roadmap documents the enterprise's performance gaps, resource requirements, planned solutions, and a summary of the current and future architecture. The Roadmap also describes the EA management process, the implementation methodology, and the documentation framework. It is a living document that is updated at regular intervals (e.g., annually) to provide version control for changes in current and future views of EA components and artifacts throughout the framework.

Future EA Summary Tab: Here is where a summary of changes to the current architecture are provided along with the EA artifacts that represent changes at each level of the EA6 Framework. It is important to show in both graphical and narrative form how the enterprise EA is changing.

EA Standards Tab: Here is where information on the EA's Technical Standards Reference Model (TSRM) is presented. As was described in Chapter 9, the technical standards for voice, data, and video products are provided in the TSRM. This can be effectively presented in the form of a table that shows the ISO/NIST/IEEE or a local standard that is approved to meet the enterprise's requirements in each of the three categories (see Figure 9-6). Then, approved COTS or custom-developed products are listed within each standard area, as well as those products that are approved for use on an interim (waiver) basis.

EA Program Tab: Here is where information on the EA program is archived, including schedules for the release of new versions of the EA, EA team information, budget information, contact information, or other relevant, similar information may be found.

EA Tutorial Tab: Here is where EA training information is archived to support EA awareness among stakeholders and other interested individuals. This is also where other EA reference information may be archived and/ or linked.

EA Site Map: This is a navigation map of the EA repository website.

EA Support Tools

Various types of commercial software applications (tools) are required to support EA documentation and analysis activities. At present, no one tool can do all of the things that are needed in the EA program, including:

- EA repository website and content to create a visual representation of the framework
- Dynamic views of the EA for a variety of users
- Archived EA products
- Management views of EA artifacts
- Strategic planning products and performance measures
- Business process documentation to answer key questions and solve problems
- Physical and logical design of data entities and objects
- Physical and logical design of voice, data, and video networks
- Linked applications and databases
- Portfolio of IT investments and asset inventory
- Configuration management documentation (EACRs)
- Project planning and tracking (cost, schedule, performance, risk)
- Security and privacy reference architectures for vendor products

Because no one EA tool can do all that is required in the EA program, a "set" of tools is required. This will include an EA modeling tool, a graphics tool, a word processing tool, a website development tool, a database, a configuration management tool, and any application development and programming tools that the enterprise needs to create or modify EA components. Figure 12-3 below provides a view of how this set of tools interrelate and how they support EA documentation product development and display via the web-based EA repository.

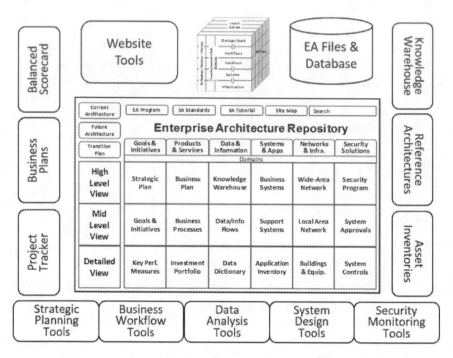

Figure 12-3. Examples of EA Tools and Applications

The following is a discussion of the contribution that various types of software tools make to EA documentation.

EA Framework Modeling Tools

These software tools are designed to use various EA frameworks that are pre-loaded and support various methodologies to develop EA artifacts throughout the chosen framework. These tools also support the conversion of EA artifacts into HTML and XML formats for increased utilization with websites and other tools. Some EA tools come bundled with web-enabled "front-ends" and databases that allow for the creation of an EA repository to store and retrieve the EA artifacts created with the tool. Some EA tools also have configuration management capabilities that support version control for the EA artifacts.

EA Repository Web-Application

This is a web-based software application that provides (1) a user-friendly graphical front end to support easy access to, and navigation of EA Artifacts in a way that relates to the chosen EA framework, and (2) interfaces with a back-end database that stores the EA artifacts. The database might be integral to the EA repository web application or might be a separate database software application (e.g., when more robust storage is required).

Web Service Development Tools

These software tools provide the capability to create a web-based EA repository that links to other web services and web sites. The development of a web-based EA repository is essential to providing easy access to the entire enterprise via a protected Intranet web site. Many EA modeling tools have web-based front ends (application interfaces) and can create EA artifacts in HTML. This allows the EA modeling tool to be directly accessed through the EA repository website.

General Graphics Tools

These software tools support general graphics design requirements and the custom creation of management views of EA artifacts. The development of briefings, HMTL pages, enterprise charts, and simple flowcharts are examples of these types of products.

Strategy Modeling Tools

These software tools support the development and modeling of EA components at the Strategic Initiatives level of the EA6 Framework. The resulting EA artifacts include the enterprise's strategic goals, supporting initiatives (programs and projects), and performance measures for the outputs and outcomes of each initiative. The Balanced Scorecard® methodology is a popular approach to developing these artifacts and several commercial tools support this methodology, including overall EA Framework modeling tools and specific strategic planning tools.

Business Modeling Tools

These software tools support the development and modeling of EA components and the Business services level of the EA6 Framework. The resulting EA artifacts include the processes and supply chains in each of the enterprise's LoBs. Business Process Reengineering (BPR) and Business Process Improvement (BPI) activities can also be documented.

Information Modeling Tools

These software tools support the development and modeling of EA components at the Information Level of the framework. The resulting EA artifacts include the logical and physical design for knowledge warehouses, data marts, databases, web sites, web portals, and data mining products. Also documented is the structure and processing of basic data elements using traditional or object-oriented modeling tools, along with the data dictionaries and object libraries that store them.

Application Modeling Tools

These software tools support the development and modeling of applications that support general operational and administrative processes and office automation capabilities throughout the enterprise that are not specific to a LoB. This includes financial systems, personnel and pay systems, e-mail, and applications that support collaboration, word processing, graphics, and spreadsheets. The resulting EA artifacts include the specifications for application capabilities, interfaces, standards, license inventories, and required support platforms. Documentation may also include the programming code for custom developed applications or modified commercial applications.

Network Modeling Tools

These software tools support the development and modeling of the enterprise's internal and external voice, data and video networks, as well as associated backbone cable plants, network operations centers, server rooms, and wiring closets. The resulting EA artifacts include the logical and physical design of the networks, performance specifications, interface points, standards, and inventories.

Security Analysis and Modeling Tools

These software tools support the development and modeling of security processes, considerations, and capabilities at all levels of the framework.

The resulting EA artifacts held to develop and model physical security, operational security, personnel security, and information security requirements and solutions as they relate to business services, information flows, support applications, and network infrastructures. These tools also support the development of security planning and management documentation including Security Plans, Security Risk Assessments, Test and Evaluation Plans/Reports, Disaster Recovery Plans, Continuity of Operations Plans, and Security Certification and Accreditation Reports.

Linked Software Applications
These software applications support other IT governance processes that integrate with the EA program. This includes capital planning, program management, and workforce planning. Being able to easily assess and relate information in these other areas of governance is essential to using EA documentation to improve communication and decision-making regarding the use of EA components in improving mission or LoBs.

The criteria for selecting an EA tool depends on the role it will play in the EA tool set. If it is an overall EA framework modeling tool, then a wide variety of capabilities are needed including the built-in support of various frameworks and modeling techniques, usability, scalability, development of management views, report generation, web interoperability, version control, security, training, licensing, and total cost of ownership.

Figure 12-5 (below and on the next page) provides an example matrix that compares several EA tools using a weighted scoring system.

EA Tool Evaluation Matrix Page 1 of 2		Tool A		Tool B		Tool C	
Tool Requirement	Grading Weight	Grade	Score	Grade	Score	Grade	Score
Framework Support							
Multiple Built-In Frameworks							
Custom Framework Creation							
Sequencing of As-Is & To-Be Views							
Creation of Management Views of EA Products							
Incorporation of EA Management Plan							
Identification of EA Performance Gaps							
Modeling Support							
Strategic Modeling							
Business Modeling							
Data Modeling							
Application Modeling							
Infrastructure Modeling							
Custom Modeling							
Symbology							
Robustness of Provided Symbols & Icons							
Custom Creation of Symbols & Icons							
Importing of Symbols & Icons							
Performance							
Usability							
Navigability							
Built-in and Custom Queries							
Built-in and Custom Reports							
Importing of Data and Products							
Integrated Web-Based Repository							
Integrated Database and Data Dictionary							
Support of Programming Languages							
Link to Capital Planning Info.							

Figure 12-5: Example EA Tool Evaluation Matrix

Page 2 - EA Tool Evaluation Matrix		Tool A		Tool B		Tool C	
Tool Requirement	Grading Weight	Grade	Score	Grade	Score	Grade	Score
Link to Project Mgmt Information							
Link to Workforce Planning Information							
Configuration Management							
Version Control							
Consistency /Completeness Checking							
Status Accounting							
Product Labeling & Dating							
Tracking Ownership of Data Entered							
Vendor							
Technical Support							
User and Administrator Training							
Product Maturity							
Proprietary Product							
Version Updating							
Vendor Stability							
Financial							
Total Cost of Ownership							
Cost Per Seat							
Licensing Flexibility							
Integration							
Supports Multiple Data Formats							
Support for Standard APIs							
Platforms Supported							
Data Interchange (XML, HTML)							
Direct Web Importing/Publishing							
Web Site Creation Capability							
Security							
User Access Controls							
Read-Only and Multi-User Controls							
Remote Access and Use							
Total Scores							

Summary of Concepts

This chapter provided a discussion of the role of an EA repository and documentation tools in the EA program. The importance of developing a web-based EA repository was stressed in that it provides easy access to EA artifacts which can assist planning and decision-making throughout the enterprise. The various types of EA-related software tools were discussed as was the idea that a set of tools are needed to support the overall EA management program and documentation process. EA tool selection criteria were also provided.

Chapter 12 Review Questions

1. What is an EA repository and how does it support the EA implementation methodology?
2. How does each column of the EA repository relate to the EA6 Framework, and what EA artifacts go into the cells of this column?
3. How does the Technology Infrastructure column of the EA repository relate to the EA6 Framework, and what EA artifacts go into the cells of this column?
4. How does the IT Security column of the EA repository relate to the EA6 Framework, and what EA artifacts go into the cells of this column?
5. What considerations should be made in developing an EA Tool Evaluation Matrix?
6. Why are management views of EA artifacts important?
7. Describe how cell names and content might change between the EA repository for a government agency and the EA Repository for a business.
8. Develop an EA Tool Evaluation Matrix and evaluate two current commercial EA modeling tools.
9. Develop the management view of information flows in a business warehouse inventory stocking system.

Chapter 13

Solution Architecture Methods

Chapter Overview

This chapter introduces the concept of solution architecture, which is a best practice wherein EA concepts and methods are used in projects to develop or improve business and technology components throughout the organization. The chapter defines terms and gives examples of the types of solution architecture projects that can occur at each level of the framework (strategy, business, data, systems, networks) as well as in the thread areas (security, skills, and standards).

Learning Objectives

> ➢ Describe how EA provides context for solution architecture projects.
> ➢ Identify key concepts and methods for solution architecture.

Introduction

Some EA practitioners separate the concept of holistic architecture from problem-solving architecture at the detailed level, which I don't believe is correct or helpful to large, complex organizations. It is as if strategic architecture has to compete with tactical architecture, which is incorrect. Holistic, strategic architecture provides the context, overviews, and enterprise-wide standards within which tactical solution architecture methods can and should be utilized. Without EA, architecture initiatives are local in origin and focus and usually don't integrate with other solutions in other business units, as shown in Figure 13-1 below. Does this sound like silios? So, let's avoid that and recognize that enterprise-level architecture and solution architecture both serve important roles in architecting the organization in a consistent manner at the macro and detailed levels, as shown in Figure 13-2 on the next page.

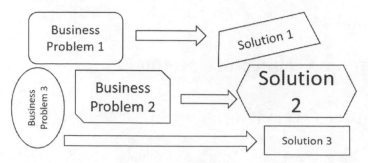

Figure 13-1. Solution Architecture without EA Context

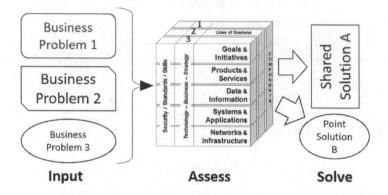

Figure 13-2. Solution Architecture Using
EA for Context and Standards

Discussion

Solution architecture is an important best practice to use when implementing an enterprise-wide architecture. The purpose of solution architecture is to use a flexible and repeatable method to receive business problems and develop component solutions in the context of EA standards. The EA standards should promote enterprise-level, shared solutions whenever possible – as this has the potential to significantly lower costs while meeting/exceeding requirements. Sometimes, business requirements are truly unique and a specific (point) solution is required – but that should be kept to a minimum.

As indicated in Figure 13-2, there are three general steps to doing solution architecture: input, assess, solve. The following are details on each step:

<u>Input</u>: All of the needs (requirements) of the organization's lines of business should be input to the EA Program Office (EAPMO) so that they can be assessed by an experienced analysis/design group with knowledge of other requests and already-available enterprise or point solutions. Each request should be assigned as a project to a lead architect in the EAPMO who will work with the stakeholders during assessment. The project is often staffed and executed by the requesting group or other outside experts with the lead architect acting as a facilitator and advisor. In this way there can be centralized awareness and decentralized execution.

<u>Assess</u>: The assessment of requirements is organized by the lead architect who works closely with the project team's stakeholder representatives and domain experts (e.g, strategic planner, business analyst, data analyst, software programmer, systems integrator, network engineer, security analyst). Timing is very important and the target timeframe for completing the assessment should be days or weeks, not months – unless it is a large-scale and/or highly complex requirement that will have a significant impact on the organization.

The requirement should be viewed in the context of the organization's strategic plan, the requesting line of business' near- and long-term operating plan, other requests in the EAPMO queue, and new technologies and trends. This provides the "big picture" of the importance and potential impact of providing a shared or point solution. Once the big picture is understood, an alternatives analysis should be performed to identify whether there are multiple realistic (viable) solutions to the problem/request. Web searches and market surveys can usually identify an initial list of potentially viable solutions, along with input from the requesting group – they are often aware of solutions that other similar groups are using, or that commercial vendors are advertising (called Commercial-Off-The-Shelf or COTS solutions).

Often, requestors will suggest/demand a specific COTS or custom solution, but the EAPMO lead architect should resist that demand and proceed with a proper alternatives analysis unless there are unique factors that dictate the selection of the requestor's solution. If there are several potentially viable COTS solutions, they should be compared from a strategic, business, data, system, security, risk, and financial standpoint using weighted measures (see Chapter 12' tool evaluation example). This analytic approach will produce a rank-ordering of the viable solutions which should support selection of the best one that fits the strategic direction of the organization and meets the tactical needs of the requestor.

Solve:
Solutions that are already being used in the organization's current (legacy) operating environment should be strongly considered for use in meeting a new request – even if the requestor's workflows have to be adjusted. It is common for requestor's to state that their requirements are unique and their workflows cannot be changed. This significantly drives up cost/risk and promotes point solutions for silo'd business units.

Unless the organization has mature expertise in developing business and technical solutions, they should utilize proven COTS products and "out-of-the-box" capabilities whenever possible. The increasing complexity of integrated supply chains and other work processes, along with the complexities of converged technologies, make it very difficult for most organizations to be successful at custom solution development and operations at all but the smallest of scales. Organizations may want to increase their internal custom solution development capabilities, but this will be expensive and full of risk as they try to keep pace with vendors who's primary function it is to develop leading-edge, well-tested and secure technology solutions that can scale, are based on open standards, and address an increasingly threat-filled external operating environment.

Relating EA, Solution, and Other Sub-Architectures

As mentioned, solution architecture solves a particular business problem for an organization or part of an organization by providing an "end-to-end" design for an EA component that integrates the in-scope business flows, dataflows, applications, and network hosting. Additionally, the design should allow the solution to scale to handle more users and transactions, as well as promote interoperability with other components through the use of EA standards at each sub-architecture domain level (e.g., supply chain, data formats, and open APIs).

Yet there are more types of business and technology sub-architectures that have become popular in the public and private sectors during the past two decades. The EA6 Framework incorporates a hierarchical set of sub-architecture "domains" to recognize the different aspects of how large, complex organizations function across multiple structural lines of business, but these other sub-architectures serve to focus and integrate design activities on a specific set of components or business units. Besides solution architecture, the other three popular sub-architecture methods are segment architectures, reference architectures, and service-oriented architectures. Figure 133 shows the relationship between EA and these sub-architectures.

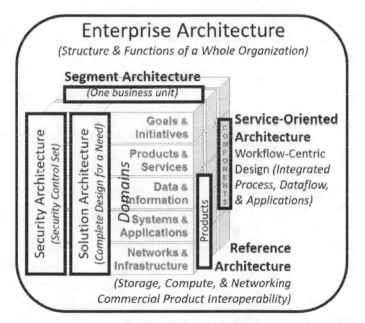

Figure 13-3. EA and Other Sub-Architecture Relationships

Agile Solution Architecture

The term "agile" has unfortunately become a buzzword for vendors that want to sell products or services. My advice for understanding and harnessing the term agile (and many other over-hyped terms) is to understand the origin and different uses of the word and select what is accurate, relevant, and helpful to you and/or your organization. So, here I am selecting the attributes of the term "agile" that address quickness and flexibility. The operational needs of many organizations change regularly at the business unit level, especially when they are regional or global in reach and their competitors are more numerous, mature, and well-resourced. This requires the organization to be both resilient when challenged, and agile when opportunities present themselves. A large, complex organization with regional or global reach is almost certain to fail if it cannot successfully adapt to frequent change. Successful adaptation draws foremost on the culture of the organization (recognizes that change is constant), then on workflow flexibility, then on new technology uptake, and then on resource availability.

Not everything in an organization has to change when a threat or opportunity comes along, and some adaptations are minor while others are major. What is usually the Same is that the timeframe for making an effective change is often tight: hours, days, weeks... not months or years. Being able to identify and implement a change in a tight timeframe is the essence of agility. The concept of agile solution architecture centers on rapidly delivering an analysis or design that stakeholders can use and will subsequently help refine.

There are many commercial approaches and support tools that seek to help multi-skilled teams form (the Agile buzzword is a "scrum", led by a "scrum master") to rapidly work over several days or weeks (called a "sprint") to deliver a basic analysis or design (called a "minimum viable product") that becomes the foundation for subsequent additions and improvements (called "iterations"). Again, my advice is to stick with simple standard terms when doing agile solution architecture – don't buy into to the hype – its expensive. Figure 13-4 below shows the typical steps in doing agile solution work:

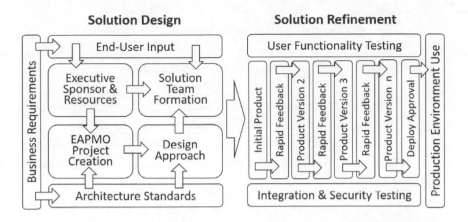

Solution Design **Solution Refinement**

In addition to following a repeatable agile architecture method that the organization gets good at, the following are some key concepts in being able to do agile solution work:

- Know what you need to develop (refine requirements with stakeholders)
- Gather the skills (experienced team leader and internal/external experts)
- Have a good team spirit (everyone contributes, frequent communication)
- If you need it in a week – first product on day 2, daily updates thereafter
- If you need it in a month – first product on Friday #1, weekly updates
- Test it for functionality and security before you deploy it
- Involve users throughout the process and do training along the way
- Document the work, submit it to the EA archive

Examples of Solution Architecture Projects

Strategic Level
- Create a Balanced Scorecard for the organization or major unit
- Conduct a SWOT Analysis for the organization or major unit
- Create an environment overview diagram for the organization or group
- Create an IT Appendix to the organization's Strategic Plan

<u>Business Level</u>
- Develop a supply-chain solution for multiple organizations or LoB units
- Conduct an alternatives analysis comparing several COTS ERP products
- Redesign a business process and identify viable workflow products
- Create a business case for a major ERP implementation
- Create workflow/process diagrams and submit to the EA repository
- Assist end-users in identifying functional requirements in workflows

<u>Data Level</u>
- Identify and document dataflows that are part of workflows
- Combine several databases into a data warehouse
- Conduct an alternatives analysis on COTS data storage products
- Develop and implement a Master Data Management Plan for a LoB
- Create and maintain a Data Dictionary and Object Reuse Library

<u>Systems Level</u>
- Create and maintain a Systems Interface Diagram for a LoB
- Conduct an alternatives analysis of COTS and custom applications
- Create and maintain an Enterprise Service Bus to connect systems
- Identify standards for application program interfaces for an ERP system
- Develop a plan for legacy applications to migrate to an external provider

<u>Infrastructure Level</u>
- Create and maintain a converged network diagram for a LoB
- Develop a solution for mobile computing and communications
- Develop a plan to migrate a legacy data center to external hosting
- Create and maintain a network disaster recovery plan and procedures

Reference Architectures (RAs) are prepared solutions for common requirements in one or more sub-architecture domains or industry and government sectors. The RA helps enterprise and domain architects to rapidly include tested solutions in their designs, which speeds up delivery time and lowers the risk of functional defects. Examples include the Java

EE architecture, AUTOSAR for automotive software, and EULYNX for railway signaling systems.

The format of a RA is sometimes a narrative document that discusses recommended designs, structures, and integration of products and services to create a holistic solution to a requirement. An example is a retail Point-of-Sale system that needs to include links to check-out registers, in-store and warehouse inventories, credit card verification, price lists, and customer loyalty programs and offers. RAs can specify combinations of particular vendor products, standards, and services that are known to work well together. RAs can also be software coding templates that utilize proven development methods for specific programming languages. RAs may specify application interface standards and networking protocols.

Segment Architectures (SAs) encompass all framework levels but are bounded by the limits of an organizational sub-unit, a specific functional area, or a component. For example, a SA may document all of the goals, workflows, dataflows, and systems in a line of business, a program office, a supply chain, or a shared service.

The value of SAs is increased if they are consistent with the higher-level enterprise architecture and more detailed lower-level solution architectures or reference architectures. This means using the Same EA approach, framework, artifacts, and methods. Using the example of the EA6 approach, one way to think of this scalability is that "there are cubes within cubes" of the framework.

Service-Oriented Architecture

Service-Oriented Architecture (SOA) became popular in the 2002-2012 timeframe as an analysis and design method that first focuses on understanding the requirements for a new or improved business workflow, and then on what the supporting dataflow(s) and software application functionality should be. SOA does not look at the entire enterprise, or at particular business units – the focus in on a workflow, also called a service.

The relationship between EA and SOA is that that EA provides context and standards for SOA workflow solutions, with a focus on the integration

of the business, data, and systems sub-architecture domains of the EA6
Framework, as is shown in Figure 13-5 on the next page.

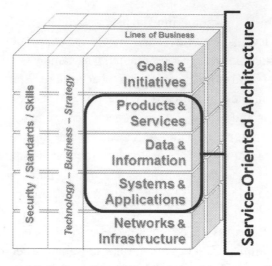

Figure 13-5. Service-Oriented Architecture (SOA)

SOA made a positive contribution to EA concepts and methods by
highlighting the close relationships (tight coupling) between the middle
three domains of the framework. SOA does not attempt to influence the
strategic planning process or the network infrastructure... the focus is on
providing integrated business/technology solution for organizational needs.
SOA also promoted application workflow and data integration through the
use of an Enterprise Service Bus, which was described in Chapter 7.

Chapter Summary

Chapter 13 introduced the concept of solution architecture, which is
basically the implementation of EA concepts and methods to find a viable
solution to an organizational need (requirement). Examples were provided
for each level of the EA6 Framework. Additionally, the concepts of a
reference architecture, service architecture, and solution architecture were
presented. The need for consistency EA and sub-architecture approaches
was stressed.

Chapter 13 Review Questions

1. What is a solution architecture?
2. How does solution architecture relate to enterprise architecture?
3. What is a reference architecture? What is a segment architecture?
4. Describe an example of a strategy-level solution architecture.
5. Describe an example of a business-level solution architecture.
6. Describe an example of a data-level solution architecture.
7. Describe an example of a system-level solution architecture.
8. Describe an example of a network-level solution architecture.
9. How do reference and segment architectures relate to an EA?

Chapter 14

Enterprise Architecture Support
for Mergers & Acquisitions

Chapter Overview

Chapter 14 discusses how EA's holistic concepts and methods can be helpful when planning for and implementing major changes in an organization's structure and functions as a result of being combined with or subsumed into another organization, which the business community refers to as Mergers and Acquisitions (M&A). This includes the use of EA in the pre-deal due diligence phase and in the post-deal organizational restructuring phase. The use of a holistic EA frameowork to enable the "likewise" comparison of two different organizations is a highlighted example, as is the use of EA artifacts to support planning and decision-making as the organizations are being merged. There are public sector equivalents to M&A (agency, which are also discussed. The chapter concludes with a discussion of other major structural events such as an organizational start-up, spin-off, and shutdown.

Please refer to M&A texts and articles for complete coverage of this subject.

Learning Objectives

- ➢ Present the major phases of a M&A initiative.
- ➢ Describe how EA can assist in private-sector M&A activities.
- ➢ Understand the value and risk areas of EA support for M&A.
- ➢ Understand the public-sector equivalents of M&A activities.
- ➢ Understand EA roles in organizational start-up, spin-off, sunset.

Introduction

Mergers and Acquisitions are a private-sector concept and set of actions for merging two "peer" organizations or acquiring and absorbing another organization. As such, there are three primary organizational viewpoints to consider in M&A: the peer/equal, the buyer, and the seller. These viewpoints have very different motivations and objectives, such as the peers feeling that there is equality, synergy, and mutual respect; a buyer getting the lowest price; and the seller getting the highest price.

M&A transactions (deals) are a way for a corporation to grow, a founder to cash-out, or a way for two competitors to come together to improve market position. M&A deals often involve large sums of money, sometimes in the billions of dollars, and therefore attract major financial institutions and business consultancies to broker and manage the process.

There is usually one or a couple of primary reason(s) for an organization and/or its principal(s) to want to engage in a M&A deal, including:

- Improve market share, revenue, or customer base
- Lower operating and/or transaction costs
- Reduce competition (if allowed by the SEC)
- Obtain patents, methods, and other intellectual property
- Obtain products, services, well-known brands/trademarks
- The owner wants to cash-out
- The owner dies (family business), kids don't want to run it
- A key executive's ego requires high-profile accomplishments

Unfortunately, the track record for M&A deals is not good in terms of achieving the primary purpose(s). Various estimates are that only a quarter to a third of the deals are successful in this way. Some value may be realized, but not the projected levels and claims of "synergy" are often not based on objective analyses. It is my opinion, that this is primarily due to an over-focus on the financial and marketing aspects of a deal and an insufficient understanding of the cultural, technological, and environmental elements. Many M&A players are motivated by fees and short-term profit and therefore think of corporation as an object - a money machine, not a collection of people, desires, and activities. As such, M&A pre-deal "make-it-happen" teams are over-represented by business executives, lawyers, financiers; and are under-represented by strategic planners, enterprise architects, risk managers, and industrial psychologists. Post-deal "restructuring" team skill sets shift significantly toward business analysts, system technologists, logisticians, and human resources…. as they try to combine and streamline as rapidly as possible.

Beyond just the financial viewpoint, a socio-technical view of both organizations is also needed to reveal areas of structure and function that can/will fit and areas that will not, as is shown in Figure 14-1 below.

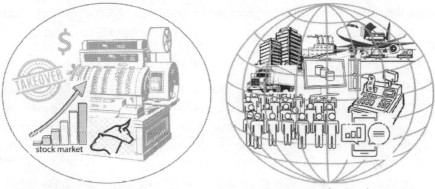

Financial View ◄─────────► Socio-Technical View

Figure 14-1. Financial and Socio-Technical Views of Organizations

The addition of holistic enterprise architects to pre-deal and post-deal M&A teams can add significant new levels of expertise in the areas of organizational dynamics, culture, restructuring, resource alignment, and technology enablement… all of which are major sources of bad post-deal M&A operating outcomes. M&A teams don't need more lawyers or financeers, they need organizational architects who can do scalable analysis and design work to support due diligence and restructuring.

M&A Phases

These are the four major phases of most private-sector M&A activities:

1. Trigger Event
2. Due-Dilligence
3. The Deal
4. Restructuring

Each phase has a different purpose and many events occur during each one, some of which may be unique to a particular deal and internal/external conditions at that time. There is always a who, why, what, when, where and how to a deal as owners, leaders, investors, regulators, stakeholders, and the M&A team provide inputs and play important roles to make a deal happen and then bring the organizations together. The following is additional information on each phase from a buyer, seller, or peer standpoint. Please note that this information is generalized and each M&A deal may have unique elements in each phase, please refer to texts and articles for more.

Phase I. <u>Trigger Event</u>.

Buyer: An investor group, a CEO, or a corporate Board decides that they want to purchase or take control of another organization to achieve a goal (money, market share, fame, patents, brands, etc.). At this point they buyer may not know with organization they are targeting.

Seller: An organization "comes into play" (becomes available or is a target of interest) for various reasons: the founder/owner wants to cash out, the head of a family business dies and the family doesn't want to run it, market conditions become very favorable or unfavorable, stock price is very high or low, the organization wants to capitalize on unique assets.

Peers: The leadership of two organizations realize that they will be more successful if they combine rather than compete. Market conditions or operating efficiencies are usually the driver for this type of realization.

Phase 2. <u>Due Dilligence</u>.

Buyer: A particular organization is targeted for acquisition and details on it are needed, or a group of "candidate" organizations are looked at to determine which one best meets the buyer's goals if it is acquired. This evaluation is called "due-dilligence" and is done to give the buyer accurate information on the finances, assets, customers, market positions, and problems/opportunities of the target organization. In opening their facilities and financials to prospective buyer(s), who sign NDAs, the seller is taking a chance on being exposed as not being well-run and therefore not commanding the best possible price. On the other had, a buyer may only want certain key assets. intellectual property, or a loyal customer base and they don't care if the target company is run well because they plan to sunset everything except the key items... think corporate raider. Also, there are regulatory rules that have to be met if the target is a publically-held corporation or if there are market competitiveness concerns.... Securities and Exchange Commission (SEC) will make that ruling, which could stop a deal from happening.

Seller: The target organization is either willing to be scruitinzed by potential buyers, in which case a Non-Disclosure Agreement (NDA) is put in place and the buyer is given access to records, people, facilities. They want to show that the organization is well-run with lots of future revenue producing potential. However, if the target organization does not want to be acquired, they will usually be uncooperative and it is up to the potential buyer to obtain information through public records and other online information. An organization that wants to be sold for the best possible price will want to have information well organized at the macro and detailed levels... but it is often that case that documentation on processes, technologies, and assets is not complete or ready for presentation to the buyer's analysts. In some cases, the analysts find that the target organization is a confused jumble of ad-hoc processes, silo'd business units, and dubious assets... collectively referred to as a "hot mess. The seller may not care if circumstances are such that they just want out, bancrupcy is nearing, or some other factor that pushes them toward a deal at whatever price or stock amount is offered.

Peers: Both organizations sign NDAs and open their financials and facilities to each other for mutual examination, looking to confirm or find areas of synergy, risk, and value. If unexpected areas of risk are found, the deal may be called off or may evolve into a purchase or hostile takeover unless this is prohibited by the SEC or mutual agreement.

Phase 3. <u>The Deal</u>.
Buyer: Once the target organization is checked for whatever elements are core to the buyer's goals, a "deal" (legal purchase) is accomplished with the help of lawyers and bankers using money, stock, or some other asset type. As in all commercial transactions, the buyer's objective is

to obtain the target item for the lowest possible price. If it is a hostile takeover, control is achieved through the purchase of voting stock and/or loyalty agreements with voting Board members, all done in the face of opposition from the takeover target's leadership who are helpless to prevent purchases on the open market (unless regulators intervene) from willing sellers of private or public stock (or pledging their Board seat) who will do this for various personal reason. If the SEC does not object, then the deal can be signed, and the buyer will want to make a big media splash to show strength and prowess in the marketplace and good intentions toward the seller organization who are about to be taken over.

Seller: As with all commercial transactions, a seller wants to get the highest possible price for their organization and this will depend on how highly the buyer values the assets based on due diligence findings. The deal results in some form of payment to a private seller's owner or a public corporation's leadership – who then keep or distribute the proceeds in accordance with legal requirements and personal desires. The seller may or may not participate in the buyer's media announcement and regardless, the signing of the deal means the end of control – the two organizations are combined and the buyer's leadership now makes the decisions. This is true even when the deal calls for the seller organization to continue to operate all or some of their business units in a semi-autonomous manner, because this is now done under the buyer's control.

Peers: Usually a merger of peer organizations involves a stock-swap, but sometimes payments are made and/or the SEC requires that some business unit(s) must be divested (sold) as part of the deal to prevent a market monopoly. The most important aspect of a peer deal is how the combined leadership team will be structured and who will hold key CXO and Board positions. This accelerates the movement into Phase 4.

Phase 4. <u>Restructuring</u>.

Buyer: It is likely that discussions regarding organizational restructuring have been going on within the buyer's M&A team since due diligence and perhaps even as part of the trigger event. One can imagine the CEO of they buyer organization saying or thinking "wouldn't it be great if we could buy XYZ company and blend their excellent supply chain with our fantastic sales and marketing goup – now that would really make us the best of class for years to come!" Even if this didn't happen, the real detailed work of an M&A deal begins in earnest as soon as legal rules allow the buyer to act on decisions about the structure and function of the new combined organization. The buyer organization is now "onboarding" the sold organization and the M&A team is usually expanded to include executives and managers of both organizations who will help make the decisions on what to keep, what to get rid of, and what new items are needed to fill gaps. This includes workflows, data/ info, systems, facilities, people, inventory, and intellectual property. It may be decided that it is best to run some similar functions and systems in parallel for a while to allow the new combined organization needed time to prioritize and execute the changes… or that the best competitive strategy is to keep operating two groups in a market area to preserve customer loyalty or keep assets under their control.

Seller: The seller's control over their organization's planning and operations will cease at whatever date/time that the deal's legal agreement specifies. The deal may call for some or all of the seller's personnel to remain on the payroll indefinitely or for a period of time. The seller organization's personnel have the best knowledge about their capabilities and challenges, which can be valuable to the buyer organization as options for restructuring are considered and decisions are made. That said, the buyer's approach to the deal may be to get rid of everything in the seller organization except key resources (e.g., customer lists, products, operating locations, subject matter experts, patents, trademarks, research labs, etc.). In either case, the buyer organization will need to identify who and what stay, what the severance will be for those who go, and how/when/where assets will be changed.

Peers: This gets tricky because there are two "equal" organizations merging into one that will have only one leadership team and will want to operate in an effective and cost-efficient manner… meaning that consolidation will have to occur unless it makes business sense to operate both the buyer and seller organizations (or parts of them) in parallel indefinitely or for a set timeperiod. An often overlooked, but very significant factor in merging two organizations are differences in their cultures – how the employees were managed, rewarded, and informed. Avoiding a "them vs us" situation is important yet will happen unless significant attention is paid to this by executives and managers for several years after the deal happens. Clear leadership (one CXO for each major role) is needed as soon as the deal is signed so that other important decisions can be made about strategic goals, business operating plans, technology enablement plans, human capital, and duplicate capabilities.

Where EA Can Help M&A Activities

As you can hopefully see, there are many points during each phase where information is needed regarding the structure and functions of each organization involved in a merger or acquisition. Providing this type of organizational analysis and design information is what holistic EA does best. Yet, the inclusion of senior enterprise architects on M&A teams is still in the very early stages. Here are some examples of where EA can help:

- Functional overviews of entire organizations or business units
- Likewise comparison of two organization's structure and functions
- Modeling of key business processes (current and future)
- Scenario-based short stories of desired business outcomes
- Alternatives analyses for structural and/or functional changes
- Facilitating standards for workflows, data, and systems
- Implementation of enterprise-level supply chains
- Transition roadmaps for systems integration, migration, or sunset
- Transition roadmaps for database/warehouse migration
- Transition roadmaps for business and technology outsourcing

Additional areas where EA can add value in M&A activities include:

- Justifying a higher sales price.
- Justifying a lower sales price.
- Communicating changes in structure and function to employees.
- Providing a common rallying point for the new combined group.
- Facilitating cultural change.
- Identifying key areas to measure integration success.

EA's Role in Public Sector Equivalents to M&A

Mergers and Acquisitions is fundamentally about bringing two business organizations together, and this type of activity occurs in government as well at the national and local levels. The trigger motivations are different (new or changed missions, budget changes, political desires) and the deal is different (law or policy), but the organizational convergence and restructuring challenges are largely the same – structure and function changes at the enterprise and business unit levels.

There is no manual or standard for restructuring a government agency, each instance is unique, as are the influencing factors (public needs, political agendas, available resources, and timeframes). Sometimes the actions are prescribed in law or related implementation policy, often not. The process for using EA to assess the structure and function of involved agencies is largely the same as with two private sector organizations: use the same holistic EA framework to identify, document, and compare strategic goals and initiatives, business processes and assets, and enabling technology. From this should come a transition plan that is the authoritative reference for when and how consolidation, alignment, or replacement should occur. As always, the biggest challenge will be with people who come from different organizational cultures and ways of doing things.

A city council may decide to combine the fire department and emergency medical department or merge their tax and licencing departments into the County's equivalent organizations to save money. A national government may face a crisis and feel the need to realign agencies to improve mission capability in a key area, such as happened in the creation of the U.S. Department of Homeland Security when a dozen agencies with domestic security missions were transferred from other departments in 2012 to form the third largest federal department with over 240,000 employees and a $47 billion annual budget. The transition was not easy as organizational roles, procedures, systems, and cultures had to be reviewed, aligned or replaced.

As with any organizational change in either the public or private sector, the value of EA is maximized when it is supported by the executive leadership team (through law or policy) as "the" authoritative source for standards and plans, and when the same holistic EA approach is used by all organizations.

EA and Start-ups, Spin-offs, and Shutdowns.

Holistic EA is focused the structure and functions of an organization throughout the lifecycle of startup and expansion, spin-offs and restructurings, mergers, and final shut-down, as illustrated in Figure 14-2. Most business organizations exist for only a few years or decades while religious groups, governments, and universities tend to exist for hundreds or thousands of years. In either case, structure and function are dynamic features that must change in response to different internal and external influences – referred to as flexibility, agility, or resilience. If the organization cannot or does not want to change – referred to as being inflexible or brittle – then major problems arise in being able to accomplish strategic goals, fulfill its mission, optimize resources, and/or compete in the market. In addition to this Chapter's discussion of how EA can be helpful during M&A activities, the following are general observations on how EA can be helpful to organizations during other periods of their lifecycle.

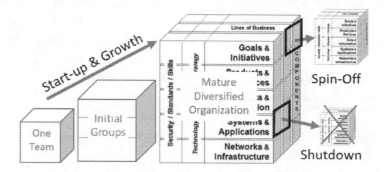

Figure 14-2. Organizational Lifecycle Examples

EA for Start-ups: The creation of a new organization is an exciting time and there is often a focus on the initial products and services, not standards for structure and function. This is usually because the initial organization is small, does not need lots of infrastructure, and there is not much divergence in terms of how inidividuals and teams are accomplishing things. The advantages of smallness will continue until different business units start to emerge that have some level of autonomy, and the number of people and operating locations grows. Beyond about 50 people and 5 locations it becomes difficult to keep everyone directly informed and in sync. So, the normal thing is to create groups and ask each one to self-manage to whatever degree the leadership culture is comfortable with. This reduces the oversight burden but increases the potential for these groups to do things differently. So, here is where organization-wide standards need to come in, with regard to work processes, data sharing/safeguarding, systems administration, supply chain management, and facility operations... which align with the EA domains that you have been reading about in this book. EA should not be implemented as a burdensome monolithic control, it should be introduced as a way to keep the organization operating effectively and efficiently, as well as promoting flexibility and scalability as the organization grows.

EA for Spin-offs: This is an interesting situation wherein part of an organization is "spun-off" and made completely or partially autonomous. It could be a small or a large part of an organization, but in either case the new organization's operating boundary is clearly identified and this is what will serve to separate the culture, structure, and functions as it begins its own lifecycle. That said, it is normal for a spun-off organization to inherit and continue standards for workflows, dataflows, systems, and how they deliver products and services. This can be good or bad depending on the effectiveness and efficiency of what is inherited in the context of the size, priorities, and operating environment of the new organization. The "spin-off" event should be looked at as an opportunity to adopt a different structure and best-in-class processes and supporting systems. EA can guide this, provided that the new organization values holistic planning – which hopefully they will as they recognize that agility and scalable solutions will always be needed to survive and thrive in their market niche. In the case of partial autonomy, the spun-off organization will often still have to adhere to the EA standards of the overall group, unless the organization decides to try to become an example of a new approach and set of best practices for the rest of the group to follow... an interesting way to promote cultural change.

EA for Shutdowns: Most every organization, especially businesses, have a lifespan of only a few years or decades... government agencies and universities tend to go on for many decades or a few centuries. There are exceptions, but many businesses are privately owned and operate for a few years until they are sold or shutdown due to a variety of reasons. Businesses that grow into large, diversified public corporations often last for decades or several centuries, but that is becoming rare as global market convergence and constant innovation make many commercial markets extremely competitive and this drives a relentless quest for mission effectiveness and cost-efficiency. This in turn leads to elimination of "middle tier" distributors as e-commerce and global delivery move producers and consumers into a more direct relationship... called disintermediation. Too bad for the local mom-and-pop convenience store or the retail malls that are closing by the dozens each year as we all can order most anything online and have it delivered within hours or days. Parts of organizations (Lines of Business - LoB) come and go much more often, which can have major or minor impacts on the overall group depending on how important, large, or inter-twined that LoB was with the other LoB that will continue on.

So, is EA important when an organization shuts down? Yes, a bit – mainly where there are government regulations on what information must be retained or archived and how that is to be done, by whom, and for how long. EA can also help by providing standards and schedules (transition roadmap) for an orderly shutdown of work processes, systems, and facilities. This can include the sale or transfer of assets to other organizations where particular methods must be followed.

Chapter Summary

Chapter 14 discussed how EA's holistic concepts and methods can be helpful when planning for and implementing major changes in an organization's structure and functions as a result of being combined with or subsumed into another organization, which the business community refers to as Mergers and Acquisitions (M&A). This includes the use of EA in the pre-deal due diligence phase and in the post-deal organizational restructuring phase. The use of a holistic EA framework to enable the "likewise" comparison of two different organizations is a highlighted example, as is the use of EA artifacts to support planning and decision-making as the organizations are being merged. There are public sector equivalents to M&A (agency, which are also discussed. The chapter concluded with a discussion of how EA can help during other major structural events such as an organizational start-up and growth, restructuring, spin-offs, and shutdown of all or parts of the group.

Chapter 14 Review Questions

1. What are the four primary phases of Mergers and Acquisitions?
2. List three types of M&A trigger events.
3. Give an example of how EA can help during due diligence.
4. Give an example of how EA can help during restructuring.
5. How can EA help organizations as they grow in size?
6. How can EA help an organization that is a spin-off?
7. How can EA help an organization or LoB that is shutting down?

Chapter 15

The Future of Holistic Enterprise Architecture

Chapter Overview

This chapter provides thoughts on future trends and issues in the practice of holistic enterprise architecture.

Learning Objectives

- ➢ Identify areas where EA can help in various sectors
- ➢ Discuss gaps and opportunities in global EA practices.

Introduction

EA continues to grow in use by corporations, governments, non-profit groups, and academic institutions. While there are similar benefits to be gained by each sector, the drivers are quite different. In the private sector, profit drives most planning and decision-making, and EA is an optional activity. In the public sector, citizen service delivery is the primary driver, money is a use-or-lose resource, and EA may be an activity mandated by law. However, outweighing these differences is the basic similarity that public and private sector enterprises are social entities based on patterns of human interaction, which therefore must deal with issues of purpose, legitimacy, culture, goal achievement, and the sharing of information.

Discussion

It is my observation that the basic trend for holistic EA is continued global growth. This view is supported by 1) the number of high-paying EA jobs that are constantly being offered; 2) the increasing number of major corporations and government agencies that are using holistic EA to promote organization-wide solutions; and 3) a steady stream of professional conferences on EA, articles in publications, and references to ongoing

EA programs in the literature and websites of public and private sector enterprises. Systems-level approaches are too limited in that they often do not emphasize human factors or business drivers and tend to produce stovepipe views of the enterprise's processes and IT resources. Executives and government leaders now want more holistic and robust views of their enterprises, presented in ways that they can drill into the information to gain insights, see performance gaps, promote communication, and enhance decision- making. As stated at the beginning of the book, EA is the one meta discipline that can provide a dynamic perspective of the whole enterprise in ways that are meaningful to all stakeholders.

As the field of EA continues to grow, the following are some of the future trends that we will likely see:

1. Corporations use EA for competitive advantage.
2. EA becomes an essential element in mergers and acquisitions.
3. IT resources/services become commodities, forcing new EA models.
4. National and local government levels integrate EA activities.
5. EA standards around the world increasingly mature and align.
6. Cybersecurity uses EA artifacts in selecting/implementing controls.
7. The Military uses EA to improve Joint capabilities.
8. Artificial Intelligence remakes organizational structures.
9. Academia grounds EA practices in social and management theory.
10. The profession of EA matures and is recognized as a career field.

1. Corporations Use EA for Competitive Advantage

Many if not most large size businesses have technology architectures that describe their IT systems, data flows, and network infrastructures, but they may not have enterprise architectures that incorporate strategy and business. The initial concepts of EA that were developed by John Zachman and Steven Spewak are fairly well known in the private sector, as is the TOGAF, but full implementation of these ideas in businesses remains uneven. Mid-size and smaller businesses often forgo any ongoing IT systems documentation and regard holistic EA as too expensive to undertake and maintain.

The problem with all of this is that these businesses, regardless of size, cannot "see themselves" and therefore are less agile. By this I mean that they cannot make consistently informed decisions on business and technology that reflect an understanding of current capabilities and future goals. The result are meetings to pass information or make decisions wherein people are trying to describe needed change, rather than being able to show the areas needing change via the EA views. I do believe that "a picture is worth a thousand words", and businesses should realize that an updated EA repository is invaluable in terms of increasing enterprise effectiveness by decreasing the amount of time it takes to articulate a requirement or make a decision, and decreasing the amount of misinterpretation of the ideas and requirements being presented. EA also helps to mature the enterprise in terms of being able to field technology solutions that are more aligned with strategic goals, doing so in less time and with higher quality. Finally, holistic EA helps to free a business from the proprietary solutions of vendors. By knowing its own current and future business and technology requirements, and being able to map those to open standards, the business has more leverage with commercial vendors to be able to obtain solutions that meet the enterprise's needs, and not be forced to inherit the vendor's prioprietary standards.

Private sector companies do not publish their approaches to architecture. It is understandable that businesses would not want to share the internal blueprints of their enterprises. However, that creates a dilemma for them in terms of wanting to obtain good examples of EA from others to guide and benchmark their own efforts. One way for private sector businesses to get EA examples is to establish non-disclosure and teaming agreements with other businesses that have similar operational and technology issues. Obviously, competitors in the samee market sector would not want to do this, but benchmarking partnerships can be effective between businesses in different industries if the EA issues are similar.

It would be beneficial to the private sector if general descriptions of EA approaches are shared in trade publications and academic case studies. For example, case studies of EA in the banking, manufacturing, insurance, retail, transportation, and freight industries would be helpful to all businesses. Understanding how technology is leveraged to improve business performance at an enterprise level is what these EA case studies could reveal. Beyond this, comparative studies of holistic EA practices between industry sectors would also be helpful to understand what the common areas of value are and to highlight EA management practices that work. Because of the lack of detailed private sector EA case studies, there is an opportunity for a business to gain notoriety if they were willing to share their approach to EA and specifics on how EA is adding value at the bottom line. Hopefully, case studies will emerge in coming years.

2. EA is Essential to Mergers and Acquisitions

One of the primary ways that large private sector companies continue to grow is through mergers and acquisitions (M&A). Two critical success factors for M&A activities are the preliminary analysis (known as "due diligence") and post-agreement decisions on which business units, systems, and processes will continue as part of the new combined organization, and which will be eliminated. EA can play a significant role in both of these activities – and the greatest value is seen when a mature EA programs are present in both organizations. This is because a mature EA program provides extensive, consistent visibility into all areas of the company through standardized documentation and resource optimization.

With regard to due diligence for an acquisition, the most important element is the valuation of the company to be acquired. Companies that want to be acquired, or are forced into an acquisition – and that do not have a good way to show their capabilities and assets - make it harder for the acquiring company to make accurate assessments of areas of strength and weakness, and put a monetary value on business units and the target company as a whole. A mature EA program should provide the documentation and scalable views needed to do that assessment. This could result in a change in the total valuation estimate (and purchase price) by tens or hundreds of millions of dollars – in an upward or downward direction. An EA program would have paid for itself many times over when positive financial impact on this scale is the result. Upward valuation is what the company being acquired wants, downward valuation is what the company doing the acquisition wants – and again, EA documentation helps to produce a more accurate picture on both sides, that helps analysis, and ultimately helps in finding accurate valuations and fair purchase prices.

With regard to pre- and post-merger analyses, EA documentation can provide essential information on strategic initiatives, business processes, information exchanges, data formats, applications and interfaces, systems, networks, and security solutions. All of this is needed to make decisions on which business units, processes, systems, and other resources will be kept and which will be eliminated. EA may also be able to provide insight into similarities and differences between corporate cultures, which is an extremely important aspect of successfully combining two organizations in one enterprise that maintains a strong competitive position. Mergers and acquisitions have been known to totally fail because cultures could not be brought together, or important systems and processes could not be migrated into an effective and cost-efficient end-state operating environment. The price of the failure of part or all of a merger or acquisition can be in the millions or billions of dollars. Knowing that having a mature EA program with enterprise-wide adoption can play a significant role in reducing the chance of that failure makes the decision to invest in EA a no-brainer – yet many enterprises choose not to do this because they are resistant to standards and/or want the locus on control to remain at the business unit, program, and system levels. Companies can survive without EA as long as they are not challenged with mega-events such as mergers, acquisitions, major changes in market conditions, or new disruptive technologies.

3. IT Services/Resources Become Commodities - New EA Models

The cost of computing services and associated software and hardware, when compared to the capability it delivers, has come down consistently and dramatically during the past twenty years. The advent of cloud computing, client-server architectures, and mainframe computing are examples of the unusual trend in IT, wherein an industry makes quantum leaps in performance on a regular basis…. and it is Moore's Law that best captured the underlying dynamic that has been fueling this performance increase. In 1965, Gordon Moore, co-founder of Intel Corporation, observed that the number of transistors per square inch on an integrated circuit had roughly doubled every year since the integrated circuit had been invented, and he predicted that this trend would continue. Only now, are we seeing a slowdown as the dramatically increased cost of further miniaturization is becoming unacceptable to global manufacturers.

That said, the increases in raw computing power that resulted from circuit miniaturization have made the development of new software and IT services during the past decade that would not have been able to be supported or fielded on a wide-spread basis. Large software programs a decade ago were in the 200-300 kiLoByte range, and today are in the hundreds of megabyte and gigabyte range. Data storage was also revolutionized several times over during the past forty years as the type and capacity of internal, external, and portable hard drives have increased many fold. The capacities of the largest internal hard drives of five years ago are now found in low-end "thumb drives" and insertable storage card that are no bigger than a postage stamp. Internal and external hard drives are soon to pass the terabyte level – moving into petabytes at very affordable prices (hundreds of dollars). The end result of advances in storage, processing, and networking has been a convergence effect that causes the performance of many mid-range IT products to be more than what the average user needs, and the price reductions of these non-leading-edge products have made them commodities whereby it is often more cost effective to replace an IT resource than to have it repaired (e.g., laptop, tablet, printer, hard drive, monitor, switch, modem, or smart phone).

What this means for holistic EA is that IT has become ubiquitous and enables many more business functions than it did a decade ago. The reliability and cost effectiveness of IT resources is therefore essential to the viability of those business services, and EA methods are one of the critical success factors for ensuring that IT functions properly and in harmony with the business operating environment. Artificial intelligence, machine learning, and robotic process automation serve to accelerate the impact of widespread IT enablement of core processes in every organization.

There is a debate continues over whether IT resources are strategic in nature or are common consumables. I suggest that IT resources are both. Leading-edge IT resources such as web services and manufacturing controls can provide an enterprise with strategic competitive advantage…. in terms of helping an enterprise to be first to market with products, finding and exploiting market niches whose opportunity windows can open and close in a matter of hours/days/weeks, and in driving down costs while holding quality at acceptable levels.

How holistic EA deals with these trends will be seen in adjustments to documentation frameworks and implementation methodologies, similar to what drove the development of the EA6 Framework presented in this book.... which primarily was capability gaps in other previous EA approaches that were created as IT advancements occurred, or as issues such as security became more prominent.

4. Government Integration and EA

The use of EA use in the global public sector is growing due to legal mandates for EA programs at the national level, and adoption of EA as a best practice by local agencies. Performance- and market-based approaches to measuring government services have emerged during the past decade.

Customers of government services want the national and local levels to increasingly integrate, so that it is easier to do things. In the U.S., opposition to this general expectation is the fundamental characteristic of our form of government that protects individual and State's rights, promotes a market-based economy, and seeks to limit Federal power. As such, there will always be a desire for independence and choice that counterbalances expectations for unified approaches to government services.

Having recognized the need for a diversification of government power, it is still possible to achieve better service to citizens and industry through standardized and integrated processes that are supported by ever- improving technologies. Whether that government service involves national or homeland defense, financial assistance, healthcare, rulemaking, licensing, enforcement, or disaster response; harmonized approaches between national and local government agencies are needed. Holistic EA is a particularly good way to achieve integration, as the definition of "enterprise" is such that particular service areas can be focused on with different government stakeholders. For example, first-responder effectiveness is largely dependent on information exchanges between all levels of government. A detailed set of current views of an EA for this government service area would be invaluable to operational effectiveness, and a detailed set of future EA views that were collaboratively developed would promote cross-agency cooperation and identify the funding and other resources that will be needed so that the changes can be planned for in forthcoming agency budgets. In a second example, integrating information on the Internet regarding government services is already occurring, but much work needs to be done so that simple searches for things like healthcare benefits do not yield a plethora of confusing and sometimes contradictory or outdated information. Smart searches and smart responses to on-line questions about government services are needed and holistic EA can promote the development of information sharing strategies at all levels of government.

One of the things that will be needed to support an integrated approach to government services is an agreement on EA frameworks and implementation methodologies. This is already happening, as is evidenced in the U.S. by the development of a State-level approach to EA through the National Association of State Chief Information Officers (NASCIO). The development of this approach was supported through a grant from the U.S. Department of Justice.

The problems with integrating government services do not stop at the national border, as they are increasingly global in scope. International trade, humanitarian relief, communications, politics, and defense treaties all rely on a robust global IT infrastructure. This infrastructure is comprised of a myriad of voice, data, and video capabilities that are carried on an equally diverse group of ground, air, and space telecommunications networks. EA on a global basis is emerging among governments and multi-national corporations as agreements are reached on IT resource connectivity and interoperability. While the diversity of communications paths will not diminish any time soon, the protocol for information exchange has become the Internet, the first apolitical, non-proprietary communications medium that has reached a global "critical mass" of participation. The growth of Internet providers and participants will continue to be significant, as will be the development of Internet-capable voice, data, and video applications. This will accelerate the need for regional and global EA programs among Internet service providers, telecommunications carriers, and commercial product developers.

5. Maturing Global EA Standards

While there are widely accepted standards for technical documentation and modeling techniques, a standard nomenclature for EA frameworks that incorporate business and technology functions continues to emerge among and between the major standards enterprises. Many of the rapidly developing object-oriented and component technologies are being combined with new delivery concepts based on web-services and related data standards (e.g., J2EE, .NET, SOAP, REST, UDDI, WSDL, XML, JSON, HTTP, XHTTP, XBRL) which create new more robust common IT operating environments... topics that are at the forefront of discussions.

Perhaps the area of greatest need for standards is the lexicon of this emerging profession. There are a number of EA frameworks and methodologies (e.g., EA6, TOGAF, MDA), and each one brings with it new terms or re-definitions of old terms. The lack of a standard base of terminology allows for the continuing proliferation of approaches and prevents meta-concepts from emerging, which serves mainly to confuse enterprises that are implementing and/or maintaining EA programs. Within the European Union, the UEML (Unified Enterprise Modeling Language) has been developed by the CIMOSA Association along with the CIMOSA Reference Architecture. In the past few years, the terms and modeling concepts of the UEML have been accepted by the European Commission. However, this standard language for modeling has not been adopted in the U.S., nor has it transcended to the level of EA. The terms and concepts introduced by John Zachman remain the de-facto standard in the U.S. for EA practices. It is the resolution of these types of differences in language and approach that will move EA forward.

6. Cybersecurity Uses EA to Lower Risk

As organizations continue to use various forms of IT to enable key processes, they will face continuous challenges in providing proper levels of security for processes, systems, and data within and between lines of business. This is because of the increasing complexity of IT hardware and software as well as the continuing lack of adherence to good cybersecurity practices by an organization's personnel at all levels. These two factors have the effect of continually giving a significant advantage to attackers over designers and defenders. The ultimate threat is an employee with "elevated" cybersecurity access rights who deliberately allows unauthorized access to organizational systems and data – called the "insider threat." More common though, are authorized "normal" users who don't use effective cybersecurity practices, which allows external hackers to gain entry and do bad things to the organization. Better designs and standards will help to counter this, and EA can help by promoting the integration of cybersecurity and data privacy controls into business workflows and technology solutions in all LoBs.

7. The Military Uses EA to Improve Joint Capabilities

National-level military organizations are some of the largest and complex enterprises in the world. It is also an enterprise that is increasingly dependent on information to perform its warfighting and peace-keeping missions. Tthe U.S. Department of Defense (DOD) developed the DOD Enterprise Architecture Framework (DODAF) in the 1990s to standardize the way that DOD agencies and military commands are modeling their IT resources, but they seem to be de-emphasizing the DODAF as an authoritiative reference, which I hope is not the case. Enterprise-wide operating and support capabilities in DOD exist through the senior staffs and major military commands. The increasingly integrated requirements of these enterprises will require DOD to continue to develop enterprise-wide planning approaches, as exemplified by the DODAF. The current DODAF approach focuses on systems, not organizations, which is a problem.

One of the most pressing considerations that the military has to keep in mind when using holistic EA is to avoid creating "single points of failure", a type of vulnerability that a consolidation of systems and capabilties present. I always recommend using holistic EA to create the right level of "planned replication" (disaster revovery) capabilities and move out of the common situation of "unplanned duplication". If the duplication in IT resource capabilities is completely eliminated, then there will most likely be a reliance on fewer sources of IT products and solutions. The potential to create "single points of failure" in systems and applications is increased when duplication is totally eliminated. For example, if DOD were to totally rely on a single commercial operating system, then security vulnerabilities become critical in terms of potentially enabling hackers to take down large parts of the DOD warfighting capability. For this reason, holistic EA needs to promote a risk-adjusted level of interoperability and functional duplication, and the subsequent cost inefficiency be viewed as acceptable in order to reduce IT vulnerabilities. DoD has also been working on an international Unified Defense Architecture Framework (UDAF).

8. Artificial Intelligence Remakes Organizational Structures

Artificial Intelligence (AI), also called Machine Learning, is an increasingly significant element in how organization's harness various types of technology to re-engineer workflows and dataflows within and between LoBs and with external partners. Robotic Process Automation (RPA) is an interesting implementation of machine learning, whereby integrated scts of robotic hardware and software are enabled/allowed to develop, implement, use, and improve the way that organizational products and services are delivered. Software applications that are designed to perform work semi-autonomously are referred to as "Bots" and are increasingly being treated like organizational employees as they are assigned ID numbers, undergo performance checks based on key output metrics, and get re-skilled through software code upgrades that come from both human and machine programmers. RPA improvements can result in tremendous reductions in cycle time, increase quality and consistence – which will likely result in new organizational structuring as functions change. For example, reviews of insurance claims, thc handling of service calls, routing of packages, and screening of job applicants are already being subjected to RPA improvement.

9. Academia's Contribution to EA

I have been a university-level instructor in IT since 1998 and it is my observation that the trend with regard to EA in the academic sector continues to be slow growth. Universities are participating in standards bodies (e.g., IEEE, ISO, and CEN), and development groups (e.g., the Object Modeling Group - OMG). However, the real contribution that academia should make to EA is theory, and that is largely being ignored.

The EA frameworks and modeling approaches that are in use in the public and private sector were largely developed by government groups and commercial practitioners. The social sciences, management sciences, and physical sciences all have a contribution to make. In that EA is about the documentation of complex social enterprises and how they use technology to improve performance, there are many areas that academia can and should comment on. This includes the ability of particular EA frameworks to capture enterprise resources, requirements, performance gaps, and cultures. Also, determining the true qualitative and quantitative value of EA to enterprises is a question that is perhaps best answered by academics with no vested interest. Multi-disciplinary methods to evaluate the effectiveness of EA approaches are also needed.

Perhaps the most telling aspect of academia's lagging contribution to EA is the lack of undergraduate and graduate level courses in this area of practice. Systems analysis and design (SA&D) courses remains a staple of programs in business, information studies, public administration, operations research, and computer science (there are over 20 textbooks on this subject in active use). However, there are very few courses on EA, and only a handful of practitioner books exist. Academia should recognize EA courses as the logical extension of SA&D courses, and that employers will accord higher value to graduates who understand enterprise requirements for integrated business and technology at both the systems and enterprise levels. More textbooks need to be written on EA to tie this discipline to other management and technical disciplines. Additionally, more case studies are needed of EA use in public and private sector enterprises. Finally, the *Journal of Enterprise Architecture* began publishing in August 2005 (I was the founding Editor), and continues as a global publication, which promotes scholarly research and writing on EA.

10. EA as a Career Field

EA is a profession that has levels of capability that will increasingly be supported by training/education programs. It takes 15-20 years of experience to qualify a senior enterprise architect, and up to 10 years to become proficient as a domain architect for business process improvement, systems design, service-oriented architecture, data architecture, network engineering, and security architecture.

As the founder of an EA training and certification program at Carnegie Mellon University in 2005, I have observed that several similar groups have been established in the U.S. and internationally during the past several years. I believe that the trend in EA certification is one of continuing growth as the number of EA programs in business and government grows. While academia needs to focus on developing EA-related theories, courses, and case studies, professional training groups need to provide EA Certification programs. The training and certification of Chief Architects to lead EA programs is essential for the advancement of the profession. Equally important is the training of other participants in the EA process including data architects, network architects, solutions architects, and IT program managers. A number of EA conferences and seminars continue to be offered each year, and there are several EA certification groups. That said, more is needed in terms of basic and advanced EA training programs.

Concluding Thoughts

Holistic EA is a discipline within the larger practice areas of business management, public administration, information management, and computer science. EA has remained important to C-suite executives and major program managers who depend on multi-unit/system integration and supply chains to be successful in meeting organizational goals. Experienced senior enterprise architects care like quilt-makers as they use scalable, consistent methods to model large, complex organizations that reveal performance gaps and resource overlaps across the organization. To plan and operate at a systems level is to look at requirements and capabilities in isolation and thereby sub-optimize the enterprise's operating potential.

Holistic EA is one of the three most powerful governance processes that a CXO has to use in implementing change (the others are strategic planning and capital planning). When used together, these processes can improve communications about current business and technology capabilities and can provide the information that executives and managers need in order to make good decisions about investing in future resources, including IT.

There is a need for holistic EA frameworks that include and integrate strategic, business, and technology planning, such as the one that is presented in this book. There is often a lack of recognition in other frameworks of the role of strategy and business in EA planning, as well as the incorporation of a component and service orientation at all levels. Seeing goals, measures, processes, information flows, applications, and networks as interchangeable components is a unique contribution that the EA6 Framework makes. Additionally, this approach can serve to connect and integrate the use of other more specialized (domain specific) frameworks and models for business, data, applications, networks, etc.

Architecting enterprises is a challenging endeavor, especially large, complex enterprises. The challenge comes in many forms, including executive support, sufficient resources, choices of methodology, and stakeholder buy-in. For these reasons, many EA programs are not given priority and therefore produce less value than they are capable of. Yet, as advances in the Digital Age continue to fuel globalization, technology convergence, and mobility; enterprises will be forced to continually evaluate at their strategies for success and develop agility to remain successful in rapidly changing competitive operating environments.

As the world grows "smaller" through instant voice, data and video communications; same-day travel to anywhere; and next-day package delivery the ways that we work and play are changing significantly. Understanding our roles and responsibilities as individuals and groups is important from a social, health, economic, political, and faith standpoint.

The last thought I would like to leave you with is that holistic EA is the only management and technology discipline that has the potential to create agility and resource optimization across an entire enterprise. Full recognition of this value is still in the future – which makes EA a relative secret – such that it can be used to gain and sustain competitive advantage.

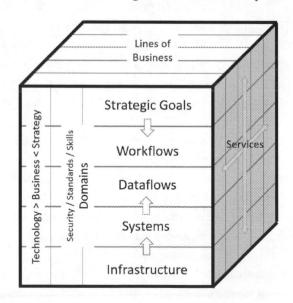

Appendix A

EA6 Cube Framework

The following four pages provide a complete set of faces for the EA6 Cube Framework, first as a group to show how they are oriented, and then as larger individual images. These images can be printed and assembled to create a cube framework model which can help in understanding concepts and relationships. These images can also be download at www.btmgllc.com.

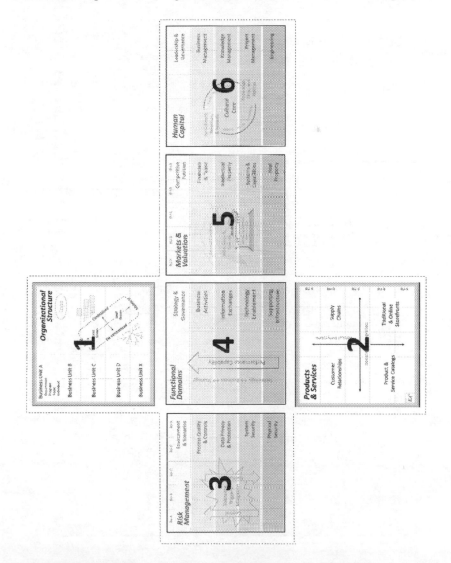

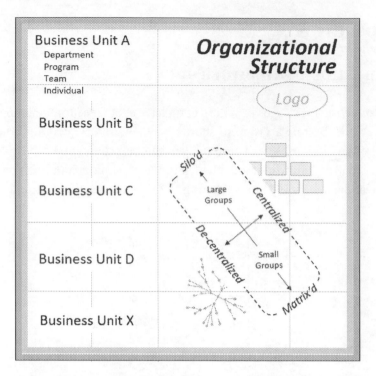

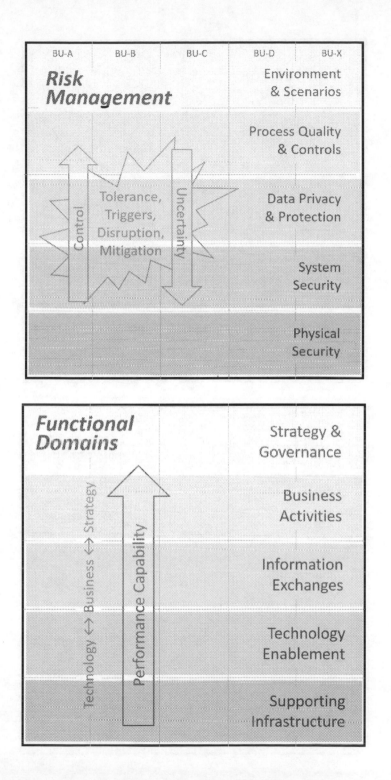

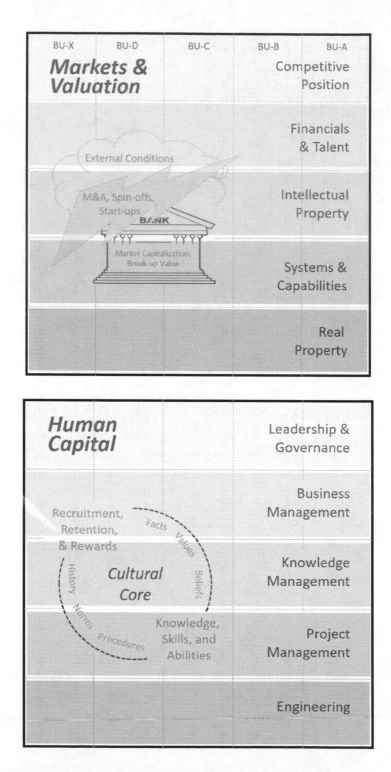

Appendix B

Developing a Business Case for an Enterprise Architecture Component

The following is an example format for developing business cases for investment in EA components.32 The purpose of the business case is to identify sufficient value in a proposed investment to merit the expenditure of resources including people's time, the enterprise's money, facilities, equipment, and other assets.

As part of the capital planning and investment control processes described in Chapter 10, the following procedure is used to identify requirements for EA components and develop a business case to justify the investment of enterprise resources to implement a solution:

1. **Requirement Identification.** A requirement for IT support is identified in an enterprise line of business (LoB), which is brought to the EA team for evaluation.
2. **Existing Solution Check.** The EA team determines that an existing EA component cannot meet the requirement.
3. **New Solution Business Case Development.** The sponsoring LoB determines that the IT requirement is of sufficient importance to merit the cost of developing a business case, and does so using the following format:
   a. **Describe the requirement** in terms of the gap in operational or administrative performance it represents to the LoB and the enterprise.
   b. Describe the **impact to the enterprise** if the performance gap created by the requirement is not resolved. Include the strategic, business, and technology impact.
   c. **Alternatives Analysis**: identify three or more viable alternative solutions (if at least three exist).
   d. Perform a **Cost-Benefit Analysis** for each alternative on a lifecycle basis to identify and financially quantify all of the direct and indirect costs and benefits, including qualitative items such as improvements in communication, morale, and competitiveness.

e.   Perform a **Return on Investment** calculation for each alternative.

f.   Perform a **Net Present Value** adjustment for each ROI calculation to account for anticipated cost increases over the investment's lifecycle due to inflation.

4.   **New Solution Business Case Evaluation**. The business case's alternatives are evaluated by the Architecture Working Group (AWG) for the correctness of the analysis, and alignment with the EA at each level of the framework. The Capital Planning Working Group (CPWG) then reviews the business case for the correctness of the financial analysis. A coordinated recommendation is made to the executive-level Capital Planning Board (CPB) as to whether the business case should be approved or disapproved for funding and implementation.

5.   **New Solution Business Case Approval**. The CPB reviews the business case in the context of the enterprise's overall investment portfolio using criteria that identify value from a strategic, business, and technology perspective:

a.   Strategic Value: Does the investment in the proposed new solution align with and contribute to the enterprise's strategic goals and initiatives? Are the outcome measures of success clearly identified?

b.   Business Value: Does the solution effectively close the operational or administrative gap in LoB performance? Does the proposed investment generate a sufficient level of return compared to other competing investment requests? If this is a mandatory requirement (e.g., meets a regulatory requirement), has the most cost efficient and operationally effective approach been identified?

c.   Technology Value: Does the solution provide an effective technical solution? Is the solution aligned with EA standards, and if not, has a waiver been recommended by the AWG? Can the solution also support other LoB requirements in the common operating environment?

6.   **New Solution Implementation**. If the business case is "selected" (approved) for funding by the CPB, the proposed solution becomes an implementation project that is managed by the sponsoring LOB. The project is reviewed by the CPB at key milestones and/or periodically as part of the capital planning process' "Control Phase" oversight of all projects. These CPB Control Reviews focus on the proper management of cost, schedule, and performance within the project (e.g., ±10% of baseline estimates).

When the project is completed, the CPB, AWG, and CPWG participate in a post-implementation review to identify lessons-learned that can help in the operations and maintenance of the EA component, and in maturing and improving overall project management practices in the enterprise. On a periodic basis throughout the EA component's lifecycle, the CPB reviews the value of providing ongoing funding for the operation and maintenance of that EA component. In this way, the entire business and technology operating environment is evaluated for continuing value.

The idea of standardized IT investment business cases was introduced by the U.S. Federal Government's Office of Management and Budget (OMB) in 2005 in the form of an "Exhibit 300" template, as described in OMB's Circular A-11. This Circular is updated annually to provide federal agencies with budget planning and submission guidance. One section of Circular A-11 is devoted to IT Capital Planning and Investment Control (IT CPIC) due to the significant amount of Federal Government spending each year in this area, which grew from $20 billion to over $90 billion for unclassified IT systems and services during the period of 2004 to 2019. In 2016, OMB replaced their Exhibit 300 business case template with a "standard investment" template to provide consistent reporting in areas of common (commodity) IT services, including email, helpdesk services, storage services, data center operations, and desktop devices. In 2017, OMB endorsed an industry standard for commodity IT service costing, called the Technology Business Model (TBM). An advantage of TBM is that is provides linked categorization taxonomies for business services, technology towers, and cost pools, which for the first time promotes standard reporting from both the CIO and CFO functions of an organization, which improves the tracking and authoritativeness of business activities and related technology enablement, as shown below. Additional information on the latest version of the TBM model can be found at www.tbmcouncil.org.

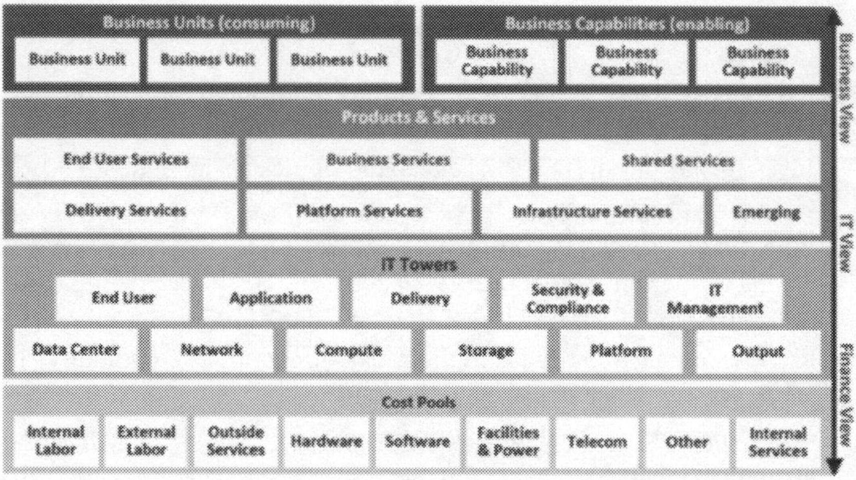

The Technology Business Model Taxonomy

Glossary of Terms

Actionable. EA documentation and data that is useful to executives, managers, and support staff for resource planning and decision-making.

Architecture. A systematic approach that organizes and guides design, analysis, planning, and documentation activities.

Architecture Segment. A part of the overall EA that documents one or more lines of business, including all levels and threads.

Artifact. An EA artifact is a documentation product, such as a text document, diagram, spreadsheet, briefing slides, or video clip. EA artifacts document EA components.

Artificial Intelligence. The ability of a computer or robot to perform tasks associated with intelligent beings such as problem solving, perception.

Business Case. A collection of descriptive and analytic information about an investment in resource(s) and/or capabilities.

Capital Planning. The management and decision-making process associated with the planning, selection, control, and evaluation of investments in resources, including EA components such as systems, networks, knowledge warehouses, and support services for the enterprise.

Change Management. The process of setting expectations and involving stakeholders in how a process or activity will be changed, so that the stakeholders have some control over the change and therefore may be more accepting of the change.

Component. EA components are those plug-and-play resources that provide capabilities at each level of the framework. Examples include strategic goals and measures; business services; information flows and data objects; information systems, web services, and software applications; voice/data/ video networks, and associated cable plants.

Composite. An EA artifact that uses several documentation modeling techniques and/or represents several types of EA components.

Configuration Management. The process of managing updates to EA components and artifacts, ensuring that standards are being followed.

Crosscutting Component. An EA component that serves several lines of business. Examples include email systems that serve the whole enterprise, and financial systems that serve several lines of business.

Culture. The beliefs, customs, values, structure, normative rules, and material traits of a social organization. Culture is evident in many aspects of how an organization functions.

Current View. An EA artifact that represents an EA component or process that currently exists in the enterprise.

Data. Data items refer to an elementary description of things, events, activities, and transactions that are recorded, classified, and stored, but not organized to convey any specific meaning. Data items can be numeric, alphabetic, figures, sounds, or images. A database consists of stored data items organized for retrieval.

Enterprise. An organization or sub-activity whose boundary is defined by commonly held goals, processes, and resources. This includes whole organizations in the public, private, or non-profit sectors, part(s) of an organization such as business units, programs, and systems, or part(s) of multiple organizations such as consortia and supply chains.

Enterprise Architecture. The analysis and documentation of an enterprise in its current and future states from an integrated strategy, business, and technology perspective.

Executive Sponsor. The executive who has decision-making authority over the EA program and who provides resources and senior leadership for the program.

Framework. The EA framework is a structure for organizing information that defines the scope of the architecture - what the EA program will document and the relationship of various areas of the architecture.

Future View. An EA artifact that represents an EA component or process that does not yet exist in the enterprise.

Governance. A group of policies, decision-making procedures, and management processes that work together to enable the effective planning and oversight of activities and resources.

Horizontal Component. A horizontal (or crosscutting) component is a changeable goal, process, program, or resource that serves several lines of business. Examples include email and administrative support systems that serve the whole enterprise.

Hyperconvergence. The use of a single vendor's hardware and software products to create an integrated, software-defined data compute, storage, and network platform.

Information. Information is data that have been organized so that they have meaning and value to the recipient. The recipient interprets the meaning and draws conclusions and implications.

Information Technology. A type of resource that supports the creation, analysis, sharing, archiving, and/or deletion of data and information throughout an enterprise.

Internet of Things. The globally interconnected grid of voice, data, and video networks that host end-user (edge) devices for people and organizations.

Knowledge. Knowledge consists of data or information that have been organized and processed to convey understanding, experience, accumulated learning, and expertise as they apply to a current problem or activity.

Knowledge Warehouse. A knowledge warehouse is the component of an enterprise's knowledge management system where knowledge is developed, stored, organized, processed, and disseminated.

Line of Business. A distinct area of activity within the enterprise. It may involve the manufacture of certain products, the provision of services, or internal administrative functions.

Machine Learning. Algorithms and statistical models that computers use to perform a tasks without instructions by relying on patterns and inference.

Methodology. The EA methodology defines how EA documentation will be developed, archived, and used, including the selection of a framework, modeling tools, and on-line repository.

Mission Statement: A succinct description of why the enterprise exists.

Network: A connected set of facilities, equipment, and transmission media/ waves that enable the exchange of voice, data, or video signals.

Performance Gap. An identified activity or capability that is lacking within the enterprise, which causes the enterprise to perform below desired levels or not achieve strategic or tactical goals.

Program. An ongoing endeavor that manages existing processes/resources or oversees development of new processes/resources via projects.

Project. A temporary endeavor undertaken to create a unique product, service, or result.

Robotic Process Automation. The use of hardware and software robots (bots) to re-design and improve the speed and effectiveness of business processes.

Stakeholder. Everyone who is or will be affected by a program, activity, or resource. Stakeholders for the EA program include sponsors, architects, program managers, users, and support staff.

System. A type of EA component that is comprised of hardware, and software, and activities that has inputs and outputs.

Vertical Component. An EA component that is contained within one line of business. Examples include a system, application, database, network, or website that serves one line of business.

Virtualization. Software applications that emulate hardware devices, logically partition operating systems, or manage other applications as groups.

Vision Statement. Succinctly describes the competitive strategy of the enterprise.

Subject Index

Endnotes

1   Bernard, S. (2004). <u>An Introduction to Enterprise Architecture</u>. Authorhouse, Bloomington IL.

2   Maslow, A. (1943). "A Theory of Human Motivation". *Psychological Review*, 50 (4) 370-96.

3   Galbraith, J. (1974). R. "Organization design: An information processing view." Interfaces 4.3.

4   Leavitt, H. (1965). "Applied Organizational Change in Industry: Structural, Technological and Humanistic Approaches" in: <u>Handbook of Organizations</u>, edited by J.G. March. Rand McNally.

5   Bernard, S. (2001). "Evaluating Clinger-Cohen Compliance in Federal Agency Chief Information Officer Positions" PhD Dissertation, Virginia Polytechnic Institute & State University.

6   Thompson, J. (1967). <u>Enterprises in Action</u>. New York: McGraw-Hill.

7   Cameron, K. & Quinn, R. (2011). <u>Diagnosing and Changing Organizational Culture: Based on the Competing Values Framework</u> (3rd edition). San Francisco: Jossey-Bass.

8   Day, J. & Zimmermann, H. (1983). "The OSI Reference Model." *Proceedings of the IEEE*. Volume 71, pages 1334-1340. December 1983.

9   Cerf, V. & Kahn, R. (1974). "A Protocol for Packet Network Intercommunication". *IEEE Transactions on Communications*. COM 22, No. 5, pgs. 637-648.

10 Nolan, R. & Mulryan, D. (1987). "Undertaking an Architecture Program." *Stage by Stage*. Volume 7, Number 2. March/April 1987.

11 Allen, B. & Boynton, A. (1991). "Information Architecture: In Search of Efficient Flexibility." *MIS Quarterly*. December 1991.

12 Zachman, J. (1987). A Framework for Information Systems Architeccture. *IBM Systems Journal*, Vol. 26, No. 3.89.

13 Zachman, J. & Sowa, J. (1992). "Extending and Formalizing the Framework for Information Systems Architecture." *IBM Systems Journal*. Vol.31, No. 3. 1992.

14 Spewak, J. (1992). "Developing a Blueprint for Data, Applications and Technology: Enterprise Architecture Planning," Boston: QED Technical Publishing Group.

15 Zachman, J. (2011). Zachman Framework for EA: The Enterprise Ontology. zachman.com

16 Humphries, A. (1965). SWOT Analysis, SRI Inc.

17 Nielson, R. (2002). "Strategic Scenario Planning at CA International." *Knowledge Management Review*, Issue 12, January/February 2000.

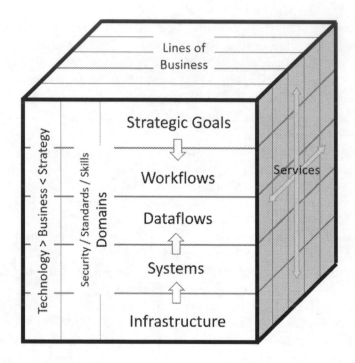

Printed in the United States
By Bookmasters